T0305784

Megacorporation

When the scale and scope of influence that a corporation wields is so great that it eclipses that of nearly all other corporations combined, it attains megacorporate status. Glen Whelan proposes that, amongst the current big tech cohort, it is only Alphabet, the parent company of Google, that can be categorized as such. In advancing a novel philosophical perspective, and aspiring to an amoral ideal of analysis, Whelan reveals Alphabet's activities to be informed by the ideology of infinite times, consequently transforming how we experience the past, present and future at personal and social levels. By shining a light on such corporate existential impacts, *Megacorporation: The Infinite Times of Alphabet* opens up a new field of research that makes the philosophical analysis of business and society an everyday concern. This novel study on corporate social influence will appeal to readers interested in Big Tech, business and society, political economy and organization studies.

Glen Whelan is Course Lecturer at McGill University. His work focuses on the social influence of corporations, and of high-tech corporations in particular. He regularly publishes in journals such as *Business and Society*, *Business Ethics Quarterly* and the *Journal of Business Ethics*.

Business, Value Creation, and Society

SERIES EDITORS:

R. Edward Freeman, *University of Virginia*
Jeremy Moon, *Copenhagen Business School*
Mette Morsing, *Copenhagen Business School*

The purpose of this innovative series is to examine, from an international standpoint, the interaction of business and capitalism with society. In the twenty-first century it is more important than ever that business and capitalism come to be seen as social institutions that have a great impact on the welfare of human society around the world. Issues such as globalization, environmentalism, information technology, the triumph of liberalism, corporate governance, and business ethics all have the potential to have major effects on our current models of the corporation and the methods by which value is created, distributed and sustained among all stakeholder–customers, suppliers, employees, communities, and financiers.

Megacorporation

The Infinite Times of Alphabet

GLEN WHELAN

CAMBRIDGE
UNIVERSITY PRESS

CAMBRIDGE
UNIVERSITY PRESS

University Printing House, Cambridge CB2 8BS, United Kingdom

One Liberty Plaza, 20th Floor, New York, NY 10006, USA

477 Williamstown Road, Port Melbourne, VIC 3207, Australia

314–321, 3rd Floor, Plot 3, Splendor Forum, Jasola District Centre, New Delhi – 110025, India

79 Anson Road, #06–04/06, Singapore 079906

Cambridge University Press is part of the University of Cambridge.

It furthers the University's mission by disseminating knowledge in the pursuit of education, learning, and research at the highest international levels of excellence.

www.cambridge.org
Information on this title: www.cambridge.org/9781108428026
DOI: 10.1017/9781108626095

First published 2021

A catalogue record for this publication is available from the British Library.

Library of Congress Cataloging-in-Publication Data
Names: Whelan, Glen, author.
Title: Megacorporation : the infinite times of Alphabet / Glen Whelan, Copenhagen Business School.
Description: Cambridge, United Kingdom ; New York, NY : Cambridge University Press, 2021. | Series: Business, value creation, and society | Includes bibliographical references and index.
Identifiers: LCCN 2020041330 (print) | LCCN 2020041331 (ebook) | ISBN 9781108428026 (hardback) | ISBN 9781108448635 (paperback) | ISBN 9781108626095 (epub)
Subjects: LCSH: Alphabet Inc. | Internet industry–United States. | Conglomerate corporations–United States. | Big business–Social aspects–United States. | Social responsibility of business–United States.
Classification: LCC HD9696.8.U64 A494 2021 (print) | LCC HD9696.8.U64 (ebook) | DDC 338.7/61025040973–dc23
LC record available at https://lccn.loc.gov/2020041330
LC ebook record available at https://lccn.loc.gov/2020041331

ISBN 978-1-108-42802-6 Hardback

Contents

Figures

Tables

Preface

It's only April, but it's already clear that 2020 is going to go down in history as a bad year. As I write these words, many people are unexpectedly dying from the coronavirus (COVID-19) pandemic, and many more are suffering from the social distancing and loss of livelihood that has come with it. As the pandemic continues to unfold, politicians and public health professionals will be held to account for their (mis) handling of the crisis, and a significant number of businesses, and many other organizations, will go bankrupt as their cashflows dry up.

Whilst many feel great sorrow, and essentially powerless, in the face of such tragedy, others appear to be, if anything, emboldened by it. Not for the first time in his life, Eric Schmidt, the former executive chair and CEO of Google and executive chair of Alphabet, provided a case in point, when, during his (livestreamed) presentation on 14 April to the Economic Club of New York, he bullishly proposed that the pandemic should make us all 'a little bit grateful that these [Big Tech] companies got the capital, did the investment', and built the communicative 'tools that we're using now', more than ever, during the lockdown.

Unsurprisingly, the megacorporation that Schmidt remains third-largest shareholder of, Alphabet, appears similarly inclined to make sure that it doesn't let the current crisis go to waste. Despite facing revenue losses that could total in the tens of billions of dollars – losses that would fatally wound almost any other enterprise – Alphabet has quickly sought to strengthen its status. So it was that, on 27 March, less than a month after announcing that it was providing $25 million in ad credit to the World Health Organization and government agencies, Alphabet announced that it was providing more than $800 million – in the form of various credits, investment funds and direct financial support – 'to small- and medium-sized businesses, health organizations and governments, and health workers on the frontline of the global pandemic'.

Along with this financial support, the megacorporation's most important asset, Google, has teamed up with Apple to create contact tracing technology that could enable health agencies to reduce the spread of the virus (whilst purporting to maintain the highest privacy and security standards possible). Alphabet's Verily and DeepMind are similarly engaged too, with the former collaborating with US health authorities to expand access to COVID-19 risk screening and testing, and the latter sharing computational predictions of protein structures that could aid in the development of a vaccine or cure. And it goes without saying that Alphabet wants to ensure that everyone is healthy, happy and productive during the lockdown. Thus, teachers, parents, workers, meditators, artists, journalists and so on can all find a wealth of Alphabet-funded resources designed to help them achieve their goals whilst staying isolated.

As this snapshot in time indicates, Alphabet's Google, and its various other assets (e.g. YouTube), are a defining feature of the current era. But as this snapshot also indicates, Alphabet is anything but satisfied with its present dominance, and is clearly looking to expand. If this expansion proves successful, then Alphabet will not just maintain but will further strengthen its megacorporate status. Any success in such regard will also result in the ideology of infinite times – the concern to indefinitely extend our pasts and futures – exerting more influence than it already does on people worldwide. Despite the importance of such possibilities, they both remain not just underexplored but more or less unidentified. The present book is therefore concerned to conceive, and help make sense, of them. As alternative framings of these possibilities can no doubt be made, my hope is that the ideas contained in the pages that follow will prove to be, if not indisputable or indispensable, then at least of interest to some.

Acknowledgements

I'd like to thank the three editors of this series – Jeremy Moon, Mette Morsing and Ed Freeman – for their willingness to take on this book, and for everything else they have done for me over the years. Many other colleagues and friends have helped out in different ways whilst the book was being conceived and completed. In particular, I'd like to thank Laure Cabantous, Michael Etter, Jean-Pascal Gond, Michelle Greenwood, Dirk Matten, Lauren McCarthy, Andreas Scherer, Dennis Schoeneborn, Andreas Rasche and Steen Vallentin. As the idea to write this book came together whilst I was a Marie Skłodowska-Curie Fellow at Copenhagen Business School from 2014 to 2016, it would be remiss of me not to acknowledge the European Commission for their generous funding. And despite the geographic distance separating us, I still receive, and am very grateful for, the support of my parents, Carolyn and Paul, and my siblings, Brett and Karen. Finally, I wouldn't want to have written this book without Hélène, Louis and Evelyn in my life; it's been fun completing the book with you all at home.

1 | *Introduction*

The introduction identifies the book's two main contributions – the explication of the megacorporate concept and of the infinite times ideology – and situates the work with reference to current discussions of Big Tech. In doing so, it is first emphasized that whereas current discussions of Big Tech often adopt a critical, and even a moralizing, tone, the present work strives to comply with an ideal of amoral analysis. The following sections then detail two supplementary contributions that the book makes to the scholarly fields of business and society and organization studies. The first of these domain-specific contributions relates to the book advancing a philosophical perspective, and the second to its demonstrating that corporations can shape social considerations of much broader importance than is commonly recognized. After this, the book's very simple method of construction and its three-part structure are described. The chapter concludes with a brief summary.

Beyond Big and Bad: An Amoral Analysis

The first two decades of the twenty-first century are notable for the emergence of Big Tech. Whilst open to interpretation, this term is generally used to refer to a select number of American corporations, i.e. Apple, Amazon, Facebook, Google and Microsoft, and their various activities. Further to their often being ranked as the world's largest corporations by market value, these firms are collectively referred to as Big Tech due to their being a major part of daily life for a great many people. On any given day, for example, people around the world will use an Apple device to post a message on Facebook, purchase a product on Amazon, conduct a search on Google and write a document with a Microsoft program.

Given the assumption that those with great power often fail to discharge their responsibilities, it is to be expected that the 'Big Tech' label has quickly come to possess a negative connotation. Thus, Wu (2018) has suggested that Big Tech is a social, political and economic curse, and Foer (2017) has warned that Big Tech constitutes an existential threat. Likewise, Zuboff (2015: 81) has voiced her concern that Big Tech is responsible for the emergence of the 'Big Other': 'a new universal architecture existing somewhere between nature and God . . . that records, modifies, and commodifies everyday experience . . . with a view to . . . monetization and profit'.

The critiques that these three authors have advanced, along with others of a broadly similar mind (e.g. Morozov, 2011), are often well founded. Yet, in their concern to resist 'the ideas that fuel these companies' (Foer, 2017: 8); to 'struggle for democracy' and diminish 'private power' (Wu, 2018: 138); and to mobilize 'in the name of humanity and the future' (Zuboff, 2019: 41), such authors tend to overlook, if not deliberately obscure, a variety of more general, and very fundamental, impacts that Big Tech is having on lived reality.

With the present work, I propose that the idea of a megacorporation can help to further reveal such considerations. Whilst the term 'megacorporation' is itself far from new, I am unaware of any sustained effort to detail its meaning. Given as such, the first contribution I make with the present work is to conceive of the megacorporate concept. In short, and as the prefix 'mega' indicates, I posit that a megacorporation is defined by its possessing a level of importance and influence that greatly surpasses that of other corporate forms, and by its influencing the lives of a huge number of people in very basic, foundational ways. Given the oversized breadth and depth of their influence, megacorporations will always be more or less limited in number. In fact, there may be times when no corporation is capable of satisfying such demanding criteria.

Apple and Facebook, for instance, are both of sufficient influence as to merit being included amongst the Big Tech brethren. Nevertheless, their respective business interests remain relatively narrow in focus – with Apple being best known for its consumer products and Facebook for social media. And whilst Microsoft and Amazon are more diverse, they likewise remain focused on developments in computing and online commerce respectively. As a result, none of these four companies can currently be considered a megacorporation.

Alphabet on the other hand, which was created back in 2015 through a corporate restructuring of Google, can be considered a megacorporation given its range of interests. In addition to Google Search, Android and YouTube, each of which have more than a billion users, Alphabet is heavily invested in the health sciences through companies such as Calico and Verily, in automated vehicles through its holdings in companies like Waymo and Uber, in urban design and development through Sidewalk Labs, and in the new space industry through its investment in SpaceX.

Whilst this breadth of investments differentiates Alphabet from its Big Tech contemporaries, it does not make it a unique corporate form. Indeed, there is a relatively significant number of corporate groups around the world that have similarly diversified, or even more diversified, investments: South Korea's chaebol (e.g., Samsung, LG) and Japan's keiretsu (e.g., Mitsubishi) spring to mind. What differentiates Alphabet from these conglomerates, and all other (groups of) corporations, then, is its capacity to shape how we construct and experience the past and the future at both the personal and social levels.

To begin making sense of this last statement, it helps to note that Alphabet's biotech subsidiary Calico is, as *Time* magazine once put it, trying to 'solve death' (McCracken & Grossman, 2013). Even if Calico's efforts prove just partly successful (by pushing death's door just a little farther back for just a few people), Alphabet will help change the experience of personal futures. In many ways, Alphabet's Google has already had such an impact on our personal pasts. The European 'right to be forgotten' ruling, which enables people to ask Google to remove links to (mis)information that would otherwise be returned when someone 'googles' their name, provides one specific manifestation of the megacorporation's influence in such regard.

Alphabet is impacting on similar matters at the social level too. By collecting more and more data on more and more aspects of domestic and communal life, Alphabet investments – such as Orbital Insight, a geospatial analytics organization that works with satellite imagery, and Nest, a smart or connected home company – are helping to build an historical store of information that changes how we can construct and conceive our social pasts. And with its various moonshots, and many other less speculative investments, Alphabet is contributing to a whole new set of means by which future human societies on Earth and beyond might be created and governed.

All of these various impacts, even those that are described as being potential at best, are controversial. In fact, one can commonly pick just one development that Alphabet is invested in, do a quick search on it and find a whole list of moral concerns. Alphabet's investment in SpaceX – which as a result of its plans to create a huge satellite internet service called Starlink has been accused of starting a project that could 'blight the night sky' for earthbound astronomers (Devlin, 2019) – provides a case in point. In addition to that, reports disclosing the presence of a hidden microphone within a Nest home security system (Amadeo, 2019) provide yet one more illustration of why so many people think of Alphabet entities as spies.

In light of this well-established, Alphabet-focused 'cacophony of critique' (Boland, 2018), the present analysis is more concerned to remain amoral than it is to moralize. Whilst I fall short of achieving this goal – in that the work is unavoidably informed by my own values – I have tried to be morally indifferent in completing the analyses, and building the conceptual constructs, that the book contains. That being said, I also think that this amoral ideal is justifiable. For whereas the concern to morally judge can narrow vision, the concern to amorally understand can broaden it.

This ideal of amoral analysis also informs the book's second contribution: the explication and elaboration of the ideology of infinite times. When conceived amorally, ideology refers to the cognitive structures that shape and limit our experiences (e.g., Jameson, 2016). It also refers to motives that – because they tend to be implicit or taken for granted – give rise to much of what we strive for and much that we want to be (Greimas, 1983: 293; Greimas & Courtés, 1982: 222). It is in this non-pejorative sense of ideology, that the ideology of infinite times is here associated with the widespread concern to indefinitely extend humanity's past and future at both the personal and social levels.

To begin with its historical aspect, the ideology of infinite times can be seen to manifest through the – currently ever-increasing – documentation of daily existence for specific individuals and whole societies. Presuming it is successfully stored and maintained, this information will provide future historians, and anyone else that is interested, with details about daily life that far exceed those that we have had on prior lives and generations up until now. And with regard to its forward-looking aspect, the ideology of infinite times is evidenced by the widespread concern to extend the length of healthy existence for individual humans and to sustain humanity's development for as long as possible.

Further to informing a whole range of activities at the individual, industrial and social levels, the infinite times ideology specifically shapes Alphabet's activities too. Without an awareness of the infinite times ideology, however, Alphabet's diverse activities and interests can seem fragmented and unrelated. What the explication of the infinite times ideology therefore does is show how these diverse ongoings come together to form a whole. It reveals that the concern to expand our temporal horizons as far as possible, both backwards and forwards, plays a key role in ensuring that Alphabet's many interests do not pull it apart.

The explication of the infinite times ideology has a number of other benefits too. First, and given that many others appear to be informed by the ideology of infinite times, the detailing of this ideology helps explain why the masses might actively support Alphabet's huge accumulation of wealth and power – an accumulation that Zuboff (2015) argues is based on an extractive relationship that people could never reasonably consent to.

The identification of the infinite times ideology also suggests that ideological conflicts will increasingly focus on the merits of human civilization and human pre-eminence. At the moment, ideological conflicts are commonly fought from a variety of political-economic perspectives, e.g., libertarian, liberal, democratic, socialist. Whatever else their differences, these political-economic perspectives are all similar in that they tend to take the merit and superiority of humanity for granted. Such assumptions, however, are likely to be increasingly reconsidered if investments by Alphabet, and other similarly informed organizations, continue. The reason why is that these investments can contribute to risks that could undermine the infinite times ideology both directly (e.g., through the risk of technologically induced extinction) and indirectly (e.g., by encouraging those opposed to the infinite times ideology to resist it).

As these initial remarks indicate, by conceiving of the megacorporate construct and the infinite times ideology, I contribute to the flourishing literature on Big Tech by showing that Alphabet is reshaping existence in ways that are more fundamental than are generally recognized. In doing so, I also make two additional contributions to the more specific fields of business and society and organization studies. These contributions relate to my proposing that scholars in these related domains can benefit from a philosophical turn and from an increased focus on how business organizations influence society. As these field-specific contributions are not of explicit concern throughout the rest of the book, I quickly detail them in the two sections below.

A Philosophical Turn

Underpinning the academic field of business and society teaching and research is the recognition that business plays a significant role within modern societies. Given that this role will often be linked to other organizations or institutions – e.g., governments, laws, religions, the non-profit sector – the business and society literature discusses other actors and structures as well. Nevertheless, the business and society literature remains focused, by definition, on the relationship between commercial activities and communal concerns (Crane et al., 2015; Greenwood & Freeman, 2017). Like other academic fields (e.g., cultural studies, international relations), the field of business and society has been informed by a number of different, and more or less long-standing, theoretical traditions. Consequently, and prior to arguing that the field can benefit from an increased engagement with philosophy, I first differentiate between the ethical, political and socio-economic theoretical traditions that currently dominate.

Ethical Theory

Ethical theory, or what is sometimes termed moral philosophy, is concerned with questions of right conduct, with the prescribing and proscribing of behaviour, and with the promotion of well-being at various levels (e.g., individual, social, environmental). So defined, ethical theory is less descriptive than it is normative: for it identifies what should or should not be done. Whilst any posited link between ethical reasoning and individual welfare/self-interest is a complex matter (Parfit, 1984), ethical theory often suggests that moral action requires some sort of self-sacrifice (Kant, 1997). Widespread notions of honesty and fairness, of equality, of familial responsibilities and so on, commonly require that individuals give up opportunities or resources that they would otherwise enjoy. Ethical theory therefore concerns itself with explaining why such notions or ideals should be complied with.

Within the business and society field, ethical theory has been used and developed to complete a number of tasks. First, ethical theory has been used to make arguments for and against the existence of business organizational forms and market institutional structures. One example is provided by Donaldson (1982: 48), who, in building on the social contract tradition, has proposed that 'hypothetical contractors in a state of nature' would consent to the corporate form's existence so long as they believed it would lead to an increase in efficiency, and benefit all affected by it. The flipside of this, of course, is that if the corporate form is not thought to meet such standards, then it cannot, according to Donaldson, be morally defended.

Second, and given the presumption that business forms do generally meet the standards set by the likes of Donaldson (1982), ethical theory has been used to make arguments for and against different types of product and service being produced and consumed by them. One clear illustration of this approach is provided by critics of the tobacco business, who propose that as 'smoking is both addictive and lethal', it is inconsistent with the common good (Palazzo & Richter, 2005: 388). Many other 'vice' or 'sin' industries, e.g., alcohol, gambling, pornography, are subjected to similar critiques (Miller & Michelson, 2013: 601).

Third, and given the presumption that both the institution of business and a great many products and services are morally justifiable, there is a body of work concerned with detailing what process standards businesses need to meet, and what responsibilities commercial actors need to discharge, in their various productive activities. The list of concerns such standards relate to is evergrowing. Amongst many other topics, standards have been developed, and responsibilities detailed, with regard to algorithms (Martin, 2019), marketing to the vulnerable (Brenkert, 1998), the amelioration of sweatshop labour concerns (Miklos, 2019), the extent of fiduciary duties (Marcoux, 2003), and women's empowerment in supply chains (McCarthy, 2017).

Political Theory

Along with the use it has made of ethical theories, the field of business and society has made considerable use of political theory and political philosophy. By and large, business and society scholars informed by the political theory tradition have sought to detail appropriate divisions of labour between business, government and civil society. In doing so, they have advanced our understanding of long-standing concerns regarding the accountability of corporations to their various constituents or publics (e.g., Clark, 1916; Dodd, 1932).

One illustration of such work is Evan and Freeman's stakeholder theory of the firm, which proposes that economic and political freedoms necessitate that stakeholders (directly) participate in corporate decision-making; that stakeholders and managers should be protected by a 'bill of rights'; and that the 'task of management in today's corporation (i.e., the balancing stakeholder interests) is akin to that of King Solomon' (Evan & Freeman, 1988: 103–105). Although stakeholder theory has changed, Freeman (e.g., Freeman, Wicks & Parmar, 2004) continues to argue that it is essential for protecting stakeholder's political (and economic) freedoms. Stakeholder theory has also come to be more explicitly associated with a libertarian political philosophy. To this end, Freeman and Phillips (2002) have proposed that one of the major benefits we would derive from the increased actualization of stakeholder principles, would be the diminishing of state regulation and the need for coercive control.

Scherer and Palazzo (2007, 2011), by way of contrast, have proposed that it is because states face increasing difficulties in regulating corporate activities and making sure they are directed towards the public good, that corporate decision-making needs to be increasingly aligned with the interests of stakeholders and civil society. The general idea is that liberal models of corporate governance, which are built on a division of labour between profit-focused corporations and (democratic) states concerned to protect and ensure the public good, are breaking down due to the globalization of economic relations and the emergence of governance gaps. In terms of theory, Scherer and Palazzo make use of a 'thin conception' (Durant, 2011) of Habermas's (1990) discourse ethics (see Whelan, 2012: 726). They build on the belief that all affected by a decision should be free to debate it to suggest that corporations should participate within multi-stakeholder initiatives that govern their activities (e.g., the Forest Stewardship Council) or that corporate boards should be comprised of representatives from stakeholder groups and civil society.

Another line of work uses theories of citizenship to make sense of corporate–society relations. This has been done in three ways: First, corporations have been metaphorically conceived as different types of corporate citizens (e.g., deliberative, republican), so as to show how different understandings of corporate social responsibility are in effect always informed, whether consciously or not, by broader political philosophies (Moon, Crane & Matten, 2005). Second, it has been argued that corporations can be conceived as administering a set of citizenship rights (Matten & Crane, 2005), particularly when the 'liberal' division of labour between business and government breaks down. Third, the idea of 'citizenship arenas' (Crane, Matten & Moon, 2008: 9–12) has been used to make sense of the ways in which social media corporations have created new spheres from within which individuals can exert influence over the political-economic actors and structures that surround them (Whelan, Moon & Grant, 2013: 780).

Socio-economic Theory

In contrast to the ethical and political theory disciplines, which tend towards the normative, the discipline of socio-economic theory tends more towards description and explanation. As its hyphenated label suggests, socio-economic theory can be found in various forms throughout the business and society field. Indeed, specific lines of work within this tradition – such as those that adopt a macro focus and investigate the influence of national legal and cultural considerations on corporate governance structures and corporate social responsibility policies and practices – constitute significant literatures in their own right (Crane et al., 2016).

One illustration of such work is provided by Kinderman (2012), who used an institutional lens to explore the co-evolution of corporate social responsibility and neo-liberalism in the United Kingdom between 1977 and 2010. Another is provided by Matten and Moon (2008, 2020), who influentially built on work in 'national business systems' (e.g., Whitley, 1997) to differentiate between an 'implicit' and 'explicit' understanding of corporate social responsibility that respectively refer to a European approach characterized by coordinated markets and collective obligation, and to a US approach characterized by liberal-market economies and individual discretion.

Unlike the just-mentioned macro-level studies, which focus on how (inter-)national considerations shape the policies and practices of corporations, meso-level studies tend to focus on how individual corporations can legitimate or justify their policies and practices in the face of conflict and reputational threats. Some of these studies, such as Helms' and Patterson's (2014) analysis of the private corporation that owns the Ultimate Fighting Championship (a mixed martial arts organization), reveal the ways in which corporations can (partially) transform society's understanding of (il)legitimacy.

Much more common, however, are studies that show how corporations comply with societies' existing understandings of (il)legitimate behaviour (Boswell, 1983). In this vein, Patriotta, Gond and Schultz (2011: 1806) built on Boltanski and Thévenot (2006) to show how various forms of justification (e.g., measures of efficiency and sustainability) helped to repair the legitimacy of corporate activities following a safety controversy 'provoked by a major nuclear accident'. Many others have drawn on institutional and resource-dependency theories to complete similar tasks (Friedland & Alford, 1991; Oliver, 1991; Suchman, 1995).

These varying strains of socio-economic analysis have advanced our understandings of how business is shaped by institutional norms and practices. Nevertheless, and as with works informed by the ethical and political theory traditions, works informed by socio-economic theory have tended to focus on relatively discrete concerns (e.g., sweatshops, corporate governance, corporate social responsibility, the safety of nuclear energy) that are of interest to relatively limited audiences (e.g., supply chain managers, financiers, civil society organizations, energy industry professionals). A philosophical perspective, by way of contrast, helps bring considerations of more general and wide-ranging interest to the fore.

Philosophy

Philosophy is generally conceived as relating to considerations of central importance to existence and experience. On the one hand, this meaning is suggested by the colloquial references that people make to their 'philosophy' when discussing the guidelines or assumptions that shape their behaviour in daily life: such as 'family first' versus 'money over everything', or 'the best defense is a good offense' versus 'you can't lose if they don't score'. On the other hand, this meaning is also suggested in more formal contexts, where philosophy is associated with questions regarding the nature of being and sentience, the possibility of knowledge and so on.

A hallmark of philosophical concerns, then, is their focus on considerations that are in some sense basic, that are in some sense unavoidable or that possess something like omnipresence. As a result, the importance of philosophical concerns – such as the a priori of cause and effect (Kant, 1998); or the explication of presuppositions that make discourse and deliberation pragmatically possible (Habermas, 1990) – transcend disciplinary divisions and demarcations. Such concerns, however, do not just transcend theoretical divisions, but those that separate the practical and concrete worlds of everyday life from the more abstract and theoretical worlds of academia as well (cf. Kieser & Leiner, 2009). In light of such, the first motivation that business and society scholars might have for taking a philosophical turn relates to it potentially enabling them to speak to, and engage with, a much broader audience.

The second reason for suggesting that the business and society field, and the related fields of organization and management studies, can benefit from a turn towards philosophy, is that it opens up new areas of research that are interesting in and of themselves. Of course, these fields already address a number of philosophical matters. Cooper's work on organization as the construction and internalization of comprehensible and fungible phenomena (e.g. Cooper, 1990) provides one example (see also, Helin et al., 2014: 15). And the existence of journals like the *Philosophy of Management*, which invites 'inquiry into the nature, knowledge, practice, limits, hopes, and possibilities of management' (Vandekerchkove, 2017: 91); and of edited collections on philosophy and organization theory (e.g. Mir, Willmott & Greenwood, 2016), suggests that self-consciously philosophical works are growing in number. This growth, however, appears to remain slow, with any growth in philosophical interests likely to have been outpaced by the apparent tendency for theoretical disciplines to split up, drift apart and become ever narrower in their specific interests (van Liedekerke & Dubbink, 2008: 278–279).

The most immediate cost that is paid for such specialization, for the multiplication of tightly focused disciplinary perspectives, is that those working in the field of business and society miss out on the pleasure of engaging with fundamental considerations. Whilst tastes will always differ, many are curious as to the underlying frameworks or abstract qualities of experienced reality, of the motives of human behaviour, or of the ways in which socialization shapes perception. So in addition to furthering the self-promoting (and somewhat ignoble) goal of increasing the field's clout, a philosophical turn could help make the field of business and society a little more fun.

Corporate-Shaped Societies

If one was forced to pick the main idea advanced by the business and society literature, one could do worse than refer to the posited need for businesses to comply with existent social understandings. Thus, the ethical tradition commonly suggests that corporations need to comply with extant norms regarding human rights wherever they operate; the political tradition that corporations need to be governed in an increasingly deliberative fashion if they are to be considered democratically legitimate; and the socio-economic tradition that corporations need to respond to reputational threats if they are to prove capable of maintaining their socially sanctioned 'licence to operate'.

This general tendency to emphasize the power that society has to shape corporations, is consistent with, and often directly informed by, trends throughout the organization and management studies literature. Institutional theorists, for example, have long focused on how external environments shape internal organizational environments, and critical theorists have explored the ways in which macro-level discourses shape corporations in a top-down fashion (Weber & Waeger, 2017).

This tendency to emphasize how corporate agency is socially shaped and constrained is also consistent with developments found throughout the humanities and social sciences, where Foucault's (1977: 31) idea of genealogical analysis as a 'history of the present' has shaped a great deal of work (Garland, 2014). Barkan's (2013) genealogical inquiry of the manner in which medieval religious thought helped give rise to ideas of corporate sovereignty, and of how subsequent transformations in US law in the nineteenth and twentieth centuries helped shape contemporary notions of corporate personhood, provides one illustration.

The point being made is that the business and society literature tends to reverse its alphabetic ordering when it comes to the apportioning of power. As various authors operating outside the traditionally defined field of business and society suggest, however, the rapid emergence of Google (e.g. Stross, 2008; Vaidhyanathan, 2011), and the rest of the

Big Tech cohort, indicate that at least a little more weight should be placed on the business side of the scales. Numerous historical cases suggest the same thing. The Massachusetts Bay Company, whose corporate charter from 1629 enabled it to operate more or less independently of British Royal oversight (Anderson 1998: 198), and to help form American ideals of association and democracy (Conway, 1998; de Tocqueville, 1945; Innes, 2001; MacMillan, 2013; Maier, 1993; Shy, 1998), provides one illustration. The English East India Company, which is discussed in more detail in Chapter 2 provides another.

A Simple Method of Construction

The two main ideas advanced throughout the present book are that (1) megacorporations are defined by their capacity to shape fundamental considerations of existence for a large number of people and that (2) the ideology of infinite times underlies the existential impacts of the megacorporation Alphabet. As I imagine is the case for many other ideas or concepts, the two just mentioned did not emerge *ex nihilo*, but from my engaging with colleagues and friends, paying attention to Google and then Alphabet, and from my consumption of media in general. No doubt, the ideas are informed by other factors too. Whatever the case, the point to note is that once I fixed on these two ideas, I used them to guide my engagement with all the materials that are referenced throughout the book. In this fashion, all the other ideas here referred to are, more or less literally, defined by the use I make of them (see Dewey, 1933: 136).

If one is willing to conceive 'method' loosely, then this approach can be considered a (purpose-driven) method (Freeman & Greenwood, 2020). More specifically, it is consistent with what I term the mélange approach to (historical) composition in Chapter 5. In contrast to the massive approach that is also detailed in Chapter 5, and which strives for exhaustiveness in its treatment of data, the mélange approach enables a user to pick and choose between the materials they utilize. Such an approach, suffice it to note, has little interest in providing the last word on original empirical sources, or in idolizing extant theoretical perspectives. But it is not interested in bastardization (of other works) for bastardization's sake either (see also, Deleuze, 1977). Rather, this very simple method of construction enables those who use it to combine and utilize different ideas and sources of data to realize their own goals.

A Three-Part Structure

In detailing and illustrating the megacorporate concept and the ideology of infinite times, the book is structured into three main sections. The purpose of Part I is to introduce and define the megacorporate concept, and to show that Alphabet is a megacorporation. Accordingly, Chapter 2 begins by proposing that a megacorporation can be differentiated from the related notions of a normal corporation, a multinational corporation and a total corporation, on two grounds. First, and unlike both normal corporations and total corporations, megacorporations are defined by the global scale of their operations. Second, and in contrast to both normal corporations and multinational corporations, megacorporations are defined by the broad scope of their influence. Having made these general distinctions, it is then more specifically suggested that, if a corporation is to be characterized as a megacorporation, then it will need to be associated with monopolistic activities, corporate social responsibility concerns, political-economic hybridity and existential impacts. As the English East India Company was associated with all these considerations, Chapter 2 argues that it provides one, particularly clear, historical illustration.

In applying the same criteria, Chapter 3 proposes that Alphabet is a megacorporation too. As Alphabet's existence is dependent – some would say parasitic – upon Google's massive profitability, Chapter 3 begins with an overview of Google's context, creation and success. The emergence of Alphabet is then contextualized by the seeming need for Google's founders, Sergey Brin and Larry Page, to 'burn' some Google cash and broaden Google's, already ambitious, organizational vision. Following this, and prior to concluding, the chapter details the first three considerations that make Alphabet a megacorporation: i.e. its monopolistic activities, its political-economic hybridity and its corporate social responsibility concerns.

The fourth and most important consideration that results in Alphabet being considered a megacorporation, its existential impacts, are the subject of Part II. The purpose of this second part of the book is to show how Alphabet is changing how we construct, experience and manage, both that which is already past and that which is yet to be. As

Table 1.1 *A Summary of Part II*

		Level of		Constructive Tendencies	
Chapter	Orientation	Analysis	Speculation	Monolithic	Multiple
4	Past	Personal	Low	Careful	Carefree
5	Past	Social	Low	Massive	Mélange
6	Future	Personal	High	Sequential	Simultaneous
7	Future	Social	High	Autocratic	Autonomous

detailed in Table 1.1, the four chapters that Part II contains are characterized by a number of differences and similarities.

To begin with the differences, each chapter is distinguished in terms of orientation (past or future), level of analysis (personal or social) and the extent to which the matters discussed are speculative (low or high). And in terms of the similarities, each of the chapters show how the changes (potentially) being wrought by Alphabet can be conceived as encouraging more monolithic developments on the one hand, and more multiple developments on the other.

To further explain, note that orientation is here said to change when an agent turns backwards to consider the past, or forwards to consider the future. Of course, the past and the future, and the present too, can be difficult to disentangle. Hence, Chapter 4 is less concerned with discussing pasts already created, than it is with the pasts that people are constantly in the process of helping create for their future selves. And Chapter 5 suggests, amongst other things, that a key motivation for engaging with social pasts is to encourage some sort of change or development in present-day societies. By way of contrast, the future orientation of Chapters 6 and 7 is simpler, in that both chapters are focused on the role technologies can, or could, play in making future existences longer.

The second main difference characterizing Part II's chapters is due to their being situated at either the personal level of analysis – which relates to identifiable individuals, albeit ones that might increase in number (as per the multiple constructive tendency – see below) or the social level of analysis – which relates to communities of variable characteristics and size: e.g. local communities, national communities, global communities (see also, Aguilera et al., 2007).

Third, the chapters of Part II are also distinguished on the basis of their being more or less speculative. Chapters 6 and 7 are conceived as relatively high in this regard given that they both refer to developments that are far from certain, such as the possibility of radically extending individual biological existence (Chapter 6) and of inhabiting other planets (Chapter 7). Most of the technologies discussed in Chapters 4 and 5, by way of contrast, are already existent. Consequently, these chapters are marked as having a low degree of speculation.

Notwithstanding these differences, Part II's chapters are also similar in that two constructive tendencies are associated with their various developments. The first tendency is termed monolithic. It is associated with phenomena that are more or less singular. This monolithic tendency results in individuals or societies being pulled together so as to create, or maintain, what amounts to one more or less integrated and homogeneous whole. The second tendency is termed multiple. It relates to efforts or concerns to keep individuals or societies in a heterogeneous state, to break them up or tease them apart, or to decompose individuals or societies into separate elements. In short, what the four chapters that comprise Part II suggest – with regard to the pasts and the futures that are being created at both the personal and social levels – is that Alphabet's existential impacts are simultaneously encouraging, or enabling of, these monolithic and multiple constructive tendencies.

With the idea of a megacorporation having been defined and illustrated in Part I and with the nature and importance of Alphabet's existential impacts having been detailed in Part II, the book concludes, in Part III, by reflecting on the main threats to Alphabet's being. Accordingly, Chapter 8 notes that, whilst the ideology of infinite times plays a key role in holding Alphabet together – by helping the megacorporation to be conceived as the custodian of our pasts and futures – it also contributes to its ultimate falling apart. The reason why is that, like everything else, the ideology of infinite times is itself finite. And in turning to a variety of more mundane considerations, the book's final chapter (Chapter 9) posits that Alphabet's megacorporate status is externally threatened by concerns to undermine its various monopolies, and internally threatened by what appears to be increasing discord amongst its employees. Whilst the exact date of Alphabet's death remains uncertain, Part III emphasizes that Alphabet will one day cease to be.

Summary

This chapter began by noting that, in striving for an amoral ideal of analysis, the present book develops and illustrates the megacorporate construct, and explicates and details the ideology of infinite times. Following this, the book's more implicit concerns of encouraging the fields of business and society, and organization studies, to take a philosophical turn, and to focus more on corporate capacities to shape societies, were outlined. Brief discussions of the book's very simple method, and of its three-part structure, were then provided. In short, this introduction has clarified my motivations for writing the book, acknowledged the broader context shaping it, and explained the constructive process that informs its final structure.

PART I

The Birth of a Megacorporation

2 | *Megacorporations*

This chapter details the megacorporate concept. It begins by noting that, whilst references to the idea of a megacorporation can be found in contemporary works of fiction, these references tend to be vague. The chapter's following section thus turns to the task of differentiating the idea of a megacorporation from three other corporate types: i.e. normal corporations, multinational corporations (MNCs) and total corporations. After this, it is proposed that, in addition to being generally characterized by their global scale of activities and broad scope of influence, megacorporations are more specifically characterized by their monopolistic activities, their social responsibility concerns, their political-economic hybridity and by their existential impact on our lives. Given these criteria, the chapter's penultimate section proposes that the English East India Company provides a clear historical example of a megacorporation. A brief summary brings the chapter to its conclusion.

From Fiction to Fact

Like the people they can be metaphorically conceived in terms of (Moon, Crane & Matten, 2005), and like the states that have often given legal force to such metaphors (Barkan, 2013), corporations can develop different capacities, and can live for variable periods of time. As a result, some corporations die soon after they are born, and never manage to exert any real influence. Other corporations, by way of contrast, can quickly come to possess capacities that outweigh those of most other organizations combined. Therefore, and just as with extraordinary or particularly charismatic individuals (Weber, 1978: 241–245), and just as with particularly prominent or hegemonic states (Mearsheimer, 2001), some corporations will always be of more consequence than others.

This idea, that specific corporations can grow to become immensely powerful actors, is one that is often found within the science-fiction genre. Most famously, William Gibson's 1984 work *Neuromancer* is filled with cities comprised of corporate arcologies and dominated by corporate giants such as Mitsubishi–Genentech, or what is presumably a merger of the Mitsubishi group – a sprawling Japanese conglomerate that has now existed for close to 150 years – and Genentech – a gen (etic) en(gineering) and tech(nology) company that was founded in 1976, and that is currently a fully owned subsidiary of Roche.

Given such illustrations, the organizations that play a central role in Gibson's work have been referred to as megacorporations (Leaver, 2003: 128; Nixon, 1992: 223). Although he does not appear to use the megacorporation label himself, Gibson – who has been referred to as a 'sociologist of the near future', and as 'probably the most important novelist' of the late-twentieth century (Poole, 1999) – has suggested the need for such a term. Hence, Gibson (2011) has stated that whereas the text in *Neuromancer* never makes the explicit suggestion that 'the United States exists as a political entity', it does point towards a 'sort of federation of city-states connected to a military-industrial complex that may not have any government controlling it'. In their turn, these city states and military-industrial complexes can be related to the 'Bigger, Globally Corporate Things' that Gibson (2012: 181) has also noted he made a 'sketchy description' of in *Neuromancer*. Moreover, and in countering the belief that his megacorporate writings are dystopian, Gibson has suggested that *Neuromancer* – which was written towards the end of the Cold War – should be conceived as an 'act of imaginative optimism. . . I didn't want to write one of those science-fiction novels where the United States and the Soviet Union nuke themselves to death. I wanted to write a novel where multinational capital took over, straightened that shit out, but the world was still problematic' (Gibson, 2011).

As these remarks indicate, the idea of a megacorporation can be found throughout much of Gibson's work. Gibson, however, is far from alone in having pointed in this direction. Indeed, the vague idea of a megacorporation has by now attained trope-like status and can be seen to inform not just the literary field (e.g. David Egger's *The Circle*, Jarett Kobek's *I Hate the Internet*) but the domain of popular culture more generally (e.g. comics, television shows, films, computer games).

Given their fictional status, it is understandable that such works do little more than allude to the megacorporate idea. On the rare occasion that an attempt at conceptual clarification is made, what tends to be suggested is that the distinguishing feature of megacorporations is that they are on the verge of replacing, or have already replaced, various policing and legal functions that we currently associate with states (Gibson, 2011). Whilst it is not wrong to conceive of megacorporations in what amounts to a hyper- or post-neoliberal fashion (Barkan, 2013; Foucault, 2008), one risk of doing so is that it results in considerations that are already well understood being revisited once again. More problematically, such conceptions tend to result in the rise of megacorporate power being made dependent on a corresponding decrease in state power, and in megacorporations being portrayed as little more than a poor relation to, or imitation of, states (see also, Atal, 2018).

It is in an effort to conceive of megacorporations on their own terms, then, that I now provide a more general discussion of the corporate form. In doing so, I begin with a brief summary of the corporation's historical emergence, and then distinguish between normal corporations, MNCs and total corporations on the basis of their scale (local or global) and scope (narrow of broad). After this, I turn to megacorporations in particular, and propose that they are marked by four characteristics.

Three Types of Corporation

The idea of a corporation as a 'legal personality separate from individual human beings ... originated in Roman law in its classical period (the first two centuries AD), was further developed in the Middle Ages in both canon (Church) and civil law, and was adopted from civil law by the Anglo-American common law tradition' (Avi-Yonah, 2005: 772). As Roman jurists apparently had an 'intense hostility to definitions and theories' (Berman, 1985: 216), the extent to which 'classical Roman Law had ... a concept of the corporation as a legal person with legal attributes (owning property, the capacity to sue and be sued)' has long been debated (Avi-Yonah, 2005: 773). Nevertheless, and along with the more general idea of legal personality, Avi-Yonah (2005: 773, 771) posits that one can discern from within these writings 'three views

of the corporation' that continue to influence thinking through to the
present day:

the aggregate theory, which views the corporation as an aggregate of its
members or shareholders; the artificial entity theory, which views the corporation as a creature of the State; and the real entity theory, which views the
corporation as neither the sum of its owners nor an extension of the state,
but as a separate entity controlled by its managers.

Further to noting that it is the real entity theory that has arguably
proven the most influential over this long time frame (Avi-Yonah,
2005: 812), it helps to recognize that the fortunes of these different
theoretical perspectives have waxed and waned along with power
dynamics more generally (Tierney, 1955: 97). By way of illustration,
Avi-Yonah (2005: 780–782) posits that Bartolus of Sassoferato
(1314–1357) leant towards the real entity view because – unlike the
artificial and aggregate theories – it could help 'independent corporations in Italy such as the city state and the Italian universities' to
maintain their independence despite the Holy Roman Empire's decline,
and the possibility of their entire membership perishing.

As these preliminary remarks suggest, the need to conceive, and
analytically distinguish between, different types of corporations, has
long been a matter of considerable importance. In light of such,
I emphasize that whilst the following discussions are concerned to
conceive of the megacorporate construct, and to differentiate it from
three other corporate forms, they do not pretend to bring the discussion of corporate types to a close.

Normal Corporations

Corporations are differentiated from other organizational structures,
such as partnerships or sole proprietorships, on a number of grounds.
In particular, corporations are marked out as a specific organizational
form due to their being separate and distinct from their owners; their
possession of limited liability; their transferable ownership and their
continuous existence.

The benefits associated with such characteristics can prove considerable and will often justify the costs of forming a corporation. Limited
liability, for example, results in a corporation's shareholders not being
personally responsible for a corporation's debts, and acts as a

significant spur to investment. Given these sorts of benefits, both for-profit and not-for-profit corporations exist in large numbers globally. Some even suggest that the business corporation, which rose to prominence in the eighteenth and nineteenth centuries (Avi-Yonah, 2005: 783–793), is the most important type of "organization in the world" (Micklethwait & Wooldridge 2003: 2–3).

As the other corporate types detailed below can also be associated with the preceding characteristics, note that for a corporation to be considered a normal corporation, it needs to remain local in scale, and narrow in its scope of impact. One example would be an incorporated construction business that builds standard homes in a given city, and that has little if any ongoing relations with the occupants thereof. Other examples would be an incorporated charity that helps feed the homeless in a given town; an incorporated non-profit that helps to start-up local businesses in a given province or state; or an incorporated retail co-operative that sells outdoor lifestyle products to members within a local, politically unified, domain.

Multinational Corporations

Unlike normal corporations, the biggest of which remain contained within one country, the existence and operations of MNCs extend across national borders. Put more technically, MNCs emerge when a parent corporation from one country makes a foreign direct investment in a child corporation from another. For a parent corporation's investment to qualify as a foreign direct investment, and not just as a portfolio investment, it has to purchase in the range of 10–25 percent of the child corporation's stock so as to ensure that it is the most powerful owner (Jensen, 2006: 22). Although ownership is important, what is more important is for a parent to control the activities of its children. Accordingly, MNCs are commonly thought to also include entities in which it is contractual relations, rather than equity holdings, that enable a parent corporation to exert significant levels of control over its children (Zerk, 2006: 53).

When people think of corporations today, it is often MNCs to which their minds turn. A main reason why is that many of the branded goods that people buy are produced by them. Nike, for instance, produces finished goods in 542 factories populated by more than 1,000,000 workers in 42 countries (Nike, Website A). It also owns or controls more than 1,000 retail stores worldwide (Nike, Website B). As this indicates, MNCs can be of significant scale. Nevertheless, and as illustrated by Nike having limited impact beyond the worlds of sport and fashion, the scope of influence of even the most well-known and powerful of MNCs remains limited.

Total Corporations

The idea of a total corporation is a play on Goffman's (2007) notion of the total institution. As well as asylums, orphanages and homes for the elderly, Goffman identified prisons, prisoner-of-war camps, army barracks and monasteries, as key illustrations of the phenomena he had in mind. Such institutions are notable due to their resulting in people living what amounts to all of their lives – i.e. sleeping, playing, working – within the same organizational confines. 'The key fact of total institutions', then, is that the same bureaucratic organization is responsible for handling the 'many human needs . . . of whole blocks of people' (Goffman, 2007: 6).

As with total institutions, the defining feature of total corporations is their capacity to shape a broad scope of considerations of fundamental importance to daily life at a local scale. Whilst Goffman (Ibid.) indicated that industrial enterprises would only embody some of the less 'totalizing' aspects of total institutions, historical developments suggest that this qualification was too cautious. George Pullman – who became rich through the Pullman Palace Car Company's building of railway sleeping car carriages, and who 'decided to build a model factory town fourteen miles' out of Chicago in 1880 (Green, 2010: 29) – provides a case in point.

The construction of the Pullman neighbourhood was informed by Pullman's belief that, just as the beauty of 'his luxurious vehicles would have a civilizing influence upon even the roughest of customers', so too would 'civilized surroundings . . . have an "ennobling and refining" effect on his workers' (Ibid.). The town's construction began with Pullman spending four years 'secretly buying up 4,000 acres along Lake Calumet's west bank', and with his then transforming what was initially a swampland area 'into the site of a giant production works with a population of 8,000, about half of them [Pullman] employees' (Green, 2010: 30). Working with architect Solon Spencer Beman and landscape designer Nathan F. Barrett, Pullman designed an '"all-brick city" that would become a showpiece for the company' (Ibid.). Along with the company's office and production facilities, the company town included a large residential area, a large market complex, a bank, a Moorish-style theatre capable of seating a thousand punters and a 'library with 6,000 volumes donated by Pullman himself. Completing the picture were a handsome hotel – which contained the otherwise-dry town's only bar – a school, parks, and playing fields. Altogether, there were more than 1,500 buildings in Pullman, all owned by the company' (Ibid.).

Parts of the neighborhood Pullman created can still be found in South Chicago. But as an example of a total corporation, it did not even make it to the twentieth century. The reason being that, in 1898 – a year after Pullman himself had died, and following a great strike of 50,000 men enraged by the Pullman Company's refusal to help alleviate the concerns of those suffering the consequences of an economic depression – the 'Illinois Supreme Court ruled that the Pullman Co. charter did not permit the holdings of real estate beyond what was required for its manufacturing businesses. The ... city of Chicago [subsequently assumed] municipal functions in 1899 and the company gradually ... [sold off] its town properties beginning in 1904' (Green, 2010: 31–33).

Many other company towns were also created in the United States (Green, 2010) and elsewhere following the Industrial Revolution. In England in 1879, Richard and George Cadbury decided to relocate their growing business, Cadbury Chocolates, 'from Birmingham's City Centre into the countryside four and a half miles away ... Situated in an area known as Bournbrook and located close to a railway and canal, the Cadbury brothers not only built a brand new factory but improved the lives of their workers by building sixteen houses. They named this new village Bournville and over time added additional homes, a school, and a hospital. By late 1900, the village had grown to 313 houses on 330 acres of land' (Cadbury World, 2016).

Chinese state-owned enterprises have been associated with such totalizing tendencies too. The Wuhan Iron and Steel Company – which is now part of Baowu Steel Group, the world's second-biggest steelmaker (Reuters, 2016) – was once responsible for a 'compound, termed "the plantation" ... [that had] 2.4 million square metres of residential space, where all 13,000 employees and their families' resided, and that included such things as 'housing, child-care, schooling,

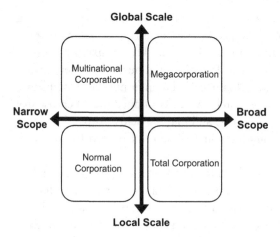

Figure 2.1 Four corporate types

health care and a variety of daily functions ... on the same premises'
(Shenker, 1996: 890). And more recent examples – such as Reliance
Industries' 'Reliance Greens', a 700-acre residential estate adjoining
two oil refineries in Gujarat, India's westernmost state; and Del Monte
Kenya's 14,300 hectare 'compound' near Nairobi, which includes a
canning plant, pineapple plantation and eight different villages– show
that total corporations can still be found in various parts of the world
today (Atal, 2018).

To summarize, it is due to their impact on all aspects of an employee's daily life – and even their afterlife if one is to believe Merle Travis's
father, whose concern that he could not afford to die because he owed
his soul to the company store, was immortalized in the 1950s hit song
'Sixteen Tons' (TEF Enterprises, Website) – that total corporations
have a much broader scope of influence than either normal corporations or MNCs.

The Characteristics of a Megacorporation

As illustrated by Figure 2.1, normal corporations, MNCs, total corporations and megacorporations, can be differentiated on the basis of their
relative scale (local or global) and scope (narrow or broad). When
viewed from this high level of abstraction, megacorporations are characterized by their overall immensity. It can also be seen that

megacorporations can be understood as either a total corporation that has gone global, or as an MNC that has significantly increased its scope of influence.

This bird's-eye view of a megacorporation is very helpful when it comes to differentiating it from the other three types of corporation. Nevertheless, when one descends from this vantage point and views it in closer detail, the megacorporate form is seen to be comprised of more specific characteristics too. As is now outlined, four are particularly important.

Monopoly

A complete monopoly exists when one firm or organization controls a market; when it is the only producer of a given product or service. Such dominant positions can first arise, and subsequently persist, for various reasons (e.g. Hutchinson, 2016: 454–481). Legal monopolies are enabled and protected by states, and often defended in public good terms. Thus, in many countries around the world, the state will legally ensure that either itself, or some other anointed organization, is the only entity that is allowed to sell or provide a given product or service. In addition to monopolies on policing functions, state or legally enabled monopolies have often existed in the energy sector, in the provision of water, in public transport, and so on.

Monopolies can also emerge when a specific firm controls all of the supplies or productive resources that are required to provide a given product or service: e.g. oranges for orange juice, bauxite for aluminium, mines for diamonds, engineers for engineering services. As this sort of control may only be feasible with protection from the state, control monopolies will often be legal monopolies. Natural monopolies – which are associated with markets where initial fixed investment costs are high and where the marginal costs of adding additional customers following such initial investments tend towards zero – commonly take the form of legally protected monopolies as well. The justification of a legal monopoly on postal services, for example, has often been based on the belief that they are natural monopolies (Panzar, 1991).

Apart from those that are state-sanctioned, monopolies can emerge through market-led innovations and technological advances. If of sufficient size and quality, such advances can result in a significant improvement in the satisfaction of a given want or need. This, in its turn, can result in monopolizing firms enjoying well above average profits. Of course, such monopolistic power will often depend on a firm being able to protect its intellectual property rights, or on its being able to prevent, or buy out, potential competitors. Many leading tech companies, such as Apple and Microsoft, have historically been associated with these sorts of monopolies. Platform monopolies are yet another form of market domination. These emerge through network effects whereby users attract more users in a virtuous circle. Such effects are often posited as the reason that Big Tech (e.g. Amazon, Facebook) has come to attain the bigness it has (Srnicek, 2017).

As these remarks indicate, many monopolies are best conceived as a sort of hybrid (e.g. platform-technology-natural). The more specific point to make, however, is that if an organization is to be considered a megacorporation, then it will need to be identified with something like monopoly power in one or more of its domains of interest.

Corporate Social Responsibility Concerns

Having been around in something like its current form for more than one hundred years (e.g. Clark, 1916), the idea of corporate social responsibility (CSR) appears here to stay. Whilst the utility of the term is yet to be universally acknowledged, and whilst its exact meaning continues to be the subject of debate, it is widely accepted that, as a general idea, if not always as an actuality, CSR possesses considerable influence. The following three points – all of which relate back to the proliferation of MNCs in the Post–World War II era (Ruggie, 2003) – help explain why.

First, as more and more people have become aware of the ways in which the policies and practices of MNCs in one part of the world may not be of the same standard as those in another, people have increasingly come to ask that MNCs 'lift their game' wherever they are perceived as lacking. As a result, MNCs that profit from sweatshops, or that profit from the incomplete protection of human rights, are often asked to ameliorate such concerns (Whelan, Moon & Orlitzky, 2009). Second, as activists have recognized that, by targeting MNCs at the top, they can potentially influence a significant number of activities and organizations below (e.g. through supply chains), CSR has come to be used as a lever to promote 'best practice': particularly when the changes sought would prove next to impossible through state or international organizations (see also, Keck & Sikkink, 1998).

Third, the emergence of new, complex and truly global concerns, such as sustainable development, are providing a major spur to current CSR practices and our understandings thereof. Whereas people have historically tended to treat social, economic and environmental concerns, as separate categories, there are clear trends towards their interrelation (Montiel, 2008: 260). Consequently, it has become easier to argue that MNCs have responsibilities with regard to issues that they may have once appeared indirectly related to at best. Links between climate change, the livestock industry, and hamburgers (e.g. McDonalds') – which previously tended to slip under the broader public's radar – provide a case in point.

As megacorporations can be roughly conceived as MNCs with a very broad scope of influence, a given megacorporation will be embroiled, more or less continuously, in CSR concerns. Similarly, the fact that many MNCs are already conceived as political-economic hybrids, suggests that any megacorporation worthy of the name will need to be widely recognized as such too.

Political-Economic Hybrid

In a sense, any corporation that focuses on the provision of goods and services, and that is somehow enabled by political structures, is a political-economic hybrid. The logic being that, if sufficient discontent were to arise amongst the masses, then the corporate form itself could be rendered dysfunctional. Likewise, and somewhat more realistically as of the time of writing, it is possible that protectionist–populist rhetoric amongst political leaders (Dutt & Mitra, 2018) could boil over, and result in significant changes needing to be made to the border criss-crossing structures that make MNCs feasible.

On top of these considerations – which relate to the simple existence of corporate forms – considerations that relate to specific products and markets can also result in corporations seeking political influence. Whatever the specific motivation, such influence can take the form of (legal) lobbying on the one hand; or of (illegal) bribes or gift-giving on the other (Lawton, McGuire & Rajwani, 2012). Whilst this second type of political influence can be found everywhere, it is often 'perceived' (Transparency International, 2018) as being most prevalent in non-Western countries (Lawton et al., 2012: 92).

Different types of corporations can also be conceived as political-economic hybrids due to their taking on responsibilities that people currently associate with states. Thus, the discharging of a whole host of 'nice' political responsibilities – such as the provision of education, health care, shelter and so on – is now commonly associated not just with state or civil society actors but also with profit-focused corporations (Matten & Crane, 2005). And like centuries of mercenaries before them, private security and military corporations are currently involved in the much 'nastier' side of politics too (Elms & Phillips, 2009).

As it has become commonplace to focus on the US government's use of private military corporations (US Department of Defense, 2018), it is important to note that other governments also make use of such services. The Russian government, for instance, has made significant use of private military companies as part of ongoing concerns in Syria. As private military companies are illegal in Russia, the companies employed by the Russian state (e.g. the Wagener Group) are formally situated or registered elsewhere (e.g. Argentina). Whilst this might seem a cumbersome way of fighting a war, it has the benefit of enabling the Russian government to 'maintain plausible deniability' of direct involvement in the Syrian conflict (Ayres, 2018).

Further to exerting influence over state structures and political elites, and further to their being directly involved in both the nice and nasty side of politics, megacorporations can be considered political-economic hybrids due to their capacity to disrupt existing class structures and privileges throughout societies more generally. Whether it is through transforming the means of production and consumption, creating new concentrations of wealth (and poverty) or building new markets, megacorporations will tend to play a central role in the transformation of extant social relations and hierarchies (e.g. Marx & Engels, 1848).

Finally, corporations are also recognized as political-economic actors due to the roles they can play in non-state (Bernstein & Cashore, 2007) and multi-actor (Moon, 2014: 87–100) governance processes. Even more directly, corporations can often be conceived as political-economic actors as a result of what they produce: e.g. arms manufacturers transform coercive capacities; social media companies our capacities for free speech (Whelan, 2017). As well as influencing state actors, and their taking on state-like functions, then, megacorporations will need to be engaged in productive activities that are readily identified as being of political-economic importance if they are to deserve their mega status.

Existential Impacts

Alongside their global scale and broad scope, their possession of monopolistic power, their links to CSR concerns and their political-economic hybridity, megacorporations are characterized by their existential impacts. Simply put, existential impacts refer to developments that alter the constraints that shape how people live their lives and experience the world. As detailed below, these constraints can manifest in conceptual and concrete form.

The conceptual aspect of existential constraints relates to our never experiencing the world independent of frames of reference. The recognition of such constraints traces back at least as far as Kant's distinction between phenomena (what we experience) and noumena (things in themselves) (e.g. Foucault, 1970: 242–244), and has subsequently taken a variety of forms. Suffice it to note that it is currently commonplace to suggest that individuals make use of institutionalized cognitive frameworks – that are temporally and/or spatially limited to varying degrees; and that have not been deliberately designed or constructed by any one person – to construct phenomena and organize their activities (e.g. Descola, 2013).

Although rarely discussed, the idea that specific corporations can impact upon conceptual constraints is not without precedent. The 'McDonaldization Thesis' – which posits that, in embodying the rationalization principles that Weber (1978) associated with modern bureaucracies, the American fast-food retailer McDonald's became an 'alluring model' that 'virtually every … sector of society' felt it should replicate – provides one illustration (Ritzer, 1996: 292).

Whereas conceptual existential constraints exist 'inside' our heads, concrete existential constraints (are presumed to) exist on the 'outside'. The importance of such constraints, which are 'independent of our own volition' (Berger & Luckman, 1966: 13) and cannot be wished away, are impossible to overstate. When put in positive terms – as Kant (1998) did in writing of the dove that flies because, and not in spite, of the air that resists it – such constraints are identified as that which make any progress possible. And when put in negative terms, as per Schopenhauer (1969), what one might say is that, in the absence of the concrete constraints that forever frustrate, a given individual, or their will, would cease to exist.

Additional to other considerations, the recognition of concrete existential constraints results in other people appearing 'as a kind of thick natural phenomenon' (Foucault, 2007: 71) that needs accounting for in daily life. Whilst such concrete constraints cannot simply 'be changed by decree' (Ibid.), they can be altered. Amphetamines like Adderall and Ritalin, which are made by Shire and Novartis respectively, can transform the learning capacities of those with attention deficit disorders. Likewise, the Cochlear implant, an electronic medical device which replaces the function of the inner ear, can enable those who are hearing impaired.

As this suggests, corporations of different shapes and sizes have long made significant profits through changing the concrete existential limits that different groups of people face. In light of such, it is here proposed that if a corporation is to be conceived as a megacorporation, then it will, alongside the other characteristics already outlined, need to impact on existential constraints for large numbers of people worldwide.

The English East India Company

Under its original guise of 'The Company of Merchants of London trading into the East Indies', what came to be known as the English East India Company received its initial royal charter on 31 December 1600 (Keay, 1991: 9). With the help of various governance changes made throughout its life, the Company remained independent until 1859, when the British government nationalized it (Stern, 2011: 209) following a 'popular revolt' sparked by the 'mutiny of disconnected sepoy regiments: i.e. Indian soldiers in the service of the East India Company' (Erll, 2009: 109). According to Dalrymple (2019: 293), the Company's response to this rebellion – which involved the 'hanging and murdering' of 'many tens of thousands of suspected rebels in the bazaar towns that lined the Ganges' – was 'probably the bloodiest episode in the entire history of British colonialism'.

As this horrific epitaph indicates, the Company proved to be more powerful than similar organizations that it originally competed with: e.g. the Dutch East India Company (Verenigde Oostindische Compagnie) that was founded in 1602 (Robins, 2012: 13). On first impressions, then, the English East India Company (the Company) was, as Dalrymple (2015, 2019) has vaguely suggested, a megacorporation. As the following discussions show that the Company was also characterized by its monopoly power, corporate social responsibility concerns, political-economic hybridity and its existential impacts, it is proposed that these first impressions are correct.

Monopoly

In the original grant of 1600, Elizabeth I provided the Company with a guaranteed monopoly of Eastern trade for a period of fifteen years. In light of 'encouraging developments', Elizabeth's successor and the first king of Great Britain, James I, used a new charter in 1609 to make the Company's monopoly indefinite and more capacious (Keay, 1991: 39). Whilst such privilege was constantly threatened and challenged, the Company managed to enjoy a number of very important monopolies in the triangular trade between Britain, China and India over the centuries.

First, the Company monopolized trade between India and England. As certain English manufactures (e.g. woolens) struggled to find any sort of significant market in India (and subsequently in China), the purchasing and import of Indian products was, for considerable periods of time – and much to the annoyance of the day's mercantilists (Khan, 1923: 52–53, 169–70) – almost entirely financed by the export of gold and silver (Chaudhuri, 1968; Chung, 1973).

Second, the Company came to monopolize all opium production in India in the second half of the eighteenth century under the leadership of Indian Governor General Lord Warren Hastings (Keay, 1991: 431). This monopoly was to prove particularly important: for it was through the selling of opium in China that the Company was able to use Indian produce, rather than bullion from England, to fund the Company's purchasing of Chinese tea (Chung, 1973). It also proved to be of significant geopolitical importance, as it helped initiate China's century of humiliation.

Third, the Company monopolized the sale of Chinese tea in England. Fuelled by the 'Englishman's newly acquired thirst', tea had become, by 1770, 'the single most important item in the Company's portfolio and the value of the China trade had come to rival that of all its Indian settlements combined' (Keay, 1991: 349). So great was this thirst that, 'sales of tea, which had averaged 6.8 billion pounds a year during the 1770s, soared to 19.7 million pounds a year during the 1790s' (Bowen, 1998: 534–535). Indeed, tea sales were still going strong fifty years later, when they once again doubled over a fifteen-year period prior to the Company losing its independence (Chung, 1973: 416). In many ways, the English obsession with tea, which continues through to the present day, is due to the Company.

Corporate Social Responsibility Concerns

One of the charges often levelled against the Company was that, whilst it benefitted from the monopoly it possessed, its home country did not. As Adam Smith (1999: 158) wrote:

since the establishment of the English East India Company ... the other inhabitants of England, over and above being excluded from the trade, must have paid in the price of the East India goods which they have consumed, not only for all the extraordinary profits which the company may have made upon those goods in consequence of their monopoly, but for all the extraordinary waste which the fraud and abuse, inseparable from the management of the affairs of so great a company, must necessarily have occasioned.

But what was even worse than all these 'bad effects ... put together', according to Smith (1999: 145), was the example being set by the leaders and owners of such a monopoly: for he feared that as their preference for expensive luxury over sober virtue trickled down, the industry they led would become increasingly 'dissolute and disorderly'. This later set of fears, in their turn, were supplemented by the belief that the ostentatious and much satirized 'nabobs' (Bowen, 2006: 16) who had made their fortunes through the 'side trades' and many corruptions the Company enabled (Smith, 1999: 166), were 'infecting the domestic political system and threatening constitutional liberties' (Bowen, 1998: 542). According to Edmund Burke (1788: 17), the 'enormous wealth' that was pouring 'into this country from India through a thousand channels, publick and concealed', was responsible for no less than the undermining of the British Empire.

Despite their significance, the concerns the Company was giving rise to in England appeared small in comparison to those it was associated with in India. Smith (1999: 155) for one, proposed that whilst the 'discovery of America, and that of a passage to the East Indies by the Cape of Good Hope, are the two greatest and most important events recorded in the history of mankind', they had resulted in little joy for the natives themselves: 'for all the commercial benefits which can have resulted from those events have been sunk and lost in the dreadful misfortunes which they have occasioned'.

And according to Burke (1783: 124–125), the underlying problem was that

[e]very rupee of profit made by an Englishman is lost forever to India ... [the Company] has erected no churches, no hospitals ... built no bridges, made no high roads, cut no navigations, dug out no reservoirs. Every other conqueror of every other description has left some monument, either of state or beneficence, behind him. Were we [i.e. the Company] to be driven out of India this day, nothing would remain, to tell that it had been possessed, during the inglorious period of our dominion, by any thing better than the ouran-outang or the tiger.

In contrast to such claims, the Company tended to tell a more positive story. To that end, and much like other organizations and departments that were responsible for England's colonial territories (Bowen, 2006: 153), the Company continuously professed 'its desire to protect the happiness and prosperity of the Indian population' (Bowen, 1998: 541). If one thinks such statements indicative of a proactive response to the recognition of real social problems, then they will paint the Company in a positive light. If, on the other hand, one perceives such proclamations as a reaction to critical concerns voiced by the likes of Burke and Smith, then the Company is more likely to be seen as having been engaged in nothing more than public relations spin.

Political-Economic Hybrid

A currently popular idea is that the adoption of explicit political responsibilities and structures can enable economic actors, and

MNCs in particular, to (re)assert or (re)construct their legitimacy (e.g. Matten & Crane, 2005; Scherer & Palazzo, 2011). For the English East India Company, however – whose most prominent responsibility concerns emerged after it became 'a territorial power in South Asia in the mid-eighteenth century' (Stern, 2011: 3) – things seem to have worked the other way around.

In a series of events that read like a Boys' Own Adventure for budding colonialists – and in duly noting that it 'had already been a form of government -... in Asia for some time' (Ibid.) – the Company was transformed between 1750 and 1770 into a Company 'state' with clear sovereign powers (Bowen, 2006: 5–10). For a great many, this transformation was a cause for concern. In a letter written in 1759, no less than Robert Clive – who led the Company's conquest of Bengal in the Battle of Plassey a few years earlier – explicitly stated that the sovereignty of Bengal was 'too extensive for a mercantile company', and that the Company should 'concentrate on that for which it was constituted – "trading to the East Indies"' (Keay, 1991: 362–363). And from amongst the Company's external critics, one can once again find Smith (1999: 164) sniping that a company of merchants was seemingly 'incapable of considering themselves as sovereigns, even after they have become such. Trade, or buying in order to sell again, they still consider as their principal business, and by a strange absurdity regard the character of the sovereign as but an appendix to that of the merchant'.

Burke (1783: 164–166) was likewise concerned that, whilst the Company had proven very successful in collecting both political and economic responsibilities, it had failed to discharge either. He thought that one could find 'no trace of equitable government' in the Company's politics, and 'not one trace of commercial principle' in its 'mercantile dealing'. Moreover, Burke believed it was 'evident beyond doubt' that the Company's abuses of the 'poor', 'oppressed', 'natives of India', were 'regular, permanent and systematical'. In other words, Burke considered the Company to be 'absolutely incorrigible' (Ibid.).

Whether consciously or not, Company employees often distanced themselves from such damning sentiment, preferring to align themselves with 'modern assumptions ... about the nation-state as the ultimate political and social community' (Stern, 2011: 8–9). Thus, at the House of Commons in 1767, the Company's secretary Robert

James declared 'that "We don't want conquest and power; it is commercial interest only we look for"'; and 'during the late eighteenth century an enormous amount of visual art, and especially paintings of East Indiamen, continued to project a powerful and enduring image of the Company as a maritime trading organization' (Bowen, 2006: 8–9). Suffice it to note that, as the Company's army is reported to have grown from 18,000 in 1763 to 102,000 in 1796 (Schmidt, 1995: 61), such de-hybridizing claims and public representations were either misguided, or entirely disingenuous.

Existential Impacts

The Company had a set of complexly interrelated impacts on both concrete and conceptual existential constraints. In terms of the former, the Company was associated with two developments – (1) the coppering of the Company's 'Indiamen' hulls and (2) navigational advances enabled by the analysis of maritime information that was collected and stored at the East India House headquarters in London (Bowen, 2006: 155) – that shortened voyage times by as much as a third in the late eighteenth and early nineteenth centuries (Solar & Luchens, 2016).

Whilst significant in their own right, such impacts appear limited relative to the more conceptual impacts that the Company had as a result of its extensive record-keeping. As even critics like Burke (1788: 51–53) acknowledged, the Company's 'government of writing; a government of record', was so 'excellent' and 'admirably fitted for the government of a remote, large, disjointed empire … that human wisdom has never exceeded it'. This structure, Burke (1788: 53) went on, was underpinned by an express covenant that obliged the Company's servants:

to keep a journal or diary of all their transactions, publick and private … [and] as a corrective upon that diary, to keep a letterbook, in which all their letters are to be regularly entered. And they are bound, by the same covenant, to produce all those books upon requisition … But, as the great corrective of all, they [i.e. the Company] have contrived, that every proceeding in publick council shall be written: no debates merely verbal. The arguments, first or last, are to be in writing, and recorded.

It is not for nothing, then, that the Company's men are said to 'have lived by the ledger and ruled with the quill' (Keay, 1991: 169); and that the resultant records – which comprise more than four hundred volumes for the years 1660–1760 alone (Chaudhuri, 1978: xv) – have been conceived as potentially inexhaustible (Keay, 1991: 169). As an 'empire of information' (Bowen, 2006: 152), the Company anticipated and perhaps 'indirectly contributed to the eventual creation of modern business corporations and the abstract concept of the "firm" as the main regulator through which the whole complex of economic production could take place' (Chaudhuri, 1978: 19). Moreover, in seeking 'better knowledge of the societies, cultures, and economies' that were brought under its control, and in being motivated 'by the firmly held belief that the possession of information represented the key to effective administration' (Bowen, 2006: 152), the Company has had a significant impact on how we make sense of, and compare, human societies.

Much of the Company's impact in this later regard originated in the latter half of the eighteenth century, when it began creating hubs of intellectual activity like the Asiatic Society of Bengal that was founded by William Jones in 1784, and that 'quickly became the most important learned society in the British colonies' (Drayton, 1988: 243). Prior to his leaving England for India in 1783, 'Jones was already a master of Arabic, Hebrew and Persian'. And, upon starting as a Company-appointed judge in Calcutta, he 'began the course of personal study that was to gather in, to rope off, to domesticate the Orient and thereby turn it into a provenance of European learning' (Said, 2003: 77–78).

To make sense of Jones' and the Company's role in the creation and diffusion of 'orientalism' – the idea that Westerners are, and that Arab–Orientals are not, 'rational, peaceful, liberal, logical, capable of holding real values, without natural suspicion' – Said (2003: 49, 78) has proposed that the law's significance must be recognized. Specifically, Said (2003: 78) has noted that prior to Jones' arrival in India, 'Warren Hastings had decided that Indians were to be ruled by their own laws'. Given that Sanskrit code of laws for practical use then only existed in Persian translation, and that 'no Englishman at the time knew Sanskrit well enough to consult the original texts', this was a considerable task (Ibid.). In playing a key role in it – and in being motivated to 'rule and to learn ... to compare Orient with Occident' – 'Jones acquired the effective knowledge of the Orient and of Orientals that was later to make him the undisputed founder ... of Orientalism' (Ibid.).

The long-lasting impacts associated with Jones' and the Company's activities do not make for flattering reading. The Company's quest for knowledge of the non-Western world can be seen to have helped justify the British belief – which appears to have been particularly prevalent throughout the nineteenth century (in the work of Company employees James and John Stuart Mill for example) – that British imperial rule was necessary to advance civilizations perceived as less 'developed' (Dodson, 2007: 66–67; Said, 2003: 14). It also appears to have contributed to the internalization of orientalism's basic thesis amongst the Orient's population itself.

As Said (2003: 25) has lamented, the investment that he made in writing *Orientalism* derived from his

awareness of being an "Oriental" as a child growing up in two British colonies. All of my education, in those colonies (Palestine and Egypt) and in the United States, has been Western, and yet that deep early awareness has persisted. In many ways my study of Orientalism has been an attempt to inventory the traces upon me, the Oriental subject, of the culture whose domination has been so powerful a factor in the life of all Orientals.

As such examples demonstrate, the East India Company has had a long-lasting, and often deeply problematic, existential impact on people around the world. As the Company was also characterized by its global scale and broad scope, its monopolistic power, its CSR concerns, and its political-economic hybridity, it constitutes a clear, historical example of a megacorporation.

Summary

This chapter has proposed that normal corporations, MNCs, total corporations and megacorporations, can be distinguished from one another on the grounds of their relative scale (local or global) and scope (narrow or broad). Additionally, this chapter has proposed that megacorporations – such as the English East India Company – are characterized by their tending towards monopolistic power in one or more of their domains; by their being consistently involved in a variety of corporate social responsibility concerns; by their simultaneously being of political and economic import; and by their having a fundamental impact on how people understand and live their lives. Given such demanding criteria, there can never be many, and may not be any, megacorporations, at a given point in time. Yet as Chapter 3 demonstrates, there is at least one megacorporation to have emerged in the twenty-first century: Alphabet.

3 | *Alphabet*

As a megacorporation, Alphabet is, by definition, an organizational agent of the highest degree. Nevertheless, it is neither entirely self-defined nor self-created. In particular, it has been shaped by the Silicon Valley context from within which it emerged. Accordingly, the chapter's first section provides an overview of the key actors and sectors that have helped define, and mythologize, Silicon Valley. Following this, Google's emergence, success and transformation are described and explained. Then, and in accord with the characteristics detailed in Chapter 2, Alphabet is shown to be a megacorporation. In contrast to As Alphabet's global scale and broad scope, monopolistic tendencies, corporate social responsibility (CSR) concerns and political-economic hybridity, all of which are described in the present chapter, the chapter's summary notes that the megacorporation's more complex existential impacts – on the extent, and our experience of, the past and the future – are focused on throughout the book's second part.

Silicon Valley

Google, and subsequently Alphabet, was founded by Sergey Brin and Larry Page. Born in Moscow and Michigan respectively, Brin's and Page's parents both had strong technological and scientific backgrounds. In light of such, and as both Brin and Page attended Montessori schools, Vise (2005: 22) has proposed that scholarship 'was not just emphasized in their homes: it was treasured'. Whilst such biographical details are interesting, what is arguably more important to the rise of Google and Alphabet is that Brin and Page met when they were PhD students at Stanford University in California's Silicon Valley.

Although the name Silicon Valley was only first coined in a three-part series that Dan Hoefller wrote on 'the semi-conductor industry in the Bay Area' in 1971 (Keeney, 2000: 3), its origins trace back to 1908, when Stanford graduate Cyril Elwell was having difficulties getting 'a spark-based radio telegraph system to work' (Sturgeon, 2000: 19). To address his problems, Elwell travelled to Copenhagen to negotiate a deal for an arc transmitter invented by Dr Vladimir Poulsen. When he came back to Stanford's hometown of Palo Alto in 1909, Elwell turned to the University for help with finance, and formed a company 'to provide wireless telephone and telegraph services on the Pacific Coast' (Ibid.).

Elwell's Federal Telegraph Corporation, or what originally went by the name of Poulsen Wireless Telephone and Telegraph, soon came to be one of the US Navy's 'darlings' due to the success of the arc transmitters it produced for shipboard use. Given considerable demand, Elwell decided to donate a 12-kilowatt arc to Stanford in exchange for access to the Stanford High Voltage Laboratory and the research and development opportunities it provided. This exchange was a good deal all round: for it enabled the Federal Telegraph Corporation to improve the Poulsen arc, the Navy its communications, and Stanford its publications (Sturgeon, 2000). Whilst interesting in and of itself, the more general importance of this foundational story is that it highlights the role of three actors that continue to contribute to the Valley's success, and that are quickly discussed in turn below: i.e. Stanford University, entrepreneurs and the US military.

Stanford University

Whilst other institutes such as the University of California, Berkeley, have also contributed to the success of Silicon Valley, it is the role of Stanford University, and of Frederick Terman in particular, that is often emphasized. The 'son of an eminent Stanford psychologist', Terman grew up on the Stanford campus and 'took his undergraduate degree there' (Leslie, 2000: 49). After a number of years at Massachusetts Institute of Technology (MIT), Terman returned to Stanford in 1925, where he 'launched an aggressive, commercially oriented programme in radio electronics' that included Hewlett-Packard's founders amongst its alumni (Leslie, 2000: 51–52; see also, Saxenian, 1994: 20). Then, more than twenty years later, and with his having spent time at Harvard's Radio Research Laboratory during World War II, Terman proceeded to become Stanford's dean of engineering in 1946.

In recognizing that the knowledge revolutionizing electronics in the post–World War II era had been government sponsored, and was publicly accessible, Terman and his team decided to make use of it (Leslie, 2000: 54). As evidenced by the creation of firms such as Varian Associates, this strategy proved very successful. Formed in 1948, Varian had interests in military and medical technologies, and was the first tenant of Stanford Industrial Park. Other, and perhaps better known, firms, such as General Electric, Eastman Kodak and Hewlett-Packard, were soon to follow. Subsequently, the Stanford Industrial Park – which is now known as the Stanford Research Park (Website), and which portrays itself as 'community of and for people who seek to invent the future' – had forty-two companies providing employment for around 12,000 people by 1965 (Quigley & Huffman, 2002: 405). By way of these and other initiatives, Terman has proven central to the building of 'a center of high technology around Stanford' (Ibid.).

Entrepreneurs

The second aspect of Silicon Valley's many successes are its businesses and entrepreneurs. Some of the current businesses to emerge from, or be located within, the Bay Area include Apple, Facebook and Tesla. As such companies are commonly considered amongst the world's most powerful and innovative, it is unsurprising that the heroes of Silicon Valley have long been 'the successful entrepreneurs who have taken aggressive professional and technical risks: the garage thinkers who created successful companies' (Saxenian, 1994: 31). These entrepreneurial heroes, however, have rarely, if ever, acted alone. In particular, they have relied on the financial resources of venture capitalists, of which Silicon Valley has historically had a 'huge presence' relative to other 'high-tech clusters around the world' (Ferrary & Granoveter, 2009: 329).

Although there is a tradition of wealthy individuals investing risk capital in the San Francisco Bay Area as far back as the 1920s, venture capital only came to take its current form when the US federal government passed the 'Small Business Act of 1958 which provided up to $300,000 in government matching money for $150,000 in investments by a person or institution wishing to establish' a small corporation (Keeney & Florida, 2000: 107). Venture capitalists take an equity stake in companies in the hope of earning huge capital gains.

Historically, their 'rule of thumb' has been that, 'for every ten investments, three are complete losses; another three or four neither succeed nor fail … another two or three return three or more times the initial investment; and one, or perhaps, two investments return more than ten times the initial investment' (Keeney & Florida, 2000: 101). In other words, venture capitalists aim at striking a 'balance between errors of omission, not investing when one should, and errors of commission, investing when one should not' (Ibid.). This sort of attitude to risk and innovation, it will be shown below, is a key aspect of Alphabet's emergence.

United States Military

The military is the third actor/sector to have played a key role in Silicon Valley. Lockheed Missiles and Space (now part of Lockheed Martin) has received significant amounts of military funding and been a significant employer of people since it first went to Silicon Valley in 1956; and the Stanford Research Institute – 'a contract research institute spun off from the university in the wake of student antiwar protests in 1970', has likewise been a long-term recipient of US Defense Agency funding (Leslie, 2000: 61, 66). Whilst Frederick Terman tended to understate the importance of Defense money when trying to package and sell Silicon Valley, it is clear that the academic-industrial-military complex has been alive and well in the Bay Area for a considerable period of time (Leslie & Kargon, 1996: 438).

As the liberal and creative culture popularly associated with Silicon Valley might seem remote from the bureaucratized hierarchies associated with the military, it helps to remember that the origins of digital computing trace back to John von Neumann's use of IBM punched card equipment as part of the Los Alamos atomic bomb project, and to his work at the Institute for Advanced Study in Princeton in the late 1940s and early 1950s that was in part funded by the US military (Aspray, 1992). It also helps to remember that the origins of the Internet trace back to ARPANET (Advanced Research Projects Agency Network), which was created by the US Defense Department in the late 1960s to save taxpayers' money by enabling researchers to make the most of computing power then available (or as the myth has it, to ensure that the US communications system could survive a nuclear attack (Naughton 1999: 85)).

Although these and other projects – such as MIT's Radiation Laboratory, which was founded in late 1940 to 'develop more effective ways to track and shoot down the bombers then plaguing Britain' – 'operated with the support of large bureaucracies', they were also 'interdisciplinary and interinstitutional collaborations' characterized by 'flexible, collaborative work and a distinctly nonhierarchical management style' (Turner, 2006: 17–19). Somewhat paradoxically, then, historical works on the development of the hacker ethic – which emphasizes free access to information over tightly held information, decentralization over bureaucracy, and revealed skills over formal credentials – clearly recognize the role of big organizations (Levy, 2010: 23–26). So too have works on the history of cyberculture, which have shown that 'flexible, conscious-centred work practices of the post-industrial society' are, to some considerable extent, the product of much more fixed and rigid organizational structures (Turner, 2006: 245).

Google

Larry Page and Sergey Brin first met on the Stanford PhD programme in the summer of 1995, the beginning of the first dotcom era. As for many during this feverish time of technology start-ups and initial public offerings (IPO) (Vise, 2005: 29; Myers West, 2019), things moved quickly for Page and Brin. In 1996 they created the new internet search technique PageRank. In 1997 they provided the search engine built on PageRank with the mathematical moniker of Google (a play on a googol – 1 followed by 100 zeros) and registered the associated domain name of google.com. Then, on 4 September 1998, they incorporated Google (Edwards, 2011: xi–xii; Levy, 2011: 21–34; Google, Website A). Along with Eric Schmidt, who prior to being named as Google's CEO in 2001 had worked at Sun Microsystems and Novell, Brin and Page agreed, one month prior to going public in 2004, to manage the company for twenty years (Google, Website A; Lashinsky, 2008).

As it turns out, they did not quite hit their twenty-year target, with all three having stepped away from management by the end of 2019, when Sundar Pichai added the Alphabet CEO role to the Google CEO role he has had since 2015 (Statt, 2019). Nevertheless, Brin and Page, and to a lesser extent Schmidt, continue to exert control over Google (and now Alphabet) through ownership of stocks. As detailed in the last annual report Google published prior to Alphabet's creation, 'Larry, Sergey, and Eric beneficially owned approximately 92.5% of our [i.e. Google's] outstanding Class B common stock, which represented approximately 60.1% of the voting power of our outstanding capital stock' (Google, 2015: 14). These ownership stakes, which have remained roughly the same since Alphabet's formation, have made Page, Brin and Schmidt immensely wealthy. At last count, Page's net worth was $50.8 billion, Brin's $49.8 billion and Schmidt's $12.9 billion – respectively placing them at 10th, 14th and 101st on Forbes' billionaires list in 2019.

Google's successes have also proven a windfall for Stanford due to it 'owning key technology used by Google', and that Google paid for in 'stock and cash for an exclusive licensing partnership, plus annual royalties' (Grimes, 2004). This licensing arrangement, which lasted until 2011, generated around $337 million for Stanford (Stanford News, 2012). As the University had earned $1.3 billion from similar licensing arrangements at the time, and given that 'Stanford's public-relations arm proclaims that five thousand companies "trace their origins to Stanford ideas or to Stanford faculty and students"' (Auletta, 2012), this has to be considered a major financial success. The fact that John L. Hennessey, Stanford's president from 2000 to 2016, was first named as a director of Google in April 2004 (prior to Google's initial public offering), and was named as Alphabet's chairman in February 2018, suggests that Brin and Page are fully appreciative of the support they have received from the University.

Along with the Stanford link, Google seeks to maintain links to the broader hacker culture of Silicon Valley. Amongst other things, Google has a long-established affinity with the Burning Man festival that was first held in 1986, and which has been held annually in the Black Rock Desert, Nevada, since 1997. The first doodle Google placed on the Google landing page in August 1998 incorporated the festival's 'stick figure in the [Google] logo announcing to site visitors that the entire staff was playing hooky at the Burning Man Festival' (Google, Website A). More recently, it has been rumored that Sergey Brin, along with Elon Musk and 'Airbnb executive and Burning Man board member Chip Conley', helped the festival's organizers purchase a sizable property in Washoe County Nevada known as 'Fly Ranch', 'where it plans to build a year-round location' (Bowles, 2016). If this turns out to be the case, then Burning Man will become even more 'Googley' than Google likes to suggest it already is (e.g. Fernstein, 2014; Turner, 2009).

In these sorts of ways, Google's success has been clearly informed by Stanford University and the broader Silicon Valley context. Nevertheless, it has also been informed by a number of more specific considerations. Three in particular – algorithms, advertising and copyright – warrant further attention.

Algorithms

'Google's first brilliant innovation was, of course, its [core] search algorithm', PageRank (Vaidhyanathan, 2011: 52). Constructed as part of Brin's and Page's PhD work, PageRank was, as the name suggests, based on Larry Page's theory that 'counting the number of links pointing to a Web site was a way of ranking the site's popularity' (Vise, 2005: 37). And in a nod to his academic heritage, the algorithm's formation was also informed by Page's recognition that scholarly works are often judged by the total number of citations, or links, they receive (Ibid.).

Providing a much-advanced means of searching what had up until then been the 'dynamic and messy ... World Wide Web' (Vaidhyanathan, 2011: 61), Google proved popular as soon it was made 'available internally to [Stanford] students, faculty, and administrators at google.standford.edu' in 1997 (Vise, 2005: 39). Whilst they failed in their efforts to interest both AltaVista and Yahoo! in what they were doing (two leading web companies of the time), Page and Brin did manage to attract the interest of angel investor Andy Bechtolsheim, who, having been convinced that their approach 'enabled Google to produce superior search results', provided them with an initial $100,000 in August 1998 (Vise, 2005: 40–48).

Whilst Google professes to believe that 'open source is good for everyone' (Google Open Source, Website), its search algorithms have long been kept as trade secrets (Levy, 2011: 56; Lohr, 2011). Whenever it has had to respond to calls to make its core search algorithms public knowledge, or at least accessible to a restricted regulatory audience (Pasquale, 2010), what the search giant has tended to argue is that, in addition to its having a keen commercial interest in keeping its results pure, it should be allowed to keep its algorithms secret so as to prevent the gaming of search results by external actors (Elgesem, 2008; Levy, 2011: 56–57). In this fashion, Google has continuously sought to suggest that its exclusive control of its core search algorithms is consistent with the public good.

Advertising

Levy (2011: 7) proposes that 'Google search is part of our lives, and [that] its ad system is the most important commercial product of the Internet age'. Vaidhyanathan (2011: 26) is even more direct when he suggests that 'Google's core business isn't facilitating searches, its selling advertising space – or rather, selling our attention to advertisers and managing both the price it charges for access to our attention and the relative visibility of those advertisements'. In short, and as indicated by Google earning around $46 billion in revenues in the fourth quarter of 2019 alone, Google is an advertiser's wet dream.

Back in 1998, however, when they were still just starting out, Brin and Page appear to have been less certain as to the merits of linking search and advertising (Vise, 2005: 85). Hence, in the first appendix to their snappily titled piece – *The Anatomy of a Large-Scale Hypertextual Web Search Engine* – Brin and Page (1998) wrote:

advertising income often provides an incentive to provide poor quality search results ... However, there will always be money from advertisers who want a customer to switch products, or have something that is genuinely new. But we believe the issue of advertising causes enough mixed incentives that it is crucial to have a competitive search engine that is transparent and in the academic realm.

As history has revealed, this mealy-mouthed statement was to quickly prove its utility for Brin and Page: for in July 1999, with more than seven million searches per day, and little by way of licensing revenues (Vise, 2005: 85), Google began to sell advertising. Moreover, they sought to address any tensions felt by making ads non-intrusive and separate from the results returned for a given search, and by convincing themselves at least, that 'information in ads could even be as valuable to users as the results Google provided from search queries' (Levy, 2011: 78).

Google appears to have taken a number of additional steps to try to account for some of Brin's and Page's initial concerns about advertising. Most notably, Google's infamous 'Don't be evil' motto, which dates back to at least July 2001 (Levy, 2011: 144; see also, Statt, 2019), can be seen to have placed some sort of moral constraints on advertising. To this end, Page and Brin used the 'Don't be evil' section of Google's 2004 IPO letter to write that: 'Our search results are the best we know how to produce. They are unbiased and objective, and we do not accept payment for them or for inclusion or more frequent updating. We also display advertising ... and we label it clearly ... similar to a well-run newspaper'. Likewise, Google's decision to go with a model in which the winner of an advertising auction 'wouldn't be charged for the amount of his victorious bid but instead would pay a penny more than the runner-up bid' (Levy, 2011: 90), can be understood not just as a great low-bid minimization strategy, but as an attempt to make Google's advertising revenues more palatable to Brin and Page.

Copyright

Whereas Google's algorithms and advertising systems are more or less directly attributable to the company itself, a third part of its success, copyright laws, are not. Amongst other considerations, the fourth of the 'safe harbors' provided by Title II of the Digital Millennium Copyright Act (DMCA) that became law in October 1998, has played a clear role in Google's profitability (Whelan, 2019). The reason being that this fourth safe harbour enables Google to avoid liability for the widespread (if not thoroughgoing) copyright infringement that it facilitates (Chandler, 2013: 661), so long as Google receives and acts upon copyright infringement 'takedown' requests from copyright holders such as record labels, movie studios and game makers (McWane, 2001: 95–96).

That the DMCA's safe harbor provisions are central to Google's success is clear from Google's vigorous opposition to the Stop Online Piracy Act and the Protect Intellectual Property Act that were debated in the US in 2011 and 2012 respectively. These proposed acts, which threatened to undermine the DMCA's safe harbor protections, ultimately proved unsuccessful. Whilst duly noting that the failure of the proposed acts is not solely attributable to Google (Benkler et al., 2013), Google – and various organizations that it has clear (historical) connections to: e.g. the Electronic Frontier Foundation, Mozilla, the New

America Foundation – numbered amongst its more prominent opponents (Whelan, 2019).

As Benkler et al. (2013: 37) have written, the culmination of the debate was marked

with an explosion of action and attention on January 18, 2012, when thousands of sites were blacked out ... Whilst Google's landing page remained operable, it offered a link to its "End piracy, not liberty" petition page. Millions of people signed on. In the wake of this massive outpouring of opposition, both the House and Senate versions of the bill were shelved.

Given that more than 4.5 million people signed the petition, *LA Times* reporter Deborah Netburn (2012) was led to remark that 'when Google speaks, the world listens'. According to David Drummond (2012), Google's former Chief Legal Officer, the company's opposition to the bills was due to their being an ineffective means of actually stopping piracy; due to their containing filtering powers that were 'on the wish list of oppressive regimes' worldwide; and due to their potential to undermine the internet industry's 'track record of innovations and job creation'. Further to this, it would seem that Google's opposition to the bills was informed by the significant threat they presented to its business model.

Whilst Google is very strongly inclined to argue that everyone benefits from the increased access to (copyrighted) content that it enables, and whilst Google clearly makes considerable efforts to comply with copyright takedown requests, the entertainment and publishing industries remain sceptical. Amongst others, Rupert Murdoch and News Corp have engaged in a long-running public relations war against Google referring to the corporation as a 'platform for piracy' run by 'cynical management' (Barber, 2014). Murdoch has also suggested, on at least one occasion, that Google is worse than the US National Security Agency (Sharwood, 2014). Such snide remarks, suffice it to note, are likely motivated by Murdoch recognizing, correctly, that Google has undermined his business.

Post-Google, Pre-Alphabet

That Google has always been an advertising company (Vaidhyanathan, 2011: 26), and that the somewhat grubby business of selling ads 'is not a business that requires a PhD from Stanford or

MIT' (Morozov, 2015), is difficult to deny. Nevertheless, it seems myopic to suggest, as Morozov (2015) does, that 'all the exciting techy areas – from self-driving cars to smart energy to health – that Google has entered over the last few years', amount to little more than an attempt to repress the 'harsh reality' that it is 'still just an ad company'.

That Google has long been more than this was suggested by Page and Brin when they compared Google to The New York Times Company and Dow Jones, amongst others, in their 2004 IPO letter. It was also suggested by their noting, in the same letter, that 'a well functioning society should have abundant, free and unbiased access to high quality information'; and that the Google Foundation that was in the process of being formed at the time (now managed by Google.org), may someday be an 'institution' that would 'eclipse Google ... in terms of overall world impact by ambitiously applying innovation and significant resources to the largest of the world's problems' (Page & Brin, 2004). Although this last suggestion has proven wide of the mark, Google.org (Website) still reports that it provides $100 million in grants to charitable causes, and that Google employees spend more than 200,000 hours volunteering, each year. Whilst Bill and Melinda Gates may not be impressed by such numbers, most people would.

Brin's and Page's interest in moonshots provides another indication that they have always been thinking in a post-Google fashion. Purportedly first used by then Google vice president Marissa Mayer in 2007 to refer to the Google Books project (Toobin, 2007), the idea of moonshots – which traces back to President 'John Kennedy's famous challenge in 1961 to safely land a human on the moon by the end of the decade' (Stross, 2008: 90) – started to become more formalized with the creation of Google [X] in early 2010 (Levy, 2013). In its turn, the origins of what is now simply termed X, trace back to Larry Page convincing the then Stanford computer scientist, Sebastian Thrun, to help out with Google's Street View mapping project some time in 2007. Subsequently, Thrun, who 'had grown disenchanted with the pace of academia', was readily convinced to 'start the self-driving car project at Google in 2009', and to then expand 'the project into a full-fledged research lab' (Stone, 2013).

Originally a 'placeholder for a better name', the meaning of X is now taken to denote solutions that 'are better by a factor of 10', or to signify a willingness 'to build technologies that are 10 years away from making a large impact' (Gertner, 2014). Unlike the classic research labs it apparently wants to be compared with, however – such as the Manhattan Project and Bletchley Park – X is not afraid of failure. Thus, one of its more famous projects, the stillborn Google Glass, was not written off as sunk capital, but framed as 'a totally new product category ... [that raises] a totally new set of questions' (Stone, 2013).

That X was always meant to be associated with 'ideas far from Google's core search business' was made clear by Brin and Page, who, in first thinking of X, 'conceived of a position called Director of Other' in 2009 (Gertner, 2014). At times, all this talk of moonshots and otherness has given Google's 'investors a touch of heartburn' (Stone, 2013). Nevertheless, when such otherness and moonshots were writ large in the creation of Alphabet, Wall Street's reaction was 'ecstatic' (Morozov, 2015).

Alphabet: A Megacorporation

If you had to pick the day when Google began publicly transforming into the full-blown megacorporation that we now know as Alphabet, you could make worse choices than Friday, 31 October 2014. For it was on this day that Larry Page, the then Google CEO, looked forward 100 years and declared, in an interview with the *Financial Times*, that 'we could probably solve a lot of the issues we have as humans' (Waters, 2014). Such an idea, Page suggested, would mean that 'even Google's famously far-reaching mission statement, "to organize the world's information and make it universally accessible and useful"', would no longer prove ambitious enough (Ibid.).

In announcing the birth of Alphabet a year later, Page (2015) made two points as to the megacorporation's name. First, he noted that he and Sergey Brin liked Alphabet 'because it means a collection of letters that represent language, one of humanity's most important innovations, and is the core of how we index with Google search!' (Ibid.). Second, Page noted that both he and Brin also liked the name because it means 'alpha-bet (Alpha is investment return above benchmark), which we strive for!' (Ibid.).

Whilst no doubt insightful, neither exclamation really manages to capture the full import of the organizational transformation as well as the name does itself. For in moving from g to a to the z, the shift from Google to Alphabet quickly communicates the megacorporation's expansive interests, and its purported motivation with 'improving the lives of as many people as we can' (Page, 2015). More pragmatically, the motivation to form Alphabet was informed by the stated need to provide clearer and more accountable corporate governance structures by separating Alphabet's Google assets from what have come to be known as its Other Bets (see below). Importantly in this last regard, Page (2015) stated that this separation would enable the megacorporation's Other Bets to continue to do 'crazy things' (that could potentially prove to be hugely profitable). With this in mind, and when noted alongside Page's prior suggestion that the basic problem Google was facing was that 'even as it pours money into new ventures, the cash keeps piling up' (Waters, 2014), Alphabet's formation can be understood as a response to the problem of excess: to the need to 'gloriously or catastrophically' (Bataille, 1991: 21) spend those surpluses that Google's ad business could no longer absorb on its own.

In separating Google from its Other Bets, Alphabet's first annual report in 2015 revealed that whereas the Google segment was responsible for (approximately) $74.5 billion in revenues and $23.5 billion in income, the Other Bets segment was responsible for $0.4 billion in revenue and $3.5 billion in losses (Alphabet, 2016). Alphabet's 2019 annual report told a similar tale: with Google being responsible for approximately $161 billion in revenue and $42 billion in operating income; and Other Bets $659 million in revenue and $4.8 billion in losses (Alphabet, 2020; The Motley Fool, 2020). Given such figures, media reports have tended to emphasize that Alphabet's Other Bets are costing it a fortune (e.g. Statt, 2018).

Alphabet's Google segment includes its 'main products such as Ads, Android, Chrome, Commerce, Google Cloud, Google Maps, Google Play, Hardware, Search, and YouTube'; and its Other Bets segment the likes of 'Access, Calico, capitalG, GV, Verily, Waymo, and X' (Alphabet, 2020: 29). As this incomplete list indicates, and as shown in more, but still partial, detail, in Table 3.1 and Figure 3.1, Alphabet has the global scale and broad scope that is suggestive of its being a megacorporation.

The manner in which Alphabet can be seen to be the result of, or as giving rise to, a sort of double eversion of Google, is similarly suggestive. In the first instance, it can be seen that, by taking the general approach that Google has applied to search and other aspects of online life, and applying it to life in general (e.g. human health/well-being,

Table 3.1 *A Partial List of Alphabet Assets*

Alphabet	
Notable Personnel	Founders and Majority Shareholders: Larry Page and Sergey Brin. As of 31 December 2019, Page and Brin had approximately 51.2% of voting rights. Page and Brin have fulfilled various leadership roles since Google's founding in 1998. Former Executive Chairman (2015–2017) and Significant Shareholder: Eric Schmidt. Owns approximately 5% of voting rights. Former CEO (2001–2011) and Executive Chairman (2011–2015) of Google. CEO: Sundar Pichai. Stanford graduate. CEO since December 2019. Started working at Google in 2004.
Mission	To solve a lot of the problems we have as humans (Suggested by Larry Page in an interview with Richard Waters in 2014).
Description	Megacorporation. Holding company for Google and Other Bets.
Asset	**Google**
Notable Personnel	CEO: Sundar Pinchai. Occupied role since October 2015. YouTube CEO: Susan Wojcicki. When she was working in marketing at Intel in 1998, Wojcicki rented her garage to Brin and Page for use as Google's first office for $1700 a month. Google Cloud CEO: Thomas Kurian. Director of Engineering: Ray Kurzweil.
Mission	To organize the world's information and make it universally accessible and useful.
Description	Includes search, email, cloud services, maps, video, home services such as Nest, hardware (e.g. Pixel phones) and so on. Makes significant profits through advertising. Google has offices located in all continents except Antarctica. Google Search and YouTube are the two most visited websites in the world. Currently has 9 products with more than 1 billion users. More than $160 billion in revenues in 2019.
	Other Bets
Asset	**Access**
Key Personnel	CEO: Dinesh Jain. Former Chief Operating Office at Time Warner Cable.

Table 3.1 (*cont.*)

	Other Bets
Mission	To connect more people to superfast and abundant internet.
Description	Gigabit internet company.
Asset	**Calico (California Life Company)**
Key Personnel	Founder and CEO: Arthur Levinson. Former CEO of Genentech. Current Chairman of the Board of Apple. Google Director from 2004 to 2009. Has authored or co-authored more than 80 scientific articles. Chief Scientific Officer: David Botstein. Anthony B. Evnin Professor of Genomics at Princeton. Winner of many prestigious awards in genetics. Prolific and very widely cited researcher. Vice President, Aging Research: Cynthia Kenyon. Discovered that a single-gene mutation could double the lifespan of healthy, fertile *Caenorhabditis elegans* roundworms.
Mission	To harness advanced technologies to increase our understanding of the biology that controls lifespan. To devise interventions that enable people to lead longer and healthier lives.
Description	Involved in interdisciplinary research in the fields of medicine, drug development, molecular biology, genetics and computational biology.
Asset	**CapitalG**
Key Personnel	Founder and General Partner: David Lawee. Former Google Vice President of Corporate Development.
Mission	To make return-driven investments in leading companies around the world and help entrepreneurs rapidly grow their investments.
Description	Growth equity investment fund. Currently invested in such companies as Airbnb, Duolingo, Lyft and Snap.
Asset	**DeepMind**
Key Personnel	Co-founder and CEO: Demis Hassabis. Chess prodigy and five-time Mind Sports Olympiad champion. PhD in

Table 3.1 (*cont.*)

	Other Bets
	cognitive neuroscience from UCL (University of Central London). In 2007 his research into neural mechanisms was listed in the top 10 scientific breakthroughs by the journal *Science*.
Mission	To unlock answers to the world's biggest questions by understanding and recreating intelligence itself.
Description	Brings together new ideas and advances in machine learning, neuroscience, engineering, mathematics, simulation and computing infrastructure. DeepMind's AlphaGo program beat the world's best Go player, Ke Jie, 3–0 in 2017.
Asset	**GV (Google Ventures)**
Key Personnel	CEO and Managing Partner: David Krane. Former roles at Apple and Qualcomm.
Mission	To back founders who transform industries and create new ones.
Description	Early stage venture capital. Currently has $4.5 billion under management, and more than 300 companies in its active portfolio. Invested in such companies as Uber, Orbital Insight and Impossible Foods.
Asset	**Jigsaw**
Key Personnel	Founder and CEO: Jared Cohen. Adjunct Senior Fellow at the Council on Foreign Relations. Previously served as part of US Secretary of State Policy Planning Staff under Condoleezza Rice and Hillary Clinton.
Mission	To identify, and find new solutions to, emerging issues that threaten our society.
Description	Previously known as Google Ideas, Jigsaw is self-styled as a 'think/do tank'. Focus on digital security and stability in international relations and global governance.
Asset	**Sidewalk Labs**
Key Personnel	Chairman and CEO: Daniel L. Doctoroff. Former CEO of Bloomberg, and Deputy Mayor for Economic Development and Rebuilding for New York City after 9/11.

Table 3.1 (*cont.*)

	Other Bets
Mission	To combine forward-thinking urban design and cutting-edge technology to radically improve urban life.
Description	Urban redevelopment company with a technology and sustainability focus.
Asset	**Verily**
Key Personnel	CEO: Andrew Conrad. Co-founded the National Genetics Institute, which developed the first cost-effective test to screen for HIV in the blood supply.
Mission	To make the world's health data useful so that people enjoy healthier lives.
Description	Develops tools and devices to collect, organize and activate health data, and to prevent and manage disease. Partners with leading life sciences, medical device and government organizations.
Asset	**Waymo**
Key Personnel	CEO: John Krafcik. Former CEO of Hyundai Motor America.
Mission	To make it safe and easy for people and things to move around. Waymo also reportedly has a motto – 'Never trust humans in cars'.
Description	Self-driving or autonomous vehicle company. In 2019, investment bank UBS speculated that Waymo could generate more than $100 billion in revenue in 2030.
Asset	**X**
Key Personnel	Captain of Moonshots: Astro Teller (Neither the title nor the name are made up).
Mission	The Moonshot Factory – To create radical new technologies to solve some of the world's hardest problems.
Description	X's goal is 10x impact on the world's most intractable problems, not just 10% improvement. Speculative start-up factory for what look like the most ambitious projects possible. Waymo and Verily both started at X.

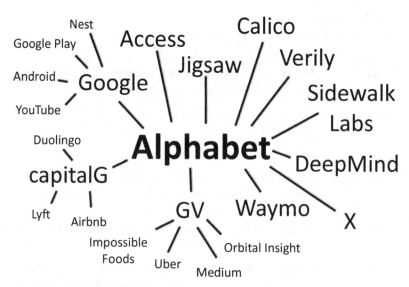

Figure 3.1 A partial diagram of Alphabet assets

home/community life), Alphabet is helping evert cyberspace. In other words, it is helping make the idea of cyberspace – i.e. of a space that is separate or distinct from 'real' or 'offline' existence – redundant (Gibson, 2007: 66). Second, Alphabet also appears to be everting Google's corporate culture and campus life (Turner, 2009) in the sense that it is spreading Google's extensive, Circle-like influence (Eggers, 2013), over its employees and users, to people around the world.

What all this suggests, in short, is that there are *prima facie* reasons for thinking that Alphabet is a megacorporation. And as with Chapter 2's discussion of the English East India Company, the discussions that follow in this chapter, and then in Part II of the book, show that these initial impressions are correct.

Monopoly

Alphabet's cash cow, Google, is a monopoly. In 2018 it was responsible for more than 5.5 billion searches a day (Duhigg, 2018), and in 2019 it was said to have accounted for 93 percent of all search worldwide (Statscounter, Website). This commanding position is the result of Google having built a better mousetrap, to its arguably having 'perfected' what search could be (Sullivan, 2016). It is also the result of network effects: of increasing numbers of Google users improving the search engine's performance, which, in its turn, attracts more users again (Srnicek, 2017).

In seeking to protect its monopoly, Alphabet does a number of things. First, elites within the megacorporation posit that Google is not really a monopoly because users are always just one click away from another service, and because their assets are under constant threat from competition. On this basis – and just as Google previously did to Microsoft, Yahoo! and AltaVista in their various fields – Google elites have long proposed that nimble newcomers could challenge, and potentially undermine, their currently dominant position (El Akkad, 2009). Second, Alphabet devotes significant resources to the lobbying of bureaucrats and politicians. In 2017, for example, Alphabet was reported to have spent more money than any other company on lobbying in Washington. Whilst not all of this money would have been devoted to fighting antitrust issues, a significant portion would have (Shaban, 2018).

Third, Google often tries to crush competitors. Crushing takes place when Google buries the websites of its competitors '12 or 15 or 64 or 170 pages down' in the list of results it returns for relevant search strings: e.g. 'books', 'email', 'maps', 'video' (Duhigg, 2018). That such placements can quickly destroy a competitor is clear given that 'the first page of Google captures 71% of search traffic clicks and has been reported to be as high as 92% in recent years' (Shelton, 2017). Indeed, the 'first five results receive 67.6% of clicks' by themselves (Ibid.).

Finally, Google also has significant form when it comes to proactively finding competitors and buying them out (Brandon, 2018). Whilst this monopoly protection strategy might sometimes prove financially enriching to the owners of bought-out companies, if a purchase is preceded by the just noted crushing tactic – which involves a company's value being deliberately diminished through very aggressive competition (e.g. by Google massively undercutting their competitor's price) or other means (e.g. by their being shifted downwards in Google search results) – then Google can buy its competitor at a significant discount (Duhigg, 2018).

Corporate Social Responsibility Concerns

Google, and now Alphabet, is consistently involved in a variety of more or less significant CSR concerns. With regard to its employees, for instance, Google has, as one of the Bay Area's most prominent employers, been placed in the sights of those who want to see a Silicon Valley workforce that is less pale and male (Wong, 2017; see also, Google, 2019; US Department of Labor, 2017). Nevertheless, some think that the problem is not that Google is doing too little to promote diversity amongst its workforce, but that it is doing too much.

Most famously, in July 2017, Google software engineer James Damore published an internal memo entitled *Google's Ideological Echo Chamber: How Bias Clouds Our Thinking about Diversity and Inclusion*. In the memo, Damore (2017) argues that Google has a left-leaning bias that inclines the organization towards: 'compassion for the weak'; the belief that 'disparities are due to injustices'; the notion that 'humans are inherently cooperative'; a preference for change and openness; and an idealist (as opposed to pragmatic) outlook. This bias, Damore (2017) argues, has also resulted in Google's diversity policies being blind towards what he posits are non-socially constructed, bio-logical differences between women and men: e.g. women tend to be more interested in feelings than ideas, women tend to be more agree-able and more neurotic. Moreover, Damore posits that this bias has resulted in Google being discriminatory towards men, and white men in particular. Consequently, Damore (2017) suggests that Google's diversity policies are wrong, and that what Google really needs is 'viewpoint diversity': a diversity of political orientations.

Damore's memo was made public on Friday, 4 August 2017. By the following Monday, it was reported that he had been fired. In her initial statement on Damore's views, Google's then Vice President of Diversity, Danielle Brown, noted that Damore's views 'are not ones "that I or this company endorses, promotes or encourages"' (Statt, 2017). Subsequently, Google's CEO Sundar Pichai wrote, in a 'com-pany-wide email entitled "Our words matter"', that 'Damore had violated the company's code of conduct, crossing "the line by advan-cing harmful gender stereotypes in our workplace ... To suggest a group of our colleagues have traits that make them less biologically suited to that work is offensive and not OK"' (Ibid.).

Google's decision to sack Damore was supported by many inside and outside the company (Eaton, 2017), largely due to the belief that his evolutionary biology arguments were flaky. Nevertheless, it also resulted in Damore becoming a martyr for the alt-right, and in Google being chastised from some philosophical quarters. The bio-ethicist

Peter Singer (2017), whose enemies have described him as 'the most dangerous man in the world' (Toolis, 1999), argued that 'Damore's view is one that a Google employee should be permitted to express' for three reasons. First, he proposed that Damore's view was neither 'twisted' or 'crazy', and that 'serious articles' in 'leading peer-reviewed scientific journals' supported it (Singer, 2017). Second, he posited that whilst employees should be 'blind' in making appointments, they should also accept that some kinds of work are likely to be more attractive to men than women (or vice versa), and thus characterized by relative homogeneity. Third, Singer posited that Damore's memo did not conflict with Google's code of conduct, as it did not harass or intimidate, and was not biased or unlawful.

Along with controversies relating to its employment policies, and further to many other concerns relating to privacy, surveillance, copyright, market domination and so on, Google has faced a number of significant concerns relating to its on-again off-again operations in China. Google first launched a Chinese language version of Search in September 2000, and by 2002 had managed to capture 'about one-quarter of the Chinese market for online search' (Lawrence, 2009: 263–264). Given this success – and in spite of difficulties from the Chinese authorities; vigorous competition from the Chinese competitor Baidu; and concerns that Google's Chinese activities were inconsistent with their old 'Don't be evil' motto (Lawrence, 2009: 254–267) – the company proceeded to announce the launch of Google.cn on 27 January 2006 (McLaughlin, 2006).

The main reason Google gave for launching Googl.cn – which the company censored as per the dictates of the Chinese Communist Party – was to provide Chinese Google users with a quicker and more reliable service than could be provided with Google.com (hosted outside of China). Moreover, the company argued that by providing the censored Google.cn, they could best fulfil their 'mission to ... [make] information universally ... accessible' (Ibid.). Google also suggested that 'continued engagement with China is the best ... way for Google to help bring the tremendous benefits of universal information access'; and that whilst some people might not consider 'a hard compromise ... as satisfying as withdrawal on principle ... we believe it's the best way to work toward the results we all desire' (Ibid.).

Having endured some exciting times in China, and having been called such things as 'evil's accomplice' (Smith, 2006), Google announced, on 12 January 2010, that it would cease censoring results on Google.cn (Drummond, 2010a). The reason given was that Google had been the target, in mid-December 2009, of a 'highly sophisticated' attack on their corporate infrastructure that originated from China, and that 'resulted in the theft of intellectual property from Google' (Ibid.). It was also suggested that the attack – which targeted at least 'twenty other large companies from a wide range of businesses' – sought to access 'the accounts of dozens of ... Gmail users who are advocates of human rights in China' (Ibid.). Whilst it took Google a while to make good on its promise to stop participating in the Chinese Communist Party's censorship regime, the company managed to come through when it started redirecting its Google.cn users to Hong Kong's 'uncensored' Google.com.hk on 22 March 2010 (Drummond, 2010b). Google's decision and consequent actions met with unequivocal support from the human rights community (e.g. Ganesan, 2010), and was quickly followed by some very supportive 'Remarks on Internet Freedom' by then US Secretary of State, Hillary Clinton (2010). The move to Hong Kong also harked back to the English East India Company's role in the first opium wars, which led to the British colonizing of Hong Kong.

Given this context, the leak of Google's plans to 'launch a censored version of its search engine ... code-named Dragonfly' for the Chinese market on 1 August 2018 (Gallagher, 2018), was always going to prove controversial. A reported application designed for use with mobile Android devices, Dragonfly would, according to reports on a document marked 'Google confidential', automatically 'identify and filter websites blocked by the Great Firewall [of China]', and return no results whatsoever for words or phrases blacklisted by the Chinese Communist Party (Ibid.). Moreover, the leak's source emphasized that 'knowledge about Dragonfly' had 'been restricted to just a few hundred members of the Internet giant's 88,000-strong workforce', and that they themselves (i.e. the leak) were personally 'against large companies and governments collaborating in the oppression of their people' (Ibid.).

Whilst not all of Google's employees would have been dismayed by the news of Dragonfly, a significant portion was, with 1,400 of them signing a petition demanding more transparency on the issue (Conger & Wakabayashi, 2018), and with seven employees reportedly resigning because of it (O'Donovan, 2018). Hence, it was in a seeming effort to assuage such concerns, that Google CEO Sundar Pichai stated that whilst the company is '"not close to launching a search product in China"', it is 'thinking about how to do more in the country' (Nieva & Musil, 2018).

Other issues – such as Google's involvement in the Maven program, an AI tool that the US military uses to interpret video images, and that could help improve drone targeting – have also resulted in petitions from Google employees, and are purported to have similarly resulted in some Google employees resigning (Shane, Metz & Wakabayashi, 2018). More generally, what such examples indicate is that Alphabet's prized possession, Google, is constantly dealing with significant CSR concerns that result in conflicts amongst its employees, users and the broader community.

Political-Economic Hybrid

In many instances, the CSR concerns that Google and other Alphabet assets are embroiled in, are, like the English East India Company long before it, due to its being recognized as a political-economic hybrid. This hybridity manifests in at least four ways.

First, it manifests through the various means by which Alphabet directly shapes governance structures. Along with the above referred to lobbying of states worldwide, such efforts take the form of involvement in non-state centric governance and regulation. To this end, Google continues to be a member of the Global Network Initiative (Website): a multi-stakeholder initiative devoted to 'protecting and advancing freedom of expression and privacy in the ICT Sector'. And following the emergence of concerns regarding Google's involvement in the above noted Maven project, Alphabet's DeepMind 'signed a pledge', along with various other AI companies and researches, 'promising to not develop "lethal autonomous weapons"' (Vincent, 2018).

Second, Alphabet's political-economic hybridity manifests through its efforts to influence political ideals. The most obvious example here is provided by Alphabet's 'think/do tank' Jigsaw, or what was, upon its founding back in 2010, known as Google Ideas. In this same year, the then Google Ideas CEO, and still current CEO of Jigsaw, Jared Cohen, published an article entitled 'The Digital Disruption' with Eric Schmidt, who was Google's CEO at the time, in *Foreign Affairs*. The main argument that Schmidt and Cohen (2010: 76, 84) advanced in the article was that, in a world characterized by connectivity and the diffusion of power, democratic governments will – in their efforts to promote democracy and human rights worldwide – need to form 'coalitions of the connected' that 'go far beyond government-to-government contacts' and 'embrace civic society, nonprofit organizations, and the private sector' too.

Third, and as Schmidt and Cohen's (2010) article made clear, Alphabet has extensive capacities when it comes to shaping some of our not necessarily violent, or less immediately violent, political capacities. These impacts are often perceived as being of both a more positive and more negative variety. Regarding the former, Alphabet entities are often thought to have helped positively transform opportunities for education, voice and organization. Through increasing the reach and speed of the Internet, for example, Alphabet assets are helping give rise to new possibilities for self-learning, identity formation and community formation. And in terms of their negative impacts, the likes of Google are – through the information they collect as part and parcel of their business – often seen to have enabled new forms of intelligence gathering and industrial-scale spying. It is for some good reason, then, that Google is often taken as the archetype of data (Myers West, 2019) or surveillance (Zuboff, 2015) capitalism. Likewise, through facilitating the distribution of fake news and propaganda, Google has come to be widely accused of enabling activities that focus on corrupting the democratic process (Cadwalladr, 2016).

Alphabet assets have also played a more or less direct role in facilitating obviously violent political capacities. From 2013 through 2017, Boston Dynamics was owned by Google/Alphabet. The Boston-based outfit is notorious for its 'unsettlingly life like robots' (Swearingan, 2017), and, given its historic ties with the military, does have more than a whiff of the Terminator about it. More generally, Eric Schmidt currently acts as Chairman of the US Defense Innovation Board. Members of the board are recruited to help provide 'US warfighters and personnel supporting them with the solutions they need to achieve' the US Department of Defense mission (US Defense Innovation Board, Website): i.e. to provide 'the military forces needed to deter war and to protect the security' of the country (US Department of Defense, Website).

It is therefore not ridiculous to suggest, along with Kobek (2016: 188–189), that Schmidt – who only stepped down from his role as executive chairman of Alphabet in December 2017 – is Silicon Valley's 'Zeus, the king of the gods':

the man behind the scenes, the unmoved mover, the guy who made deals with the government and the CIA and the NSA, the guy who worked on various Presidential commissions and had a hand in the company's Washington dealings. He loved that Google afforded him proximity to power. Like Zeus, he was weird and mysterious in a way that the others weren't. He was always there but you never knew what he was really like. And let's not get into his complicated romantic life, the servicing of which required a fuckpad on Manhattan island.

Summary

This chapter has described and contextualized Google's and Alphabet's emergence. It has also posited that the latter is a megacorporation. In doing so, the chapter has detailed Alphabet's global scale and broad scope; outlined some of its monopolistic powers and CSR concerns; and proposed that its political-economic hybridity manifests via its impact on political structures and ideals, and its impact on our more and less violent political capacities. What is yet to be described, however, are Alphabet's existential impacts. The reason why is that, whereas the preceding considerations are more or less well known, and relatively easy to summarize, the megacorporation's existential impacts are not. Given as such, the book's Part II, which is comprised of four chapters, is concerned to reveal, and help make sense of, the megacorporation's concrete existential impacts (i.e. the ways in which Alphabet is extending our pasts and our futures), and the conceptual existential impacts they encourage (i.e. monolithic and multiple constructive tendencies).

Shaping Our Pasts and Futures

4 | *Personal Pasts*

This chapter explains how Alphabet is influencing the construction and experiencing of pasts at the personal level. To provide some context, it is first noted that various key players associated with the megacorporation have suggested that privacy is (currently) dead. This death is then posited as being the result of our growing digital dossiers, i.e. the collection and storing of digital traces that can be associated with specific people. Following this, the chapter differentiates between two approaches – one more careful and the other more carefree – that individuals can employ when seeking to manage or account for the recallable pasts that are continuously being created by, and for, themselves. Finally, the chapter's summary notes that – with specific regard to its impact on our personal pasts – Alphabet's megacorporate status is not so much illustrated by the fact that many express concern about our growing digital dossiers, as it is by so many appearing to have already accepted that such growth is inevitable, and even desirable.

RIP Privacy (1760–2013)

Vint Cerf played a key role in the Internet's development whilst working as an assistant professor at Stanford University and as a manager at the US Department of Defense Advanced Research Projects Agency (DARPA) in the 1970s and early 1980s. In addition to his having thus earned the epithet, 'Father of the Internet', the widely decorated Cerf has been Vice President and Chief Internet Evangelist (his actual title) at Google since 2005 (Internet Society, 2020), where he is responsible for contributing 'to global policy development and continued spread of the Internet' (Google AI, 2018).

Whilst fulfilling these evangelical duties in November 2013, Cerf pithily suggested that 'privacy may actually be an anomaly' (Kastrenakes, 2013). In explaining his point, and as reported by Kastrenakes (2013), Cerf proposed, in what he acknowledged was an oversimplified fashion, that current understandings of privacy only really emerged with '"the industrial revolution and the growth of urban concentrations"', and with the simultaneous decrease in the prominence of (small-town) life where everybody knows what everybody else is doing. Consequently, Cerf also suggested that

the technology that we use today has far outraced our social intuition ... we are gonna live through situations where some people get embarrassed, some people end up going to jail, [and] some other people have other problems as a consequence of some of these [digitally recorded and distributed] experiences. (Kastrenakes, 2013)

Cerf's basic point relates to what Eric Schmidt and Jigsaw CEO Jared Cohen have suggested is the problem of data permanence in the afterword to the paperback edition of their *New York Times* bestseller *The New Digital Age* (Schmidt & Cohen, 2013: 274–276). On top of the recognition that, at a given point in time, multiple audiences now tend to collapse into one general mass due to the ease of accessing/distributing digital materials, the idea of data permanence emphasizes that multiple points of time, which are themselves comprised of multiple audiences, can collapse together too (Brandtzaeg & Lüders, 2018; Marwick & boyd, 2011; Wesch, 2009).

One upshot of this permanence of data, of this collapsing of contexts, is that a specific individual is now more or less directly linked to an increasingly heavy load of 'informational baggage' (Solove, 2006: 511). On this basis – and instead of associating the Internet with high levels of anonymity (Etzioni, 2019) and the inauthentic and risk-free decision-making associated therewith (Dreyfus, 1999) – many are now concerned that life on the Internet is anything but anonymous, and close to unforgettable. Many teenagers, for instance, recognize 'that there is no such thing as online privacy ... [and] that users should think of social media environments as public, not private' (Agosto & Abbas, 2017: 354). More generally, there is a growing recognition that because digital memories are very difficult to delete (Mayer-Schönberger, 2009), they can have long-lasting and 'significant real life consequences' (Petrik, Kilybayev & Shormanbayeva, 2014: 279).

Your Digital Dossier

Like prominent political figures, or characters from a John le Carré novel, many people now have relatively extensive dossiers. These dossiers include all 'the personally identifying information' associated with one's name: e.g. medical records, 'social security records, tax returns, … traffic violations … arrest records' (Palfrey & Gasser, 2008: 41). They also include information that only certain parties such as doctors, employers, or the police can access (Ibid.). A person's digital identity, on the other hand, can be conceived as that subset of a person's digital dossier that is readily accessible to all and any interested parties: e.g. what one can find out about someone by conducting a search online.

Whilst there is some merit in analytically distinguishing between a person's digital identity and their digital dossier (Palfrey & Gasser, 2008: 40), the potential for data leaks, hacks and simple human error, means that any barriers separating the two notions are permeable in practice. Accordingly, the following discussions identify three sources of information that contribute to one's dossier in general, and not just to one's current or historical identity.

Your Own Contribution

As part of daily life, many people regularly and intentionally contribute to their own dossier. This occurs whenever a person stores a digital photo of themselves, sends an email, makes a post on Twitter, uploads a video to YouTube, or likes something on Facebook. The reasons for people doing such things include their concern to preserve personal memories, to project a personal image (Marwick & boyd, 2011: 119) and to socialize and participate in the life of communities (Agosto & Abbas, 2017: 355; Palfrey & Gasser, 2008: 24). Additionally, people can make contributions to their dossier for financial reasons, or out of a concern to further their careers.

Those working in the porn industry provide a particularly clear example in this later regard. Whilst parts of the industry have been threatened by the huge array of amateur porn available online for some time now (Miller, 2012), there is still money to be made from filmed sex. According to Derek Hay, the founder of LA Direct Models which represents many of the top adult performers, 'as a standard, a female performer in a scene with an (sic) male performer could expect to earn around $1,000 … However, for some scenes this pay cheque can increase significantly, more so if it involves a sexual act the performer has not done before' (Blair, 2017). Hay goes on:

For the right girl . . . to do acts like their first anal scene, first interracial scene, first scene with three, four or five guys, those scenes could pay premium rates [up to $6,000]. A company's studios would offer a particular girl a much higher rate to induce her to accept the offer to shoot that kind of scene. That's always been the case, but in the past few years a number of different studios have put a lot of prominence on those kind of scenes and the rates offered to models to do that have increased markedly. (Blair, 2017)

Whatever the reason for their performance, these sorts of self-created pieces of 'personally identifying information' (Palfrey & Gasser, 2008: 41) are in effect 'permanently committed to the internet' and can potentially be 'replicated thousands of times and watched by millions' (Saul, 2016). Such recordings are not inherently problematic, but they can have long-lasting effects due to their tending towards the unforgettable. The basic sense of the matter, and its potential implications, was succinctly communicated by the now deceased, and at times very controversial, leading light of the porn industry Bill Margold in the 2011 documentary *After Porn Ends*. Specifically, Margold used his interview in the documentary to emphasize that there may not be

that much of a future after the x rated industry because somehow, somewhere, somebody will find you. The famous line I used to say to anybody walking into my office when I ran the biggest agency [was] what are you going to do 10 years from now when your kid brings home a magazine . . . with you laying in the middle of it with a candle shoved up your ass. You going to tell them you were playing the role of a birthday cake? It doesn't go away. (Wagoner, 2011)

The arguably staider world of academia has also provided at least one standout example of the ways in which individuals can contribute to the construction of their own dossier. The case in question dates back to April 2010, when Orlando Figes, a professor of history at Birkbeck, University of London, admitted that he had 'made some foolish errors', and 'that he was the author of anonymous reviews that praised his own works . . . whilst rubbishing that of his rivals' (Lea & Taylor, 2010).

As Figes ultimately appears to have recognized, his efforts at anonymization were amateurish at best. Unsurprisingly, they began to quickly unravel when

historians noticed reviews on Amazon . . . [that praised] Figes's books and attacked those of academic rivals. Comments under the alias "orlando-birkbeck" and "Historian" called Rachel Polonsky's book *Molotov's Magic Lantern* "hard to follow" and [Robert] Service's *Comrades* "awful", while praising Figes's study of Soviet family life, *The Whisperers*, as "a fascinating book ... [that] leaves the reader awed, humbled, yet uplifted". (Ibid.)

Although this scandal is likely to have proven difficult for Figes on various fronts – amongst other things, he originally sought to blame his wife for the comments – he has managed to keep his esteemed position. As John Sutherland, a professor of English at University College London, suggested at the time, Figes' seeming good fortune could be due to academics being "'on the whole ... pretty tolerant'". Alternatively, it could be due to Figes' publication record, and to Birkbeck needing research 'stars' so as to better ensure favourable ratings from the United Kingdom's higher education funding councils (Ibid.).

The Contribution of Others

As the rival historians targeted by Figes are no doubt aware, one's dossier can be deliberately added to by other people. When this is done by family and friends in a consensual, cautious and caring fashion, people are likely to appreciate such additions being made. Positive childhood memories, for example, can be significantly enriched by the recordings that parents make of their children's first years. But of course, there is a darker side to the contributions that other people can make, as illustrated by various privacy infringing acts.

In the first instance, other people can employ disclosure in an effort to damage the reputation of a specific person by revealing and disseminating 'truthful information about a person that impacts the way others judge' their character (Solove, 2006: 491). Outing homosexuals, despite their potentially having 'many valid reasons ... for not choosing to be open about their sexuality to every person in their life' (Stonewall, 2018), provides one clear illustration of the sorts of activities that disclosure can entail.

Like disclosure, exposure involves the revealing of (truthful) information about a given person. But whereas disclosure relates to personal details in general, exposure involves the revealing of personal attributes, activities or events that people have 'been socialized into concealing', such as 'grief, suffering, trauma, injury, nudity, sex, urination, and defecation' (Solove, 2006: 533). Exposure appears increasingly widespread, and has contributed to a host of tragic events, such as the depression and suicide of Tiziana Cantone after a sex-tape featuring her went viral following its being distributed by 'virtual friends' (Pianigiani, 2016).

Acts of identification, which associate a given individual with some sort of details, and acts of distortion, which represent a specific individual in an inaccurate or misleading fashion (Solove, 2006: 511, 547), also appear to be on the rise as a result of developments in information and communication technologies. In the first regard, recent years have seen the growing prominence of doxxing, i.e. the revealing of the (real) name and (real) location of an otherwise anonymous person with some sort of internet presence. This information could be used to identify people found in footage of a rally for white supremacists (Grey Ellis, 2017), to link porn actresses with their (non-porn) social media profiles with the help of neural network technologies (Orf, 2016), or to identify people involved in whatever behaviour is considered annoying, embarrassing, immoral, scandalous, or what have you, within a given society.

Neural network or deep learning technologies are also enabling those that want to distort another individual's dossier. Deepfakes, which use open source deep learning code libraries and resources like Google's TensorFlow to 'faceswap' a person's face into porn films, provide a case in point. Whilst still difficult for most people to use, this technology is developing very quickly, and being democratized as a consequence. This was acknowledged in a 'now-deleted subreddit' post from the purported deepfake creator Gravity_Horse, who proposed that '"as it becomes more mainstream and near impossible to tell fantasy from reality, anything is subject to being fake"' (Farokhmanesh, 2018). Or, as Cole (2017) succinctly put it, 'AI-assisted fake porn is here and we're all fucked'.

As these discussions suggest, other people can make significant contributions to a targeted person's dossier. They may or may not personally know the person they target, and they may or may not think the person they target is a public figure. Whatever the case, and whatever the motivation (e.g. greed, hate, entertainment), other people are an important consideration.

The Contribution of Corporations

Alphabet assets like Gmail, YouTube and TensorFlow, and even the likes of Alphabet's Calico, which is seeking to extend (biological) human memory, are all helping to extend the ways in which a specific person's dossier can be added to and experienced by individuals themselves, and other people. In addition to these sorts of indirect contributions, Alphabet's major asset, Google, is also making a more direct, and very significant, contribution to peoples' dossiers worldwide.

As already noted, Google is, and always has been, an advertising company. It makes money through selling targeted advertising based on search, language and location. In the process of doing so, Google contributes to the dossiers of its users. Amongst other things, Google tracks and stores the location of its users whenever they turn on their phone (if they have location tracking turned on); knows its users' entire search history (even those searches that have been deleted); and has an advertisement profile for its users based on 'gender, age, hobbies, career, interests, relationship status, possible weight ... and income' (Curran, 2018). As a result, Google is widely conceived as being in both the advertising and the surveillance business (Zuboff, 2015).

Whilst the information that Google gathers on its users is reported to not be widely shared (without consent), and whilst Google (Website B) no doubt makes significant efforts to protect its users, and itself, 'from unauthorized access alteration, disclosure, or destruction' of user information, such efforts at security could be breached. If someone manages to access another person's Google account then they could easily download all the data Google has stored on them, or what amounts to 'a diary of everything that person has ever done', at least on Google (Curran, 2018). And if someone manages to hack Google itself – like 'The Impact Team' did to the cheating/extramarital affairs website Ashley Madison in 2015 – then they would potentially have all such details for each and every one of Google's users.

Vaughan's and Martin's (2015) comic *The Private Eye* provides a snapshot of what might follow from such an occurrence. Set in the United States in 2076, Vaughan and Martin (2015) tell of a world post the bursting of 'the cloud' (which occurs sometime in the 2010s). The bursting of the cloud, or what with biblical allusions is also termed 'the flood', released everyone's deepest and darkest secrets that were stored online. As noted by the work's central character, a private investigator who has a 'Free Assange' poster hanging on his wall at home, and who answers to the name of Patrick Immelmann, nobody knows if it [the flood] was an act of war or an act of God. But for forty days and forty nights everything just poured right out for the whole damn country to see. Every message you thought was safe. Every photo you thought you deleted. Every mortifying little search you ever made. It was all there for anyone to use against you. People lost their jobs. Families were torn apart. Blah fucking blah. (Vaughan & Martin, 2015)

Whilst scant on details, the comic implies that due to the social trauma that was caused by the flood, the Internet was shut down straight away. The post-flood world is thus a post-Internet world where adults wear a variety of elaborate costumes called nyms – because they provide anonymity – in public. Only at home do adults get around unmasked. In these ways, Vaughan and Martin (2015) graphically illustrate the drama that would likely unfold if Alphabet's database of dossiers was ever to be opened up for all the world to see.

Careful

When the information that Alphabet stores on specific individuals is noted alongside that created by individuals themselves, and that which other people create about them, the need to adopt an approach to deal with the creation of (future) personal pasts, on a daily basis, already seems a pressing concern. Nevertheless, as the number of people with internet access grows beyond the approximately 4 billion people that currently have it, and approaches all 7.8 billion of the world's population, this concern will, in all likelihood, become even more important. Accordingly, the remainder of this chapter is devoted to detailing two approaches – termed the careful and carefree approach respectively – that individuals can employ in seeking to account for such matters. In particular, I propose that the likelihood of adopting either approach can be conceived along four lines: concept of self, social norms, target risk and post-disclosure management.

Concept of Self – Integrated

Despite undergoing various, more or less significant, changes, throughout their lives, many people still think of themselves as one, integrated being. Many people, for example, think of themselves as 'a separately existing entity', distinct from their 'brain and body', and distinct from their 'experiences. On the best-known version of this view, a person is a *purely mental entity*: a Cartesian Pure Ego, or spiritual substance' (Parfit, 1984: 210). Even if people do not believe in an immortal soul, they might still think of themselves as having a separate, integrated sense of self due to reasons of biology, neurology, human evolution and so on (Ibid.). Once again, these latter perspectives seem to be ones that many people currently hold in a more or less explicit fashion.

Despite their popularity, various doubts about these points of view – most of which boil down to the idea that there is no (readily identifiable) permanent self that is separable from what we experience (Hume, 1969: 240) – suggest that we should jettison the idea of a strongly integrated and continuous self. Korsgaard (1989), however, posits that this would be a mistake on the basis of a Kantian understanding of practical reason. According to Korsgaard (1989: 110), one's conception of self 'as a unified agent' is 'not based on a meta-physical theory, nor on a unity of which you are conscious'. Rather, it is based on the practical recognition that because 'you only have one body with which to act', it is a 'raw necessity' to reason, and eliminate 'conflict among your various motives' at any given point in time (Korsgaard, 1989: 111, 110). This practical unity, Korsgaard (1989: 113–114) goes on, quickly extends over time due to even the most trivial of choices or actions taking 'you some way into the future', with the result that you need 'to identify with your future in order to be what you are even now'.

When people view themselves in this practically willful way (Korsgaard, 1989: 119–120), they will tend to construct, try to predict, or account for, the values, wants and needs they will have in the future. For some people, this sort of project can extend over a lifetime, with their actions as a 15, 25 or 35-year-old being guided by their (imagined) existence at the ages of 45, 65 or 85. Consequently, those that adopt or align themselves with this sort of integrated sense of self, could find it relatively difficult to dissociate themselves from any recordings of their past that are found in their dossier, and that might somehow limit their ambition, cause them embarrassment, or prove unedifying or upsetting in some other way. The net result is that such integrated people will be inclined to adopt the careful approach to the continuous construction of their personal pasts.

Social Norms – Predictable

The likelihood of one adopting a careful approach to the construction of their personal pasts also increases with the perceived predictability of social norms. The basic logic here is that people can be stigmatized (Goffman, 1963), and made to suffer various costs (Crocker & Major, 1989: 609), when they fail to comply with what a society thinks is right and appropriate. At a given point in time, failure to comply with gender norms, professional standards, notions of public decency, or even just trends in fashion, could result in one being ostracized from their family or community; rendered unemployable; made into a social pariah; or turned into the subject of continuous ridicule. When one extends one's temporal frame of reference, and recognizes that one's dossier of historical activities, whilst perhaps in line with social norms when originally engaged in, may not be in line with social norms in the future, the positive influence that the perceived predictability of social norms has on the adoption of the careful approach to the construction of future personal pasts becomes apparent.

There are various reasons that people might think social norms predictable. People might, for instance, believe in progress, i.e. the idea that humanity is advancing, in some sort of unilinear fashion, from a state of inferiority in the past, towards a state of superiority in the future. As Nisbett (1994: 5) has detailed, this idea can be found 'from the Greeks down to the twentieth century' and is comprised of 'two closely related but distinguishable propositions'. The first is that there is a 'slow, gradual, and cumulative improvement in *knowledge*, the kind of knowledge embodied in the arts and the sciences'; and the second is that humanity's 'moral or spiritual condition on earth' is moving towards perfection (Ibid.).

Belief in moral progress in particular, tends to be conceived in terms of the move from a tribal morality towards a more universal morality characterized by greater objectivity and impersonality (Jamieson, 2002: 10). To this end, a moral index supported from different value perspectives can be constructed that conceives of moral progress in terms of 'the abolition of war and slavery', 'the reduction of poverty and class privilege', 'the extension of liberty', the 'empowering of marginalized groups', and 'respect for animals and nature' (Jamieson, 2002: 12). When one considers moral progress likely, they will be inclined to not engage in acts that, whilst currently acceptable in certain circles – e.g. the eating of animals; the teasing of transgender people – may be less acceptable twenty years hence.

Importantly, people that do not believe in progress, or in some other sort of social determinism or utopianism, can still think that social norms are relatively predictable (cf., Popper, 1994). Sociologists like Bourdieu (1977: 95) suggest that social action is as 'remote from … unpredictable novelty' as it is from 'simple mechanical reproduction'. And political scientists working on selectorate theory (Bueno de Mesquita et al., 2003) have built a framework to (try to) predict revolutionary change, regime maintenance and so on. Whatever the theoretical basis, if a person considers themselves capable of predicting social norms, then they are more likely to engage in the careful construction of their personal pasts.

Target Risk – High

Let's say that a person has a highly integrated sense of self and that they believe they have significant predictive capacities when it comes to social norms. Let us also say that this person is of the belief that, thirty years from now, their dossier is going to contain significant amounts of information that, if disclosed to the broader public, would cause them levels of embarrassment and distress that would, on balance, outweigh whatever joy and sense of correctness they felt whilst engaging in the behaviour the information relates to. To be a little more concrete, it might help to think of a person with a strange fetish or love object – such as a certain gentleman who developed 'a lifelong interest' in ejaculating whilst his thighs and testicles were tickled by ants (Ogas & Gaddam, 2012: 53). Or, and the evidence suggests this is much more common, it might help to think of a straight male who loves watching porn with massive male organs in it (Ogas & Gaddam, 2012: 40–41).

Whatever the (documented) activity that could result in fallout, the person concerned might still decide to engage in it due to their perceiving their (future) self as having a low target risk. If, on the other hand, they think they will be a high target risk in the future, then they will be much less likely to engage in such (potentially controversial) activities. Whilst other methods could no doubt be identified, or constructed from scratch, Google's current policy for adjudicating upon what is popularly known as a right to be forgotten request, or what Google

(Website C) officially terms a 'personal information removal' request, provides a helpful starting point for thinking about how a person can establish their risk of being made a target (Fleishcer, 2014; Google Advisory Council, 2015). In particular, by proposing that the general public has a legitimate interest in disclosures of information relating to prominent, public figures (e.g. leading politicians, captains of industry, film stars), and potentially in information relating to public figures conceived more generally (e.g. somebody who works as a school teacher, who coaches a local football team, who owns a popular local restaurant), Google suggests that the more public a person's identity, or the more public their role, the more likely they are to be the target of information disclosure.

Whether legitimate or not, a cursory glance at the gossip media suggests, in line with Google's criteria, that the more popular or prominent a figure is, the more likely it is that the public will be interested in information relating to them. Indeed, the case of Monica Lewinsky – who was involved in an affair with then US president Bill Clinton between 1995 and 1997; and who has now been immortalized in what is reported by Lewinsky (2018) herself to be over '125 rap songs' – demonstrates that people that would otherwise be considered as non-public figures, can come to be perceived as public figures due to their association with a particularly prominent or famous individual. Given such considerations, there is likely a positive link between one's ambition (or the ambition of someone they are connected to) and their own perceived target risk. Whilst there will always be counterexamples – such as the appropriately named, dick-pic sending, former US Congress member Anthony Weiner (Casarez, 2017) – people who anticipate their being a target risk will be more likely to take relative care when constructing their personal pasts.

Post-Disclosure Management – Difficult

The final consideration inclining a person towards adoption of a careful approach is the belief that post-disclosure management will prove difficult. The basic reasoning here is that, if one perceives themselves as having a limited capacity to account for or deal with the unwanted revealing of (problematic) personal information, then they will seek to avoid such information being generated in the first place (see Folkman et al., 1986; Rippetoe & Rogers, 1987; Rogers, 1975).

Initially, the perceived difficulty of managing post-disclosure existence could relate to a person thinking that they will possess neither the financial resources nor the technical know-how that would be needed to make the relevant aspects of one's digital dossier publicly inaccessible (see discussion in the carefree section on post-disclosure management below). More strongly, it might relate to one believing that, whatever else the Internet does, it does not forget, and that the removal of information from the Internet is, in the last instance, closer to impossible than difficult.

The perceived difficulty of post-disclosure management also relates to whether or not a person expects themselves to be emotionally capable of dealing with any fallout from unwanted information release. Unhappily, it seems that many people would also be strongly tempted to take their own life if they found themselves in a similar position to Tiziana Cantone: whose smiling comment '"*Stai facendo il video? Bravo!*" ("You're filming? Bravo!") ... became a meme, - parodied on YouTube and printed on T-shirts and phone cases sold on eBay' following the widespread viewing of her sex-tape (Warren, 2018).

This case, and many others that could be identified, point towards the ways in which the growth of digital dossiers could have a significant 'chilling effect' on the activities people engage in. Originally coined by Schauer (1978: 693) to describe the way in which activities 'protected by the first amendment' can be curtailed by 'governmental regulation not specifically directed' at the protected activities, the idea of a chilling effect is now used to refer to 'people censor[ing] themselves and avoid[ing] certain activities not necessarily out of fear of prosecution but out of concern for potential future harms due to privacy violations' more generally (Penney, 2016: 164).

In his work on public shaming, Ronson (2015: 268) gives various examples of people that have modified their life or changed their behaviour in anticipation of, or in consequence of, unwanted information disclosure. Following the public shaming of Justine Sacco, who made an ill-advised joke about Africa, AIDS and skin colour on Twitter in late 2013, Ronson (2015: 282) had a conversation with a journalist friend who told him that

he had so many jokes, little observations, potentially risqué thoughts, that he wouldn't dare to post online anymore. "I suddenly feel with social media like

I'm tiptoeing around an unpredictable, angry, unbalanced parent who might strike out at any moment," he said. "It's horrible." He didn't want me to name him, he said, in case it sparked something off. We see ourselves as nonconformist, but I think all of this is creating a more conformist, conservative age. "Look!" we're saying. "WE'RE normal! THIS is the average!"

This sort of tiptoeing is a key feature of the careful tactic, and it can, and needs to be, inclusive of not just what one deliberately says or writes for a public audience, but of one's activities in general. The websites one visits; the (Google) searches one conducts; the people one decides to (privately) have sex with; and the (private) conversations that one is willing to have with their (so-called) friends, with their colleagues, or with their family – all these (recordable) acts need to be recognized as potential parts of one's dossier. To forget as such is to risk making 'the one unforgivable mistake of the early Twenty-First Century' (Kobek, 2016: 34), and will result in any efforts to employ the careful tactic more generally, being far from robust.

Carefree

As part of their study on the online privacy and security attitudes of older teens, Agosto and Abbas (2017: 353) write of one male participant who 'justified his frequent personal sharing' by stating that: "'I post whatever I want. I don't really care what people think about me, so it is what it is. I'm not ashamed of anything.'" They also refer to one female participant who explained to them that: "'I don't worry about privacy stuff, because I don't have anything to hide.'" Whilst reported to be in the minority (Agosto & Abbas, 2017), and whilst quite possibly ill-considered, the sentiments expressed by these teenagers are nevertheless suggestive of what the adoption of the carefree tactic to the construction of one's personal past entails. Like the careful approach, the likelihood of adopting this second and opposed approach can be conceived along four lines.

Concept of Self – Disintegrated

David Hume was a central player in the Scottish Enlightenment in the eighteenth century. As has already been alluded to, he suggested that

'Tis certain there is no question in philosophy more abstruse than that concerning identity, and the nature of the uniting principle, which constitutes a person. So far from being able by our senses merely to determine this question, we must have recourse to the most profound metaphysics to give a satisfactory answer to it; and in common life'tis evident these ideas of self and person are never very fix'd nor determinate (Hume, 1969: 240).

Whilst those inclined to Kantian-influenced practical understandings (Korsgaard, 1989), or those that are (implicitly) committed to the simpler idea of one being a permanent person or individual subject, will be unconvinced by Hume's suggestion, others think it a point well made. Thousands of years of Buddhist thought, for instance, is in rough agreement with Hume's position (Collins, 1982: 255–257; King, 1999: 38; Harvey, 1995). And more recently, Parfit (1984: 273) has suggested that Hume's commentary on the question of iden-tity – which can be taken as reductively denying that 'we are separately existing entities, distinct from our brain and bodies and our experi-ence' – 'is true'.

When acknowledged, this perspective suggests that if we are to speak of a self, then we should not do so to refer to one that is continuous and long-lasting. Instead, the idea of a self should be used to refer to a series of selves that, whilst perhaps overlapping, are different in significant ways. Importantly, this view does not just result in the simple discounting of the value of one's future happiness relative to one's present happiness (Parfit, 1984: 313–314). Rather, it leads to the more 'extreme' (Parfit, 1984: 307) belief that any future sense of happiness is ultimately unknown; to the belief that even if one only looks forward 'a year hence', it is exceedingly difficult to form 'a sure forecast' of one's feelings (Sidgwick, 1874: 113).

Although associable with a passive life (Ibid.), this point of view can also be more constructively conceived as the deliberate and continuous engagement with 'the trauma of our own deaths' (McGrath, 2004: 219). Foucault – who suggested that he sought to lose himself in labyrinths of his own construction so that he could continuously emerge anew (Foucault 1972: 17) – provides one example of someone who might be so understood. Another is provided by Skin Diamond, who, having 'stopped performing in adult films to focus on her music career', is now going by her real name Raylin Joy as part of a personal re-branding process that makes no effort to hide or deny Skin's (former) existence (Saul, 2016). In short, a disintegrated sense of self tends towards the carefree approach to personal past creation.

Social Norms – Capricious

If a person believes that changes in social norms are unpredictable, then they will consider any effort to avoid the costs of non-compliance with such norms, at some future point in time, futile. A belief in such unpredictability, whilst far from widespread, is not unheard of. Work by Kuhn (1970) and Feyerabend (1970), for example, posits that scientific paradigms or theories are incommensurable, and that there is no rational way of comparing or contrasting them. They accordingly propose that the world of science cannot be characterized in terms of progress: for 'in the absence of a neutral language, the choice of a new theory is a decision to adopt a different native language and to deploy it in a correspondingly different world' (Kuhn, 1970: 277). Indeed, Feyerabend (1970: 229) suggests that the choice between competing, sufficiently wide-ranging, theories, ultimately boils down to a matter of taste. In this way, both Kuhn and Feyerabend appear to acknowledge, as critics of their work suggest they must, that scientific change is '*irrational, a matter for mobpsychology*' (Lakatos, 1970: 178).

Like the world of science, which continues to make a significant contribution to changing norms regarding sexuality, family life and so on (Swierstra, 2013), history demonstrates that the world of markets can also have a very significant impact on social norms. And just as Kuhn and Feyerabend have proposed that future developments in science are unpredictable, so too can various economists be found suggesting that future developments in the not unrelated sphere of markets, are unpredictable too.

The 'Austrian' economist Ludwig Lachmman, who has had some influence in entrepreneurship and organization studies (Chiles, Bluedorn & Gupta, 2007), and who was actually German, provides a prime example. Further to his explicit endorsement of Shackle's (1958: 105) suggestion that 'predicted man is less than human, pre-dicting man is more than human ... man in his true humanity can neither predict nor be predicted' (Lachmann, 1986: 28), Lachmann proposed that '[a]ll economic action is of course concerned with the future, the more or less distant future. But the future is to all of us unknowable, though not unimaginable' (Lachmann, 1976: 55). This belief that human society is best characterized as a kaleidoscopic 'world of continuous unexpected change' (Lachmann, 1970: 46), is underpinned by Lachmann's (1986: 28) conceiving of human thought as 'footloose' (Lachmann, 1986: 28). In other words, Lachmann appeared to believe that 'individual actors do not possess any such thing as a character': for 'only if individual actors were assumed to be completely-disjointed personalities, such that my actions tomorrow were always entirely unrelated and unaffected by my actions today or yesterday, could Lachmann's scenario of radical uncertainty ever become a reality' (Hoppe, 1997: 74–75).

Whether one agrees with such ideas or not, what they highlight is that, when a disintegrated concept of self is extended beyond one's self, and used to conceive others, it will either lead one to think, or further bolster one's existing belief, that social norms are capricious. On this basis, any person who makes such a conceptual extension, will be doubly inclined towards adopting the carefree tactic due to their considering any efforts to predict both social norms, and their own future desires, equally pointless.

Target Risk – Low

As previously indicated, one could consider their future self an unlikely future target of malicious information disclosure due to their believing that they will not occupy a social position of sufficient prominence to entice such an attack. One might also believe that, even if they were to find themselves in a position of prominence, they will be unlikely to be the target of such an attack due to the prediction that such attacks will be of reduced efficacy at some later point in time.

Technical changes might be one source of such development. This possibility is suggested by Banks (1988: 69) in one of his Culture Series books, *The Player of Games*, where he writes of a world in which technological developments have meant that

[a]nybody could make up anything they wanted; sound, moving pictures, smell, touch ... there were machines that did just that. You could order them from a store and effectively paint whatever pictures–still or moving–you wanted, and with sufficient time and patience you could make it look as realistic as the real thing ... Some people used such machines just for fun or revenge, making up stories where appalling or just funny things happened to their enemies or their friends. Where nothing could be authenticated, blackmail became both pointless and impossible.

Such a world, which the emergence of deepfakes suggests may not be limited to fiction for long (Farokhmanesh, 2018), would, in addition to being a 'post-truth' world, be a world where any potential digital 'kidnapping' or cloning (Floridi, 2006: 195) would be redundant. Thus, if one thinks that this is the path that socio-technological assemblages are likely to take, then they will also think, other things being equal, that the risk of people being targeted in the future will be reduced too.

One could also think that unwanted information releases will be diminished in the future due to changing norms. When everybody has easily revealed secrets, conventions could develop that make their revealing distasteful. Such conventions could emerge through those directly affected, or those concerned on their behalf, attacking malicious disclosers out of a 'thirst for retaliation' (Mill, 1861: 36), or on the basis of more rational reflection (Fehr & Gächter, 2000). In its turn, the perceived threat of retaliation could result in those that are tempted to directly engage in such acts coming to internalize a norm that prohibits malicious information release (Salter, 2012: 314; see also, Hume, 1969: Books 2 and 3).

Recent events involving the *Huffington Post*'s Luke O'Brien are suggestive of how this might unfold. In 2018 O'Brien doxxed New York resident Amy Jane Mekelburg, who as @AmyMec on Twitter (more than 200,000 followers), and through maintaining the Resistance Against Islamic Radicals (RAIR) website, was publicizing racist views and doxxing those she considered radical Islamists. As part of his investigations, O'Brien made the pro-wrestling entertainment company WWE aware that one of their employees, Sal Siino, who was negotiating a television deal in the United Arab Emirates at the time, was married to Mekelburg. Subsequently, a WWE spokesperson informed O'Brien (2018) that, in light of this information, Siino's employment at WWE had been terminated.

Mekelburg then retaliated by posting 'a long thread on Twitter blaming me [O'Brien] for the WWE's decision to fire Siino over her bigotry. Within minutes, her followers began calling me with threats' (O'Brien, 2018). Then, others opposed to O'Brien retaliated by doxxing 'the personal information of several *Huffington Post* employees and their families on the Internet' (Kupfer, 2018). As Kupfer (2018) goes on to rhetorically ask, 'who could have seen it coming?' More substantially, Kupfer (2018) proposes that, whether the motivation itself is ultimately deemed good, bad, progressive or regressive, as soon as one participates in the doxxing–counter-doxxing process, they contribute to the 'reckless escalation' of 'the online culture war'.

If this sentiment – that doxxing is little more than 'shame-slinging' vigilantism (Grey Ellis, 2017) – were to spread, then engaging in it will come to be increasingly conceived as shameful and vicious. Thus, if a person thinks that this turn of events is likely to play itself out in the not too distant future, then they will be a little more carefree when it comes to constructing their personal (future) pasts due to their belief that doxxing (and other similar acts) will become less common.

Post-Disclosure Management – Possible

If one presumes that people will remain targets of malicious information disclosure in the future, and even if one presumes that they themselves are likely to be specifically targeted, then they could still be inclined to adopt the carefree tactic if they presume that their capacity to manage any unwanted information spread is high. Someone might, for instance, think they will be technically capable, or able to access the technical capacities needed, to minimize any harm done by the spread of malicious information.

With this possibility in mind, Schmidt and Cohen (2013: 38) have suggested – when they were both on the Google payroll – that we are likely to see

a proliferation of businesses that cater to privacy and reputation concerns. This industry exists already, with companies like Reputation.com using a range of proactive and reactive tactics to remove or dilute unwanted content from the Internet. During the 2008 economic crash, it was reported that several Wall Street bankers hired online reputation companies to minimize their appearance online, paying up to $10,000 per month for the service. In the future, this industry will diversify as the demand explodes, with identity managers becoming as common as stockbrokers and financial planners.

Along with this possibility, which Ronson's (2015) chapter on 'The Man Who Can Change the Google Search Results' suggests is increasingly realistic for many, one might imagine that they possess the emotional fortitude to deal with whatever follows from their digital dossier. Those with experience in the porn industry once again provide a variety of helpful examples. As part of the filmed 'Real Women, Real

Stories' series in 2016, Bree Olson, who stopped appearing in porn in 2011, stated:

When I go out, I feel as if I'm wearing "slut" across my forehead. All the mean things people say to me on the internet – that's how I feel when I walk out the door ... I've gotten to a point where there are days to weeks at a time that I don't leave my house ... I get so disappointed when I meet a new friend, and it turns out they don't want to be my friend anymore ... People treat me as if I'm a paedophile. They don't treat me like I'm an ex-sex worker, they treat me like I would be damaging to children ... I wish that people would treat me like they'd treat a married registered nurse with 2.5 kids in Indiana. That's how I wish people would treat me. But it'll never happen ... I've had people recognise me off just my voice alone. Porn is the one industry where the more successful a woman is, the more she will suffer for the rest of her life (news.com.au, 2016).

She goes on:

I send a very strong message to young girls: don't do porn. As much as you want to embrace your sexuality and say "I can do whatever I want with my body", you're going to have a life of crap in front of you. You can never work with children after you do porn, you can never work in the medical field after you do porn. These are things that teenage girls don't think about. How people treat you for the rest of your life — it's not worth it (Ibid.).

In contrast to Olson, the likes of Raylin Joy appear much more capable when it comes to dealing with the potential difficulties of being recognized as working in, or having worked in, the porn industry. As Joy has stated:

the stigma that can come with porn is too much for some girls to handle ... it is not even the porn world that can really get to girls, it's the bulls**t that girls can experience from the outside world because people think they have this idea of porn and that if you are a girl who does it then you must be a little bit weird or something. For me, personally, I don't give a s**t but for some other girls they find it quite hard, so that's why they don't stick around for as long (Saul, 2016).

Alongside this posited ability to robustly manage stigma, those associated with the world of porn have also employed more conciliatory approaches to the management of their digital dossier. To this end, Padgett's (2016: 227) 'close reading' of the memoirs of four porn stars revealed 'a number of linguistic patterns and discursive strategies that are shared throughout the sample. All four follow a similar narrative arc, involving the birth of a second identity (the porn star), the navigation and mitigation of that identity as it interacts and contradicts with a primary identity, and finally the end of this duelling of identities with the rebirth of the primary "authentic" identity'.

In these and other ways, a person might believe that some version of their future self will have the wherewithal to manage any potential difficulties or obstacles they might encounter as a result of their digital dossier. If this belief is sufficiently strong, then a person could choose to adopt the carefree tactic, even if all other considerations point towards their adopting its careful alternative. On the other hand, a person with a disintegrated concept of self, and who believes that social norms are capricious, will be inclined towards the carefree tactic for these reasons alone – and will consider any attempts at predicting or anticipating the future pointless and unnecessary.

Summary

By contributing to the creation and maintenance of digital dossiers in multifaceted ways, Alphabet is helping to construct a world in which we need to consider how we manage the continuous creation of our (future) personal pasts. Whilst this is not an entirely new concern, the novel types, and sheer amount, of information that is now stored on anyone with a digital profile suggests that the matter's importance has undergone a step change.

Nevertheless, and consistent with the long line of reactionary developments throughout history, there is currently no shortage of critics suggesting that we could somehow return to prior times. In this fashion, Zuboff (2020) has recently suggested that 'a fragile new awareness is dawning as we claw our way back up the rabbit hole towards home', and away from Alphabet's (and the rest of Big Tech's) surveillance. But if anything, it seems we are currently becoming ever more transparent to the megacorporation's gaze. Suffice it to note that, to read her article on *The New York Times* site, I quickly decided to sign into a Google-controlled Gmail account so that I could access it.

Given this example, Google's chief economist and Zuboff's *bête noir*, Hal Varian, appears to have been basically correct when he proposed, back in 2014, that '"everyone will expect to be tracked and monitored, since the advantages, in terms of convenience, safety, and services, will be so great"' (Pew Research Center, 2014: 28; see also, Zuboff, 2015). The fact that Google alone now has nine products with more than one billion users – i.e. Android, Chrome, Gmail, Google Drive, Google Maps, Google Photos, Google Search, the Google Play Store and YouTube (Knight, 2019) – does not exactly undermine Varian's basic point either. Consequently, it seems naïve to think that the ongoing loss of personal privacy will be significantly reversed anytime soon. Until such a change occurs, presuming it ever does, people should at least consider the carefree and careful approaches to personal past management that have just been detailed.

5 | *Social Pasts*

Along with the masses of information that Alphabet is collecting on specific individuals, Alphabet is currently digitizing existing, and creating entirely new, data sets of broad social relevance. As a result, and as the first section of this chapter outlines, Alphabet is contributing to a world in which the problem is not too little information, but too much. The chapter then proposes that those that want to use this information to make sense of, or construct, our social pasts, can employ one of two approaches – termed the massive and mélange approaches to historical analysis respectively – to ensure that they are not overwhelmed by our ever-growing archives. Having done so, the chapter concludes by emphasizing that, by creating and maintaining this 'great library', Alphabet is already in a strong position from which to decide – like the ongoing winner of some never-ending war – who can, and cannot, write history.

An Embarrassment of Riches

In 1994, Jacques Derrida gave a lecture in London. The following year, the lecture was published with the title *Archive Fever: A Freudian Impression*. As was Derrida's want, the lecture comprised a series of enigmatic discussions on such topics as the etymology of archive, the fratricidal relationship of Christianity to Judaism, and circumcision. Despite the essay's general vagueness, the titular idea of archive fever is a relatively simple one. On my reading at least, it can be conceived in terms of three main considerations.

The first relates to the initial act of creating a store of recorded events and phenomena such as those found in a library. This act, Derrida (1995) emphasizes, is always comprised of an act of exclusion, in the sense that all recordings are in some sense partial. Interview transcripts for instance, might accurately record all the words that are spoken, and may go some way to recording the general tenor of a conversation.

Nevertheless, they might also be lacking due to their not containing a full biography of the person interviewed, or a full explication of the interviewee's mental state and personal objectives. What Derrida emphasizes, then, is that whenever one reads a series of letters, books or what have you, one is left in the dark when it comes to what the authors exclude, deliberately or not, from their analysis.

The second consideration is that an archive's extent and content, the limits of what it enables to be recalled and analyzed, is impacted upon by technology. As Derrida (1995: 18) summarizes with uncharacteristic lucidity:

[W]hat is no longer archived in the same way is no longer lived in the same way. Archivable meaning is ... in advance codetermined by the structure that archives. It begins with the printer.

The third consideration follows on from the preceding two. It emphasizes that those with an interest in historical matters can become possessed of the want or need to push back the limits of an existing (and always limited) archive. To be possessed of this *mal d'archive*, this archive fever

is to burn with a passion. It is never to rest, interminably, from searching ... It is to have a compulsive, repetitive, and nostalgic desire for the archive, an irrepressible desire to return to the origin, a homesickness, a nostalgia for the return to the most archaic place of absolute commencement. (Derrida, 1995: 57)

Given the still growing extent of its informational activities, a strong argument can be made that, if any organization has ever suffered from archive fever, then it is Google. Although Google is the most prominent example of an Alphabet company possessed of archive fever – e.g. the seventh of ten things it purportedly 'know[s] to be true' states that 'there's always more information out there' (Google, Website D) – it is far from alone. Orbital Insight's founder Jimi Crawford, for example, has, in addition to describing the company as 'Google Books for satellite images', opined that 'The biggest challenge we always face is that we never have enough imagery, we never have enough data. So we are inevitably looking to our data scientists to pull as much signal as possible.' (Crawford, Website)

Given such sentiments, it is unsurprising that Alphabet affiliates have recognized that there is a profit to be made when archive fever burns brightly amongst the general population. Nest (Website), which purports to be 'creating the thoughtful home', includes Nest Aware amongst the products and services it offers. According to its website,

Nest Aware catches everything you missed. Nest Aware continuously records what's happening, 24/7, for up to 30 days. You can scan through your entire video history – not just clips – to see what you missed. You'll also get alerts for things that matter, like when your Nest Cam spots a person, or your Nest Hello or Nest Cam IQ detects a familiar face.

By encouraging archive fever to spread, and by being directly possessed of it, Alphabet investments are major players in the 'archival revolution' (Bearman, 2015: 1). Although still very early days, manifestations of Alphabet's fever-fueled contribution are abundant. One example is provided by the Google Cultural Institute (Website), which has, for a number of years now, enabled people to digitally visit and 'explore cultural treasures' and 'discover millions of artworks, historical sites and stories' from all around the world. Another is provided by Sidewalk Labs, which began providing access to the open-source and open-data Old Toronto map tool that links to historic photographs from the City of Toronto archives on 20 March 2018. Like similar resources that combine Google Maps data with city archives from San Francisco and New York, this specific resource enables the curious to easily and immediately see how Toronto's built environment has transformed since 1850.

Further to making a huge contribution to the rapid digitization of 'historical archives of enormous significance' (Bearman, 2015: 1), Alphabet companies and affiliates are contributing to the archiving of contemporary everyday existence. Although one cannot say that everything is currently being digitized, it does appear that 'we have reached a tipping point' (Jockers, 2013: 4) in terms of generating data that seeks to be 'exhaustive and fine-grained in scope, and flexible and scalable in its production' (Kitchin, 2014: 2).

YouTube alone, whose mission is 'to give everyone a voice and to show them the world' (YouTube, Website A), is reported to have 720,000 hours, or 82.2 years, of new video content uploaded every day (Hale, 2019). And Sidewalk Labs (Website), whose tagline is 'reimagining cities to improve quality of life', have recently commenced Sidewalk Toronto, a joint venture that 'aims to make Toronto the global hub for urban innovation'. As part of a plan to promote better transport, mixed-use neighborhoods, and a new standard of sustainability, the project will be underpinned by an 'open digital infrastructure ... that provides ubiquitous connectivity for all' (Ibid.). In doing so, Sidewalk Labs appear to be raising data collection on the tangible and more intangible aspects of city living to a whole new level.

As Marshall (2017) has written:

Sidewalk Labs promises to embed all sorts of sensors everywhere possible, sucking up a constant stream of information about traffic flow, noise levels, air quality, energy usage, travel patterns, and waste output. Cameras will help the company nail down the more intangible: Are people enjoying this public furniture arrangement in that green space? Are residents using the popup clinic when flu season strikes? Is that corner the optimal spot for a grocery store? Are its shopper[s] locals or people coming in from outside the neighborhood?

Given its seemingly pronounced fear of having to live with 'a history of the world imperfectly kept' (Darwin, 1968: 316), Alphabet can be seen as helping to construct what Moretti (2009: 158) terms 'some great library' of human existence. This concern to preserve more than just a 'few chapters ... or lines' (Darwin, 1968: 316) of human cultural and scientific existence is, at the risk of significant understatement, a sizable task. And whilst it is a task that digital technologies make possible, it is also a task that digital technologies threaten to undermine.

The reason why is that changes to hardware and software can make recorded digital content inaccessible or uninterpretable. One way to avoid this predicament would be to construct what Vint Cerf terms 'digital vellum ... an X-ray snapshot of the content and the application and the operating system together, with a description of the machine that it runs on, and preserve that for long periods of time' (Ghosh, 2015). In this way, society could 'preserve every piece of software and hardware so that it never becomes obsolete – just like what happens in a museum – but in digital form, in servers in the cloud' (Ghosh, 2015).

Such a service, Ghosh suggests, would have to be provided by a company. Ghosh also notes that as 'even Google might not be around in the next millennium', we could find it difficult to 'guarantee that both our personal memories and all human history would be safeguarded in the long run'. Whilst agreeing with Ghosh on this matter, Cerf still suggests that he finds it '"amusing to imagine that it is the year 3000 and you've done a Google search. The X-ray snapshot we are trying to capture [with digital vellum] should be transportable from one place to another. So, I should be able to move it from the Google cloud to some other cloud, or move it into a machine I have"' (Ghosh, 2015).

This idea – that Google might still be around in the very distant future – is likely to be anything but amusing for many people. Nevertheless, and given Google's, and now Alphabet's, track record when it comes to hugely ambitious goals, it would not be altogether surprising if Sergey Brin or Larry Page were to come out and suggest that Alphabet should be made the custodian of all social memories, and consequently granted some sort of infinite, guaranteed, life. But even if we cast this suggestion aside for the moment, the fact remains that Alphabet is, here and now, a major constructor of humanity's great library.

Although far from complete and fully secure, this great library currently contains a huge wealth of information. As a result, it appears that we may have already reached a point where there is not too little information, but too much (cf. Floridi, 2012). Thus, and whilst archive fever is in no danger of disappearing, it does appear that it is being superseded by archive drowning as a consideration of general prominence.

This sense of drowning in data, of being overwhelmed by information's flooding abundance, is something that Borges touched on in various works. In *Funes the Memorious*, the title character finds himself physically crippled, but in possession of an infallible perception and memory, following his fall from a horse. Funes' recollections, Borges emphasizes, were anything but simple:

[E]ach visual image was linked to muscular sensations, thermal sensations, etc. He could reconstruct all his dreams, all his fancies. Two or three times he had reconstructed an entire day. He told me: *I have more memories in myself alone than all men have had since the world was a world.* And again: *My dreams are like your vigils.* And again, toward dawn: *My memory, sir, is like a garbage disposal.* (Borges, 1942a: 112)

The basic point Borges sought to make was that an ever-growing recollective accuracy can prove more of a curse than a cure; that it can contribute to a sort of paralysis; to one's existing within some sort of non-conceptual darkness. Borges (1942a: 115) therefore emphasized that, whilst Funes had managed to 'learn' 'English, French, Portugese, Latin ... he was not very capable of thought': for to 'think is to forget a difference, to generalize, to abstract. In the overly replete world of Funes there were nothing but details, almost contiguous details'.

In referring back to Alphabet, it helps to remember that the growing flood of details that it, and others, are responsible for, is the result of both qualitative and quantitative changes to the information we can record. An example of the former is provided by our already being able to access fine-grained temporal data on the public's actual reactions to controversies. Such information simply did not exist prior to social media, which resulted in prior analysis of such events being limited to sentiments expressed by notable persons and the establishment media (Etter, et al., 2018: 75). And in terms of both qualitative and quantitative change, it appears that future generations will – thanks to the proliferation of microphones and cameras in domestic spaces (e.g. Nest Aware), to recordings of online transactions, to histories of media-viewing habits, email records, and so on – have access to veritably huge stores of what Braudel (1981: 560) termed, with no pejorative intent whatsoever, 'the dust of history'.

If those concerned with social pasts are to stand a chance of benefiting from our newly constructed and archived information riches, then they will need some sort of approach that enables them to swim rather than sink therein. With what follows, I propose that two approaches – the massive and mélange approaches to historical analysis – are likely to prove increasingly popular in such regards.

Massive History

Massive history is the first approach that can be employed to tackle the ever-increasing amount of information that is recorded and stored on our social pasts. It can be conceived in terms of four factors: its attitude to data; its worldview; its technologies and techniques; and its goals.

Data – All of It

In referring to a project he was first asked to write in 1952 – and that was subsequently published in French in 1979 as the three-volume *Civilisation matérielle, économie et capitalisme, XVe–XVIIIe siècle* – Braudel (1981: 25) noted: 'I wanted my study to cover the whole world if such a thing could be done.' Around twenty years later, Moretti – who 'was very influenced at a certain point by the Annales School' of which Braudel was arguably the leading light (Hackler & Kirsten, 2016: 5) – wrote of his ultimately similar desire to look beyond the (canonical) literature or style of any given region, and to begin work on the 'problem' of 'world literature' (Moretti, 2000: 55).

Moretti's concern to address the problem of world literature stemmed from his recognition of 'what Margaret Cohen calls the "great unread"', of the fact that whilst many people have read a great many books, no one has (or could) read them all: for 'there are thirty thousand nineteenth-century British novels out there, forty, fifty, sixty thousand—no one really knows ... And then there are French novels, Chinese, Argentinian, American' (Ibid.). Moreover, Moretti's concern stemmed from his belief that, 'if you really want to understand literature, you can't just read a few books or poems over and over ("Hamlet", "Anna Karenina", "The Waste Land"). Instead, you have to work with hundreds or even thousands of texts at a time' (Rothman, 2014).

As Moretti's colleague Matthew Jockers (2013: 7) has detailed:

Instead of conducting controlled experiments on samples and then extrapolating from the specific to the general or from the close to the distant, these massive data sets are allowing for investigations at a scale that reaches or approaches a point of being comprehensive. The once inaccessible "population" has become accessible and is fast replacing the random and representative sample.

Although more elaborate forms of data will prove increasingly analyzable at scale, the likes of Jockers and Moretti have hitherto focused their analyses on simple types of metadata – such as the information that library catalogues contain about a book's author(s), publication date, place of publication and subject matter. They have also tended to base their analyses on data sets that, at most, number in the thousands (Jockers, 2013: 35–36).

By way of contrast, a project that the Google Books team was involved in, and that was published in *Science* in 2011, involved the analysis of '5,195,769 digitized books containing ~4 percent of all books ever published' (Michel et al., 2011: 176). This analysis, which was conceived in terms of 'culturomics', sought to extend quantitative and precise measurement into the world of culture. The study focused on 'the question of how often a given 1-gram or n-gram was used over time. A 1-gram is a string of characters uninterrupted by a space; this includes words ("banana", "SCUBA") but also numbers ("3.14159") and typos ... An n-gram is a sequence of 1-grams, such as the phrases "stock market" (a 2-gram) and "the United States of America" (a 5-gram)' (Ibid.). Usage frequency was then 'computed by dividing the number of instances of the n-gram in a given year by the total number of words in the corpus in that year' (Ibid.). In this fashion, the study was able to establish that the 'use of "slavery" peaked during the Civil War (early 1860s) and then again during the civil rights movement (1955–68)' (Ibid.).

Whilst this study has its faults – e.g. n-gram counting does not allow for meaning usage to be disambiguated (Jockers, 2013: 120–122) – the fact that it was even completed (close to ten years ago now), remains impressive. So too does the fact that anyone can now use Google's Ngram Viewer to do similar analyses. By way of illustration, those interested in basketball might be interested to note that between 1990 and 2000, the frequency with which 'NBA' (National Basketball Association) was found in the English corpus slightly exceeded 'NFL' (National Football League). And those interested in late twentieth-century continental philosophy might have their suspicions confirmed when they see that, within the English corpus once again, the frequency of 'Derrida' mentions began outstripping 'Habermas' mentions around 1985.

Worldview – Objective

The ideal worldview for the massive historian is an objective one. The purpose, according to Braudel (1981: 25), is to 'see and to let others see, by allowing' the material drawn upon 'to speak for itself'. In a post-Kantian world where 'representational theories of truth' would seem to have been 'put to an end' (Hacking, 1979: 383), this sentiment can seem misguided and naïve. Nevertheless, the ideal of letting data speak for itself remains very appealing, and can, in a variety of obvious ways, be seen to work in everyday life.

The postal system, as discussed by Burke (1941), provides a case in point. Through a system involving the identification of a name, apartment number, building number, street, city, country and often a postcode, it is possible for one person to address a letter to another person half way around the world, and be relatively certain that this person will receive the correspondence. Thus, by 'filling out those few lines [on an envelope], you can effectively isolate one man among ... billion[s]' (Burke, 1941: 140). Rather than seeking to describe the person's character and appearance, two things that are open to interpretation, one simply focuses on describing facts that all can readily agree upon, and that can be termed, for all intents and purposes, objective.

The objective ideal is to extend such semantic meaning beyond the postal system and '*to evolve a vocabulary that gives the name and address of every event in the universe*' (Burke, 1941: 141). Such a vocabulary would avoid much (and potentially all) confusion. To illustrate, the perfect 'semantic definition of a chair would be such that, on the basis of the definition, people knew what you wanted when you asked for one, a carpenter knew how to make it, a furniture dealer knew how to get it, etc.' (Burke, 1941: 141–142).

John Wilkins (1614–1672), one of the founders of the Royal Society, a natural philosopher, and an important player in the Anglican church in his day, was famously inspired by such a goal. In his *An Essay towards a Real Character and a Philosophical Language* that was published in 1668 by the Royal Society – and which is now readily accessible thanks to it having been digitized by Google – Wilkins (1668: The Epistle) sought to construct a 'Universal Language' that would provide 'the shortest and plainest way for the attainment of real Knowledge'. He also hoped that his efforts would 'contribute much to the clearing of some of our Modern differences in Religion, by unmasking many wild errors, that shelter themselves under the disguise of affected phrases'.

Wilkins' Universal Language provides one of the many threads that Neal Stephenson weaves together in *Quicksilver (Baroque Cycle 1)*. At one point, for example, he writes of Wilkins revealing – in conversation with one of the book's main characters Daniel Waterhouse – that he had begun work on the *Essay*, on what he terms the 'Universal Character ... the Alpha ... A candle in the darkness' (Stephenson, 2004: 116). Daniel then asks Wilkins:

"Is this anything like Comenius's project?" Wilkins leaned across and made as if to box Daniel's ears. "It is his project! This was what he and I, and that whole gang of odd Germans— Hartlib, Haak, Kinner, Oldenburg— wanted to do when we conceived the Invisible College [predecessor of the Royal

Society] back in the Dark Ages. But Mr. Comenius's work was burned up in a fire, back in Moravia, you know." (Ibid.)

John Amos Comenius was a Moravian philosopher and educator known for being one of the earliest champions of universal education, and for advocating Pansophy: an approach promoting universal wisdom in knowledge and ethics. The fire to which the fictional Wilkins refers, is seemingly that which burnt down Leszno, in Poland, during the First Northern War in 1656. Comenius had been working in Leszno since 1654, and tragically 'lost many of his unpublished manuscripts' as a result of the fire (Atwood, 2015). Wilkins' own project was almost lost to the same fate in the Great Fire of London in 1666. But as it turned out, and no doubt thanks to a great deal of work by Wilkins and his team, the Great Fire only pushed back its publication a few years (Wilkins, 1668: The Epistle).

Although Borges (1942b) himself does not make the link, it is not difficult to imagine him using this fire as a metaphor for what he considered the ultimate futility of such projects. For Borges, this is very simply illustrated by Wilkins' scheme – which is comprised of forty top-level categories or classes (Wilkins, 1668: 387) – placing the whale 'in the sixteenth category: it is a viviparous, oblong fish' (Borges, 1942b: 231). To drive his point home, Borges (Ibid.) makes no lengthy excursion into the whale as mammal literature. Rather, he writes that the 'ambiguities, redundancies, and deficiencies' of Wilkins' project

recall those attributed by Dr. Franz Kuhn to a certain Chinese encyclopedia called the Heavenly Emporium of Benevolent Knowledge. In its distant pages it is written that animals are divided into (a) those that belong to the emperor; (b) embalmed ones; (c) those that are trained; (d) suckling pigs; (e) mermaids; (f) fabulous ones; (g) stray dogs; (h) those that are included in this classification; (i) those that tremble as if they were mad; (j) innumerable ones; (k) those drawn with a very fine camel's hair brush; (l) etcetera; (m) those that have just broken the flower vase; (n) those that at a distance resemble flies.

The preceding passage has inspired mirth in many, including Foucault (1970), who claims that it inspired him to write *The Order of Things*. But despite Borges' generally dismissive attitude, he was still gracious enough to recognize that Wilkins' system contained moments of ingenuity. Whatever the case, the point to emphasize is that some sort of universally agreed upon system by which to organize existence would achieve Braudel's objective aims of letting the facts speak for themselves. It would also further Moretti's (2003: 68) concern to construct a 'more rational literary history'.

Tools and Techniques – Count and Learn

In wanting to objectively analyse 'everything' related to a specific event, or to a more expansive *longue durée* (Braudel, 1958: 27–28), massive historians have to use computers. Time is the most obvious reason why. If, for instance, one wanted to read the six thousand English novels that were published in nineteenth-century Britain and remain available today, then it would take 'sixteen and a half years ... to get through them all' presuming that one could read one book a day (Jockers, 2013: 19). And in illustrating the same point, albeit in a more ridiculous fashion, it is noted in the Google Books team analysis referred to above, that if you wrote out the 'English language entries from the year 2000 alone ... in a straight line, it would reach to the Moon and back 10 times over' (Michel et al., 2011: 176).

The simplest use that massive historians can make of computers is counting. Whilst very basic, this technique can still prove suggestive. To this end, the Google Books team showed that mentions of 'pizza' and 'pasta' have gone through the roof since the 1950s, whereas mention of 'hamburger' has enjoyed a lesser, but steadier, climb since around 1920. They also showed that, whereas 'men' was far more commonly mentioned than 'women' from 1800 to 1950; 'women' came to be mentioned more than 'men' around the year 2000 (Michel et al., 2011: 181). As such counts might be dismissed off the bat as nothing more than superficial, it should be remembered that they are not altogether dissimilar to the counts that saturate the works of Braudel: e.g. his figures outlining the weight of bread and the price of grain in Venice from 1575 to 1603 (1981: 142).

Besides simple counting, massive historians can employ supervised machine learning (DiMaggio, 2015; Etter et al., 2018). There are two main steps. First, a set of data is coded by researchers: e.g. for sentiment or style. This data is then split into a 'training set' and a 'test set' so as to generate and validate a model that is predictively accurate – such as a model that is able to identify a specific style of music with a specific artist (e.g. metal with Black Sabbath, funk with James Brown). Once the model has learnt to classify the test set to a degree of accuracy deemed sufficient, it is then used to classify an un-coded data set: e.g. associate Prince with pop. In this way, the machine learns to classify materials that can prove exceedingly difficult for humans to classify – whether for lack of resources or lack of skill.

Massive historians can also use unsupervised machine learning techniques. In contrast to supervised learning – which involves a pre-coded or classified data set to train the machine – unsupervised learning involves algorithms that 'experience a dataset containing many features ... [and] then learn useful properties' of its structure (Goodfellow, Bengio & Courville, 2016: 105). Amongst other things, machines can learn to cluster data in ways that are not evident from existing classification models (Murphy, 2012: 10–11): e.g. a hitherto unidentified group of demographically diverse consumers that buy similar products and services. Unsupervised learning is more difficult for researchers to validate, in the sense that they are not measured against a pre-established classification system (DiMaggio, 2015: 2). But it has a number of benefits. Perhaps the most obvious is that, by observing the world, rather than 'being told to name every object' in it, it is closer to how humans and animals learn (LeCun, Bengio & Hinton, 2015: 442). It also enjoys cost benefits due to it not requiring a 'human expert to manually label the data' (Murphy, 2012: 10). Given such considerations, leading researchers in machine learning (LeCun et al., 2015) and the social sciences (DiMaggio, 2015) suggest unsupervised learning will grow in prominence.

Goals - Description and Explanation

The first and most basic task of those who employ the massive history approach is description. Through the use of machines that count and learn, massive historians can try to provide an objective summary of the most complete or largest data set possible. The Google Books team's analysis provides a good example by describing shifts in the use and spread of (ir)regular verbs, and of the changing temporal dimensions of fame (Michel et al., 2011). So too does Moretti's (2009) description of how the median length of British novel titles dropped from 15–20 words in 1740 to just 6 in 1850; and his showing that (hegemonic) genres (e.g. epistolary novels, gothic novels, historical novels) produce 'more or less the same number of novels per year', tend to last for between 25–30 years, and only rise in prominence once a 'previous wave [or genre] has begun to ebb away' (Moretti, 2003: 77).

Back in 2008, the then editor of *Wired* magazine Chris Anderson, made the provocative suggestion that description might be all that we need in the petabyte [10^{15} bytes] age. He proposed that this, our contemporary period, is

different because more is different. Kilobytes were stored on floppy disks. Megabytes ... on hard disks. Terabytes ... in disk arrays. Petabytes are stored in the cloud. As we moved along that progression, we went from the folder analogy to the file cabinet analogy to the library analogy to — well, at petabytes we ran out of organizational analogies. (Anderson, 2008)

More stridently, and as is clear from the article's title, Anderson posited 'The End of Theory: The Data Deluge Makes the Scientific Method Obsolete'. He used Google to illustrate his basic point by writing

Google conquered the advertising world with nothing more than applied mathematics. It didn't pretend to know anything about the culture and conventions of advertising – it just assumed that better data, with better analytical tools, would win the day ... Google's founding philosophy is that we don't know why this page is better than that one: if the statistics ... say it is, that's good enough. No semantic or causal analysis is required. (Ibid.)

This sort of pure empiricism can seem attractive. But as more prudent observers have noted, it is unworkable because we always frame (Kitchin, 2014: 5), and always need to frame (Borges, 1942b), data. Indeed, without some sort of conceptual structure – e.g. the idea of a cluster, the simple idea of 0s and 1s – we cannot make sense of anything.

The less banal problem with Anderson's (2008) position is that it obscures the prospect of using massive data sets to generate new theories (Goldberg, 2015: 3). Rather than focusing on atheoretical description (Anderson, 2008), then, massive historians can actively seek out 'facts contrary to what we should expect' – and develop new theories that explain such anomalies (Peirce, 1901: 94–95). Such a 'mystery driven', 'breakdown' or abductive approach has often been associated with singular or small-number case-study research (Alvesson & Karreman, 2007). Massive historians, however, can apply it to huge data sets. As a result, they can avoid the generalizability concerns that plague those who try to develop theories off limited, illustrative case-study examples (Eisenhardt & Graebner, 2007: 27).

More broadly, much of the excitement that big data and machine learning has created in the humanities and social sciences, relates to their contributing to entirely new questions, and what amounts to entirely new fields of study, emerging. Whilst portmanteaus such as 'culturomics' (Michel et al., 2011), and bold assertions of 'a new "science"' (Moretti, 2000: 55), are not to everyone's taste, it does seem that the general phenomenon being pointed towards – here termed massive history – can 'revolutionize historical social science' (Bearman, 2015). And as Zeng and Greenfield's (2015) use of the Google Ngram Viewer to analyze cultural evolution in China will suffice to illustrate, Alphabet entities are clearly enabling of the approach's development.

Mélange History

Mélange history is the second approach that can be employed to tackle the ever-increasing amount of information that is recorded and stored on our social pasts. As with massive history, it can be conceived in terms of four factors.

Data – Appropriate

When confronted by the growing mass of digitized social records, the mélange history approach dictates that one treats these records like 'a buffet' (Dennett, 2007: 248). Whereas the massive approach encourages those interested in social pasts to engage with as much data as possible, the mélange approach encourages one to be much more selective as to the materials they build upon. Moreover, the mélange approach encourages the historian to think in terms of 'post-production' (Campanelli, 2015: 73); to be willing to appropriate and transform data for their own ends.

In emphasizing the potential for artefacts to be used in ways that may have been unwanted, unimaginable or both, for their original creators, the act of finding, selecting and then combining different pieces of information and media, is conceived as both industrious and artistic. In fact – and as indicated by the currently ubiquitous talk of (data) mining (Christopher, 2015: 207) and (data) curation (Wanono, 2015: 399) – such acts are already commonplace. Given that such developments are still quite recent, Claude Lévi-Strauss's notion of the bricoleur, and Michel de Certeau's notion of tactics, can appear prophetic.

Lévi-Strauss (1966) used the notion of bricolage to highlight the ways in which a given set of tools and materials could be used in a multitude of ways. In contrast to the engineer, who has 'as many sets of tools and materials or "instrumental sets" as there are different kinds of projects'; the bricoleur makes use of materials and tools that, whilst 'specialized up to a point', do not have 'one definite and determinate use' (Lévi-Strauss, 1966: 17–18). Thus, when starting a new project, the bricoleur will collect or revisit a selection of materials to identify those pieces that can be directed towards the achievement of their current aims and goals. The fact that the bricoleur's materials were not originally created with the bricoleur's purpose in mind, means that any given part of a new construct, will tend to be, or need to be, replaceable. It also results in any inherent meaning of a given piece of material being abstracted away and replaced by one derived from its 'potential use'. Consequently, the bricoleur experiments with different materials to 'discover' which combination thereof best aids the achievement of their task (Lévi-Strauss, 1966: 17–19).

This capacity to select objects and materials from amongst those already created, to turn the 'actual order of things' to one's 'own ends', was referred to by de Certeau as '"popular" tactics' (de Certeau, 1984: 26, 2). Tactics are popular in the sense that 'everyone' can employ them from within the 'space of the other', or within 'enemy territory' (de Certeau, 1984: 36–37). To illustrate, de Certeau referred to the manner in which employees make use of company time and resources to pursue their own personal projects: e.g. write a letter, make a piece of furniture (25–26). Accordingly, and much like Lévi-Strauss, de Certeau emphasized that the meaning of a given set of materials 'are neither determined nor captured by the systems in which they [originally] develop' (xvii).

As these points suggest, massive and mélange historians differ due to the former focusing on the manifest meaning of data sets that are treated as wholes (Jockers, 2013; Kitchin, 2014: 8; Mohr, Wagner-Pacifici & Breiger, 2015: 2; Moretti, 2000), and the latter on acts of appropriation that interpret and construct meaning with texts and materials that are treated as fragmentable and incomplete. In other words, the mélange historian utilizes pieces of what has already been 'transmitted and displayed in the media universe' (Campanelli, 2015: 75), and redeploys them as part of their own design.

World View – Contextual

Alongside other titles such as *Road to Equality*, *Monet Was Here*, and *Treasures of Lyon*, the Google Arts & Culture website listed, in May 2018, *Black History and Culture* amongst its featured themes. Further to the assembled collection of 'artworks, artifacts and stories from cultural organizations across the United States', the theme contained a variety of commentaries. One of these commentaries – by Shameless Maya: a YouTuber and social media influencer/brand promoter – focuses on Black Female Icons. In her talk, which was filmed for Google Arts and Culture (2018) to celebrate Black History Month in February 2018, Maya states:

I feel like we were deleted from textbooks.
I feel like our story was stripped from us.
We weren't allowed to write.
We weren't allowed to read and now this is our time to tell our stories that haven't been told and I'm so passionate about seeing more of those in things that are accessible, like television, like movies because we're constantly looking out to look back in and if we don't see those stories, if we don't hear them we lose a sense of our identity.
And in order to know where you're going, you have to know where you came from.

With the preceding statement, Maya neatly illustrates the basic way in which mélange history is associated with a contextual world-view. In contrast to massive history's objective worldview, which aims to let any material or data drawn upon 'speak for itself' (Braudel, 1981: 25), the contextual worldview recognizes that the data or materials focused on are conditioned by the place and time in which they are utilized.

In emphasizing and explicating their context, the mélange historian could be said to be making a virtue of necessity: for a text can only ever have meaning 'through its readers; it changes along with them' (de Certeau, 1984: 170). Consequently, de Certeau (1988: 56) also thought that, even when a given piece of historical research strives towards the 'general or extensive' – as in the case of massive history – its author will never prove 'capable of effacing the *specificity* of the place, the origin … This mark is indelible'. One's 'way of speaking', one's 'patois', is always marked by one's 'relation to a given place' (Ibid.).

Rorty (1989: 21, 50) makes much the same point when he posits that we cannot simply escape 'the language of our ancestors' or easily 'rise above the contingencies of [our] history'. More positively, Rorty suggests that if people are to prove capable of altering or redirecting the course of [their] history, then they will first have to confront their own contingency by tracking their 'causes home'. In this way, Rorty posits that people will be in a much stronger position to (re-) create their 'own mind and language rather than let the length of … [their] mind be set by the language other human beings have left behind' (27).

In short, the contextual worldview can be seen as not just necessary, but as empowering, for the mélange historian. Rather than simply enabling an individual or community to look back so as to extrapolate where they are going, it enables individuals and communities to construct historical self-knowledge and redirect their futures.

Tools and Techniques – Remix

The ability to appropriate resources that document social pasts has been hugely enabled by digitization. By and large, this relates to the ease of searching for digital materials online, and to the copying or stealing of digitized materials being 'costless'. Such developments have been continuously resisted by incumbent powers in the content industries. Others, however, encourage such developments due to their enabling a further break in the divide that separated producers (professionals) and consumers (amateurs) in the age of mass media (e.g. Benkler, 2006).

Lawrence Lessig is the most famous champion of such changing dynamics, and of what is often referred to as 'remix culture' (Navas, Gallagher & burrough, 2015: 1). In one of his books on the topic, Lessig (2008: 28) advocates '"Read/Write" ("RW")' over '"Read/ Only" ("RO")' culture. Whereas RO culture is associated with the simplest and most basic acts of consumption, Lessig suggests 'think: couch'; RW culture is associated with people 'creating and re-creating the culture around them' by 'using the same tools the professional uses' (Ibid.).

In effect, RW culture is conceived as a horizontal world populated by more or less equal actors, or makers, who simultaneously produce and consume. It is also associated with a rapidly advancing

ecology of RW Media … [that] remix, or quote, a wide range of "texts" to produce something new. These quotes … happen at different layers.… remixed media may quote sounds over images, or video over text, or text over sounds. The quotes thus get mixed together. The mix produces the new creative work – the "remix". (Lessig, 2008: 69)

Given that Lessig makes a lot of positive references to YouTube throughout this 2008 work, which is itself entitled *Remix*, it is not surprising that the book's publication followed Google's November 2006 pledge of US $2 million to the Stanford Centre for Internet and Society that Lessig founded (Whelan, 2019). That being said, Lessig (2008: 256) does seem to have been correct when he suggested that YouTube has, arguably more than any other organization, provided a platform from which to make 'remix(es) publicly available'. Moreover, by providing users with infrastructure, succinct information and various tools, the likes of YouTube – and other organizations like Creative Commons (which Lessig also founded) – have been key players in helping those that remix materials avoid infringing on extant copyright laws.

A very literal example of how remixing can construct social pasts is provided by Göran Olsson's (2011) *The Black Power Mixtape, 1967–1975*. The footage used in the film was originally broadcast on 'Swedish primetime' and was found by Olsson in the basement of the Swedish broadcast corporation (Mumin, 2011). The footage includes interviews with, and recordings of presentations by, Stokely Carmichael, an influential player in the SNCC (Student Nonviolent Coordinating Committee); Angela Davis, a leader of the Black Panther Party; and Eldridge Cleaver, who, amongst other things, was the Minister of Information and Head of the International Section of the Black Panthers.

Along with the use he made of footage from half a century ago, Olsson included contemporary comments from some of the original protagonists, such as Angela Davis, and from politically 'conscious' musicians such as Erykah Badu, Talib Kweli and Questlove. The film also builds upon a rich and prominent soundtrack from the era. In combining all these elements, Olsson wanted to open up 'new possibilities for filmmakers in terms of ... archival footage, voiceovers and music' (Mumin, 2011). Furthermore, Olsson proposed that

there is a relation between moving images and music that is very, very strong. When music works in rhythm with the moving image, that's the best you can get. And if you could add some social or human level into that mix ... add some politics or social issues or consciousness into that dance between music and film, you should be very happy. But it's easy. It's very easy to do because editing is so great ... you can change the face of work and it's so easy. (Mumin, 2011)

Whilst Olsson's suggestion that (re)editing multimedia is 'very easy' is currently an overstatement, the ongoing democratization of music-mixing technologies – which has long been the source of hand-wringing amongst interested parties (Lhooq, 2017; Swift, 2015) – suggests that the general direction in which he points is correct. So as remixing technologies get easier to use, and as footage materials increase in number and accessibility, we should expect more actors interested in social pasts to employ remix tools and techniques.

Goals – Development

One possible motivation for adopting the mélange tactic is social change or development. In contrast to the massive historian, whose focus on describing and explaining history is at best indirectly concerned with changing the future course of events, the mélange historian can focus on using the past as a means by which to direct the future. To paraphrase Marx, the mélange historian can try to change, and not just interpret, the world (Marx, 1845: Thesis XI).

The concern to use historical or 'ancient materials' to develop new forms of community, or to fortify existing ones, has been highlighted by Hobsbawm (1983: 6) with the notion of 'invented traditions'. Such inventions 'throw considerable light on the human relation to the past' and are – in their 'use [of] history as a legitimator of action and cement of group cohesion' (Hobsbawm, 1983: 12) – more or less common-place. 'Even revolutionary movements back ... their innovations by reference to a "people's past" ... to traditions of revolution' (Hobsbawm, 1983: 13). Such invented traditions have also been inte-gral to the flourishing of nationalism worldwide; and have, whether 'consciously or not', long been the stock-in-trade of (professional) historians who dismantle and restructure 'images of the past which belong not only to the world of specialist investigation but to the public sphere of man as a political being' (Ibid.).

This concern with (re)invention or (re)development can have varying purposes. Nevertheless, it is perhaps most interesting, and most influential, when it seeks to broaden a community or make it more inclusive. For Burke (1941: 144), such a task involves the thinking up of new poetic meanings that 'are related to one another like a set of concentric circles, of wider and wider scope'. Burke (1941: 148) also posits that this sort of poetic movement – from the particular to the general – works not by trying 'to cut away' or 'abstract, all emotional factors', but from 'the maximum heaping up of ... emotional factors', by 'playing them off against one another, inviting them to reinforce and contradict each other'.

The remix technique is particularly well-suited to constructing such contradictory messages. It can also be used to highlight the risks associated therewith, as Olsson does in *The Black Power Mixtape, 1967–75*. Most notably, Olsson includes interview footage with Courtney Callender at The Studio Museum in Harlem from 1973. In the selected footage, Callender raises the concern that

This whole kind of falling in love with black things for a short period of time is essentially racist. It still is hypothesized on a great sense of separateness and a sense of treating black activities as a kind of curiosity. Either benign or threatening, one or the other. When its threatening, you know, oh my god they're going to riot or something. When its benign, let's let them paint or draw or sing or dance or whatever they want to do until we get tired of it. Until we the white community get tired of it. That whole structure is essentially racist. (Olsson, 2011)

The tension Callender explicates is evident throughout Olsson's mixtape, and is further illustrated by Olsson's choosing to use footage of a Harlem bus tour following Callender's statement. The footage shows (white) passengers being told by their tour guide that the bus tour operators '"do not want anyone to visit Harlem for personal studies ... This neighborhood is only for black people. Not even the better – if I may use that wording – the better Colored people visit this area because of the risk of being mugged"' (Olsson, 2011).

By so explicating the risks of cultural appropriation and the fetishizing of difference, and through his use of Swedish footage of the life and times of American revolutionaries more generally, Olsson sought to extend the contextually specific meaning of the Black Power movement to a broader audience. He made this clear at the end of his interview with Mumin (2011) when he states:

Angela [Davis], Stokely [Carmichael]— are great, great people. I think they deserve a lot of respect — not for fighting for their cause only, but also fighting for democracy. Because what these people did, to me, was that they put energy into the process of democracy and that's very important. Not only for Afro-Americans, or for any ethnic groups, but to all individuals ... It's not about skin color; it's about standing up for your rights.

Summary

The preceding has posited that, through creating, and providing access to, previously unimaginable stores of information, Alphabet is in effect necessitating that those who seek to analyze or construct our social pasts adopt something like the massive or mélange approach to historical analysis. The reason why is that, despite their clear differences, both approaches are similarly well-suited to managing the vastness of information that the historically curious are increasingly confronted by.

Although Alphabet entities currently provide access to significant parts of the great library they are continuously building, there is no guarantee that they will continue to do so in the future. The data that is being collected by the likes of Orbital Insight, Nest and Sidewalk Labs, for example, could easily be kept in-house, or only be made accessible to select parties. Even when information is not tightly constrained in terms of access – as is currently the case with YouTube – Alphabet entities are in a privileged position from which to analyze and utilize the data they collect and store. The sorts of analyses that YouTube currently does through its Culture & Trends arm – e.g. its provision of details on viewing patterns at different geographic levels over varying timeframes (YouTube, Website B) – can therefore be seen as but the earliest stage in the development of Alphabet's history-constructing capacities.

More generally, what the considerations of this and Chapter 4 combine to suggest, is that Alphabet is very strongly motivated to become – and in some ways already has become – the custodian of our personal and social pasts. Whilst Alphabet does not yet dominate the future in the exact same way, Chapters 6 and 7 suggest that the megacorporation is doing its best to ensure that it is just as powerful when we turn away from historical concerns, and look towards those which are yet to come.

6 | *Personal Futures*

This chapter proposes that, through its various investments, Alphabet is contributing to developments that could significantly extend our lifespan via biological and digital means. In doing so, the chapter first provides a very brief overview of Ray Kurzweil's desire to live 'forever'. Whilst acknowledging that at least some people are likely to always remain ready to die – given their desire to ascend (to heaven), egalitarian concerns, bioconservative tendencies or fear of boredom – it is posited that most people would, along with Ray Kurzweil, choose to (radically) extend their personal future if given the choice. In light of such, two approaches to managing such extended personal futures – termed the singular and sequential approaches respectively – are detailed. Finally, the chapter concludes with a brief summary, and by noting that the life extension business could prove even more profitable than Alphabet's current money printing machine: Google advertising.

Who Wants to Live 'Forever'?

Ray Kurzweil began working for Google as a director of engineering in January 2013 (Hof, 2013). This appointment, which has been described as one of Larry Page's more 'surprising initiatives during his second stint as the company's CEO' (Simonite, 2017), appears to have been informed by three overlapping considerations. First, it is seemingly informed by Kurzweil's impressive record for invention, which began with his building 'a computer to analyze and compose classical music' when he was a teenager from Queens, New York, in the 1960s (Cowan, 2011). Following this, and amongst many other accomplishments, Kurzweil helped to generalize optical character recognition technologies; 'invented the modern synthesizer, passing the musical equivalent of a Turing Test by generating sound indistinguishable from a grand piano'; and 'developed and commercialized the first large-vocabulary speech recognition software' (Ibid.).

Second, Page's decision was influenced by Kurzweil's writing of the 2012 book *How to Create a Mind*. In this work, Kurzweil proposes 'that all functions in the neocortex... are based on systems that use a hierarchy of pattern recognition to process information. Each layer, he argues, uses the output of the ones below it to work with increasingly complex and abstract patterns' (Simonite, 2014). Although some of Kurzweil's critics have suggested that his theory is at best 'generic', and at worst uninformed and entirely lacking in 'novel insight' (Marcus, 2012), Kurzweil himself has noted that he was '"basically recruited"' by Larry Page '"to bring this thesis to Google"' after he had '"made the case that applying this model to machine learning would make it very good at understanding language"' (Simonite, 2017).

Third, Page's decision to appoint Kurzweil was likely informed by the latter's work as a futurist. Whilst no less than Bill Gates has referred to Kurzweil as '"the best person I know at predicting the future of artificial intelligence"' (Cadwalladr, 2014), not everyone is convinced that Kurzweil has some sort of privileged insight into future happenings. In particular, Kurzweil's tendency to evangelize on the 'singularity' (Kurzweil, 2005) – 'a theoretical moment in the future when computers would achieve a critical mass of artificial intelligence and wake up and change everything' (Kobek, 2016: 190) – has led some to suggest that he is 'the god of lies', the 'king of the most intolerable of all intolerable bullshit' (Ibid.).

As Kurzweil gets closer to what most assume will be his (biological) death (he was born in 1948), it is to be expected that more and more people will take joy in pointing out the craziness of his widely reported desire to live 'forever' (i.e. to continue living indefinitely – for he is yet to suggest that he wants to be re-born at the beginning of time). Consequently, Google, and the other Alphabet assets and initiatives that Kurzweil is linked with – such as Calico, the 'solving death' company that Kurzweil encouraged Bill Maris, the founder and former CEO of Google Ventures, to establish (Friend, 2017); and Singularity University, which Kurzweil co-founded, and which Larry Page and Google have supported in various ways (Popper, 2013) – could like-wise come to be increasingly ridiculed by association.

Without wanting to deny that such ridicule can be fun, and that the calling of bullshit can serve a serious purpose, the present chapter suggests that, given Alphabet's resources, the various ways in which the megacorporation is currently seeking to extend our personal futures are worthy of attention. But before turning to a discussion of such matters, it is necessary to first note that, for a number of different reasons, people might decide that they are not interested in indefinitely extending some version of their current life at all.

Ready to Die

When considering the idea of consciously deciding to die, or of refusing some sort of help that would extend one's existence, one's mind generally turns to those that are suffering from an insurmountable depression, from immense pain or that are going through, or have had to endure, some sort of tragedy. In addition to people suffering from these sorts of immediately painful concerns, however, it is possible to identify another four, potentially overlapping, groups of people, that would appear to have relatively more positive reasons for turning their back on life-extension technologies, and who are ready to die.

Ascensionists

Many people believe that, following their death, they will ascend to some sort of heaven. Those aligned with the Abrahamic religions of Judaism, Christianity and Islam, for example, often believe in some sort of divine and transcendent world that is ultimately separate from, but somehow discernable or imaginable through, the immediate, real and secular phenomena that we associate with earthly life (Cumpsty, 1991: 123). Once they are born again and welcomed into heaven, these people expect to live forever (Belshaw, 2015: 323; Williams, 1973: 83).

Historically, this promise of heaven has functioned as a strong motivation to adhere to a set of rules established by what is believed to be the one and true god (as reported by those with divine contact or awareness). Moreover, it has served as a source of comfort for those that live by such rules in the current world, but that feel they have been treated unjustly or otherwise suffered therein. In short, the belief that 'the manifest injustices of this world will be superseded by the cosmic justice of the next', has given people hope that the 'sufferings of the innocent and the triumphs of the vicious' will be divinely rectified (Scheffler, 2013: 67). Thus, ancient apocalyptic traditions in Jewish and Christian thought were associated with the belief that God 'would raise up the dead in purified... immortal... [and] glorious new bodies [that] would enable the righteous to join the angels in the Kingdom of God' (Geraci, 2010: 19). And traditions of martyrdom throughout the Abrahamic religions have emphasized that those willing to comply with the word of God in the face of adversity, or to fight for the word of God against adversaries, would be blessed with eternal salvation (Hatina, 2014: 19–37).

On top of believing that justice will be served, and that they will be reunited with those they have already lost (Scheffler, 2013: 67), ascensionists have tended to believe that the afterlife will be something like the best imaginable, or an amazingly good, version of earthly lived reality (Belshaw, 2015: 323). In this fashion, early and medieval Islamic traditions promised that those that actively sought to sacrifice their life 'for God and the faith' would get 'a seat of honor in paradise next to the prophets and the righteous'; 'be wreathed in a crown of honor... whose every jewel is worth more than this world in its entirety'; and be 'married to seventy-two virgins with beautiful eyes' (Hatina, 2014: 43).

Ancient apocalyptic visions and strenuous notions of martyrdom, however, are not necessary for one to believe they will ascend to a world that is much better than this one. Many contemporary Christians, for instance, appear to believe that heaven can be attained by demonstrating relatively moderate self-control, and by engaging in relatively non-demanding acts of charity. More generally, the point to emphasize is that, for those that believe in a more or less glorious afterlife, the prospect of extending their present one indefinitely, should, even if their current life is a good one, seem relatively unappealing. What is more interesting than simply imagining religion 'in a world without death' (Harari, 2015: 25), then, is imagining a professed believer having to decide between (1) the more or less certain continuity of a relatively well-off present existence and (2) their dying and, fingers-crossed, ascending to meet their maker.

This sort of Pascalian wager, whilst no doubt less pronounced when related to a choice between heavenly salvation and an earthly life that is not eternal, but merely longer than that which is currently expected, still suggests that true believers should be less inclined than non-believers towards extending their lives. Indeed, the willingness of ascensionists to give up 10, 20, 30 or more years, of potential extra life, could be quite strong if – like egalitarians – they believe that their access to such additional years is the result of, and likely to somehow exacerbate, social inequalities.

Egalitarians

The idea that high-tech developments might unfairly privilege some over others is as old as the hills. The lyrics of Gil Scott-Heron's 1970 track, *Whitey on the Moon* – which was released one year after (the white) Neil Armstrong became the first human to set foot on Luna's surface – articulates the basic concern:

> A rat done bit my sister Nell; with Whitey on the moon.
> Her face and arms began to swell; and Whitey's on the moon.
> I can't pay no doctor bills; but Whitey's on the moon.
> Ten years from now I'll be paying still; while Whitey's on the moon.

Just as Heron was critical of Whitey's Apollo 11 moon landing back in 1969, more recent developments in biotechnology, and the related field of bioethics, have been similarly criticized for having a Whitey focus: i.e. for dealing with problems of concern within the 'developed' world. In particular, it has been asked: 'given the problem of unequal death, can we morally afford to invest in research to extend life?' (Pijneburg & Leget, 2007: 585–586).

That we continue to live in a world of unequal death is readily apparent. At the beginning of the century, life expectancy in Australia, Japan, Sweden and Switzerland was greater than 80 years. By way of contrast, life expectancy in Angola, Malawi, Sierra Leone and Zimbabwe was less than 40 years (Dwyer, 2005: 460). Given this stark inequality, some suggest that instead of devoting more resources to such 'luxuries' (Benatar, 2003: 391) as extending the already relatively long average lifespan of those that are lucky enough to live in richer countries, we should increasingly direct our 'political, financial and scientific powers' (Pijneburg & Leget, 2007: 586) towards projects that help increase the average lifespan of those that live in less advantaged places (Dwyer, 2005).

Besides these more immediate inequality concerns, there is the potential for life-extension technologies, and other technologies by which we might 'upgrade', to give rise to inequalities that, if not new in kind, are new in degree. To illustrate, the 2,000 or so billionaires that are currently listed on the Forbes billionaire list could use their immense resources to monopolize life-extension and life-enhancement technologies to become 'superhumans [that] will enjoy unheard of abilities and unprecedented creativity, which will allow them to go on making many of the most important decisions in the world' (Harari, 2015: 404). If the rest of us were not so 'upgraded', then we would seemingly become little more than an 'inferior cast dominated by... the new superhumans' (Ibid.).

In a similar vein, there is the fear that, 'assuming aging-intervention and life extension are both effective and widespread in their uptake, then those who are chronologically precedent [i.e. older]... will have no incentive to make way for the young, and indeed... may be positively driven by their faculties and abilities to remain incumbent in positions of power and authority indefinitely' (Horrobin, 2005: 19). This basic problem is 'most stark when one adds to the scenario the conjecture that at least some of these persons will be of bad character' (Ibid.) and immensely powerful. Nevertheless, it is also a concern that anyone who has ever been in a more junior position is likely to be keenly aware of. Just think, that well-established 'colleague' that so obviously dislikes you, and that you just know is forever making reject recommendations on your oh-so-well-thought-out papers, might never retire. But in putting these more selfish thoughts to one side, the point to emphasize is that, if a person truly values equality, then there are a number of reasons to think that they should be willing to take any resources they currently control away from projects that might unduly extend or upgrade their own existence; and redirect them towards extending the much shorter expected lifespan of those that live in less prosperous parts of the world.

Bioconservatives

In addition to the equality risks they give rise to, and to their potentially delaying or preventing one from realizing divine profits, some think that life-extension (and life-enhancement) technologies are 'dehumanizing' (Bostrom, 2005: 203). Such people can be termed bioconservatives (Ibid.), and have been associated with the suggestion that 80 years

is a conceptually manageable lifespan, with individuals living not only through childhood and parenthood but long enough to see their own grand-children, and permitted a taste of each sort of relationship. It is a world in which one's direct family lineage is connected by both genetics and personal experience, not so attenuated by time that relatives feel unrelated. Generation and nurture, dependency and reciprocated generosity, are in some harmony of proportion, and there is a pace of journey, a coordinated coherence of meter and rhyme within the repeating cycles of birth, ascendancy, and decline—a balance and beauty of love and renewal giving answer to death that, however poignant, bespeaks the possibility of meaning and goodness in the human experience. All this might be overthrown or forgotten in the rush to fashion a technological project [that would radically extend our lifespan]. (The President's Council on Bioethics, 2003: 197)

Despite having some intuitive appeal, this general argument can, relative to the aforementioned arguments regarding equality, be quickly dismantled due to it falling 'foul of a standard objection in philosophy…"the naturalistic fallacy"' (Horrobin, 2005: 10). In short, the argument makes the problematic suggestion that any efforts that humans make to alter or amend their lived reality are unnatural, and therefore incorrect (Horrobin, 2005: 11). Additionally, the argument appears to assume that one's current expected lifespan, which is clearly determined by our current 'ways of life and… medical technology', possesses an intrinsic moral worth that belies its epiphenomenal status (Schloendorn, 2006: 194).

In various works, Nick Bostrom – a self-professed 'transhumanist' Oxford philosopher, and current fellow at Alphabet DeepMind's Ethics & Society research unit – has taken the bioconservative perspective apart. In a paper written with Toby Ord, Bostrom has advanced the idea of the 'reversal test' so as to overcome the 'status-quo bias': i.e. a bias that results in one tending to perceive potential technology-enabled enhancements to human existence in a negative light (Bostrom & Ord, 2006). When the reversal test is applied to the possibility of genetically engineered cognitive enhancements, what it suggests is that if a given person presumes that using this same technology to reduce human intelligence would be a bad thing, then it is they who bear the argumentative duty of explaining why this same technology could not be used to increase it (Bostrom & Ord, 2006: 664–665).

As Bostrom and Ord (2006: 677) go on to note, in the 2003 report produced by the US President's Council on Bioethics, Leon Kass and his team came 'tantalisingly close to considering a Reversal Test' when 'the report reflects: "Yet if there is merit in the suggestion that too long a life... might diminish its worth, one might wonder whether we have already gone too far in increasing longevity... [and] further suggest that we should, if we could, roll back at least some of the increases made in the average human lifespan over the past century"' (The President's Council on Bioethics, 2003: 196). But in immediately backing away from such a possibility, what the Council emphasized was that, whilst they did identify various 'possible problems with substantially longer lifespans, we have not expressed, and would not express, a wish for shorter lifespans than are now the norm' (Ibid.).

Bostrom and Ord (2006: 677), suffice it to note, were unimpressed by this failure to apply the reversal test. More positively, Bostrom (2005: 213) has elsewhere suggested that what bioconservatives need to recognize is that,'[i]n the eyes of a hunter-gatherer, we might already appear "posthuman". Yet these radical extensions of human capabilities – some of them biological, others external – have not divested us of moral status or dehumanized us in the sense of making us generally unworthy and base'. He accordingly posits that 'should we or our descendants one day succeed in becoming what relative to current standards we may refer to as posthuman, [then] this need not entail a loss [of] dignity either' (Bostrom, 2005: 213).

Ennuists

The final group of people that might refrain from making use of technologies that could help them (indefinitely) extend their existence, are ennuists. As the label indicates, such people are self-interestedly worried that an extended existence would come to be characterized, more or less quickly, by a general lack of interest, excitement and novelty. 'Live fast, die young', might be taken as their motto. Within the relevant literature, it is possible to identify two aspects to the ennuist position.

First is the boredom argument associated with Williams' (1973) discussion of *The Makropulos Case*: the title of a play written by Karel Čapek in 1922. As per Williams' (1973: 82) summary, Čapek's play tells the story of

a woman called Elina Makropulos, alias Emilia Marty, alias Ellian Macgregor, alias a number of other things with the initials "EM", on whom her father, the Court physician to a sixteenth-century Emperor, tried out an elixir of life [at the age of 42]... [After another 300 years of existence] Her unending life has come to a state of boredom, indifference and coldness. Everything is joyless: "in the end it is the same", she says, "singing and silence". She refuses to take the elixir again; she dies.

According to Williams (1973: 89), EM's decision to die was entirely justified: for 'an endless life would be a meaningless one... There is no desirable or significant property which life would have more of, or have more unqualifiedly, if we lasted forever'. More pointedly, what Williams (1973: 95, 100) posits is that, if we presume that some more or less extensive retainment of character is necessary for us to speak of a person continuing to exist as the same person, then such a person will, sooner rather than later, come to 'have had altogether too much' of themselves. Indeed, and in duly noting that at the time of writing he was 42 – just as EM was when she received the elixir– Williams (1973: 90) is unambiguous in stating that EM's problem was 'a boredom connected with the fact that everything that could happen and make sense to one particular human being of 42 had already happened to her'.

Whilst the empirical merit of Williams' argument is difficult to discount without having spent 300 years in one's middle ages (according to current lifespan expectations in rich countries), many have suggested that Williams' own demeanor and middle age appear to have led him to overgeneralize what was his own subjective outlook (e.g. Belshaw, 2015; Nussbaum, 2013). Nevertheless, Williams' argument, that at some point in time the life of those with a relatively stable character will become unbearably repetitive, and no longer worth pursuing, is rarely dismissed out of hand. Instead, the general approach that people have employed in countering it, is the relaxing of its qualifications. Hence, Belshaw (2015: 330) has emphasized that there is no reason to presume that we need place such strict constraints on how our character can or might change (Belshaw, 2015: 330); and Nussbaum (2013: 40), that whilst future versions of ourselves might engage in activities that are very different to those we currently engage in, this need not result in our assuming that we would be entirely unrecognizable to either ourselves or others.

The second and related part of the ennuist platform can be termed the lost urgency argument. The President's Council on Bioethics (2003:

186), for instance, has suggested that many 'of our greatest accomplishments are pushed along, if only subtly and implicitly, by the spur of our finitude and the sense of having only a limited time. A far more distant horizon, a sense of essentially limitless time, might leave us less inclined to act with urgency. Why not leave for tomorrow what you might do today, if there are endless tomorrows before you?' Similarly, the fact that one would have an extended period of time in which to do things, would seemingly reduce, and potentially remove entirely, any pressure that one feels to get things correct first time round: such as 'choosing the right partner in life' (Belshaw, 2015: 334). This overcoming of 'temporal scarcity' (Scheffler, 2013: 99) could also make it very difficult for people to establish priorities and make decisions. Should one devote themselves to playing the piano, developing their football skills or to years of learned scholarship?

If temporal boundaries are taken away, then the felt importance of these sorts of 'life choices' would likely be reduced. In fact, there is the possibility that decisions that many currently consider momentous – e.g. getting married, moving countries, changing careers – would come to seem trivial (Belshaw, 2015: 334). For ennuists, then, an extended lifespan may be less than desirable not just out of a fear that one will soon come to have 'seen it all', but out of the much more immediate fear that, without one major driver of current action – i.e. temporal scarcity – we will be entirely underwhelmed by the nihilistic indecisiveness of it all from the very start.

Sequential You

Whatever their ultimate merit, one or more of the above considerations would likely result in at least some people turning their back on the opportunity of (significant) life extension, and in their choosing to leave their current bodily or earthly existence behind. A great many more people, however, would – as myths like the Fountain of Youth indicate – join Ray Kurzweil, and choose to continue their current existence for as long as possible. Given the potential market for such developments, it is to be expected that Alphabet is involved in efforts that aim to significantly extend our existence by halting the deterioration of functional capacities associated with biological ageing (i.e. senescence). More specifically, and in contrast to the subsequently discussed possibility of our being digitally replicated (and altered), the following suggests that this possibility of biological life extension-will prove particularly attractive to those who are willing to patiently pursue projects, and who believe their continued existence is substrate dependent.

Substrate – Dependent

In and of itself, life extension need not be a good thing. To risk stating the obvious, when people express a desire to live longer, they are expressing their desire to live a life that is not just longer, but that is similar or better in its overall goodness to the life they have already lived. In short, people want to stay alive so that they can experience and enjoy more good things (however defined). If people are to prove capable of such experiences, then they will need to be conscious. Despite it having been the subject of a veritable mountain of scholarly (and popular) attention, definitions of consciousness continue to prove vague, and a little disappointing. Searle provides a case in point when he notes that *'consciousness... consists in all of one's states of awareness... sentience or feeling'* (Searle, 2017: 327).

Somewhat more helpfully, Searle goes on to associate consciousness with all those qualitative states, or 'qualia', that are experienced by a given individual, and that have a 'subjective or a first-person ontology'(328). As Searle apparently likes a refreshing beverage, he uses an alcohol-infused illustration to make the whole idea a little more concrete when he writes:

Right now I am consciously thinking about my desire to drink a cold beer. This conscious thought is real in the sense that it cannot be shown to be an illusion or reduced to something else. It is subjective in the sense that it has a first-person ontology, and the conscious thought is qualitative in the sense that it has a certain qualitative feel to it, and it is definitely intentional in the sense that it is directed at or about beer drinking. (Searle, 2017: 331)

Given the 'overwhelming amount of evidence' that 'all our conscious states, from feeling thirst to experiencing mystical ecstasies, are caused by brain processes', Searle conceives of his position on consciousness as 'biological naturalism' (330–331). Thus, and whilst acknowledging that it may one day be possible to build 'an artificial machine that... [would be] conscious', Searle is very clear that consciousness is currently 'a biological phenomenon' that is limited to 'humans, and other animals' (Ibid.). As a result, Searle's position on consciousness can also be conceived in terms of substrate dependence: for it holds that consciousness arises from within, and is subsequently dependent on, the 'wetware' or 'meatsacks' that comprise our corporeal being.

Whilst Kurzweil (2002) does not appear to see much merit in Searle's biological naturalism, or in his famous Chinese room argument against strong AI (Searle, 1980), he is still seeking to extend his personal existence by slowing down his biological ageing. To this end, it has been reported that Kurzweil 'swallows some ninety pills a day', including Metformin, 'a diabetes drug that has made elderly diabetics live longer than a healthy control group'; Basis, a product that 'promises "metabolic repair and optimization"'; 'a coenzyme called Q10, for muscle strength; and phosphatidylcholine, to keep his skin supple' (Friend, 2017).

By slowing down his ageing, Kurzweil hopes to reach an 'escape velocity' (Ibid.) that will enable his existence to continue until some-time around 2045: when he thinks that he will no longer need to continue existing within, and will ultimately be hindered by, his meatsack. But in leaving such speculation aside for the moment, the immediate point to make is that, just like its famous employee Ray Kurzweil, Alphabet is currently invested in slowing down, if not solving or ultimately curing, biological ageing.

Calico, an acronym for California Life Company, was originally launched in 2013 following a significant investment overseen by Google Ventures co-founder and then CEO Bill Maris. According to Harari (2015: 28; see also, Brooker, 2015), Maris can be considered an 'immortality true-believer' given his hypothetical suggestion that, '"If you ask me today, is it possible to live to be 500, the answer is yes".' Although somewhat more restrained in its language, the com-pany Maris helped establish, Calico, is not exactly hiding its light under a bushel when it notes, on its website, that 'we're tackling aging, one of life's greatest mysteries'. More fully, it notes that,

Calico is a research and development company whose mission is to harness advanced technologies to increase our understanding of the biology that controls lifespan. We will use that knowledge to devise interventions that enable people to lead longer and healthier lives. Executing on this mission will require an unprecedented level of interdisciplinary effort and a long-term focus for which funding is already in place. (Calico, Website)

Given the hyperbole that surrounded Calico's launch, it is interesting to find at least some of the initial scepticism regarding its prospects diminishing. Regalado (2013), who titled his initial article on the company's prospects: *Google to Try to Solve Death, LOL*, provides a case in point. For little more than three years later, he could be found writing, in a more measured than cynical fashion this time, that Calico is, 'in effect, an elite university research group housed within a corporate bunker, doing mostly basic science' (Regalado, 2016). Further to other details, Regalado notes that Calico's chief scientific officer, David Botstein, is a well-known – and very well cited one might add (200,000 and counting on Google Scholar) – 'Princeton geneticist whom Calico recruited out of near retirement'. According to Botstein:

Calico is exactly what Google intended: a Bell Labs working on fundamental questions, with the best people, the best technology, and the most money. "Instead of ideas chasing the money, they have given us a very handsome sum of money and want us to do something about the fact that we know so little about aging. . . It's a hard problem; it's an unmet need; it is exactly what Larry Page thinks it is. It's something to which no one is really in a position to pay enough attention, until maybe us. (Regalado, 2016)

Calico's activities are secretive (Friend, 2017). But on the basis of publications associated with leading personnel, it appears that much of the company's efforts are dedicated to identifying genes that can extend lifespans, in worms, flies, rats and eventually humans (e.g. Kenyon, 2010). Additionally, it is reported (Regalado, 2016) that the company is looking for a 'biomarker' – such as a molecule within blood – that would provide an estimate of how long a person has left to live, and that would shift along with changes in drug consumption, diet or some other measure. If this proves successful, then drug manufacturers and others could establish the impact of various initiatives that seek to halt or reduce ageing, without having to wait a lifetime for an answer.

To people that want to live for a longer period of time, and who presume that their continued existence, or consciousness, is substrate dependent, Alphabet's investments in the likes of Calico and Verily – a life-science company with more modest lifespan improvement goals: e.g. reversing heart disease, developing bioelectronic medicines (Verily, Website) – are very good things. Whilst such investments are unlikely to result in the megacorporation 'solving death', they do provide a simultaneously competitive and cooperative focal point that could help spur the whole field onwards. So even if these efforts prove just partially successful, Alphabet would help add years, going on decades, and even centuries if Maris is to be believed, to the time that those with the requisite resources can expect to stay alive.

Personal Projection – Orderly

Unlike ennuists, who suggest that life is already too long, many others think that their lives are much too short. A key reason why is that meaningful goals can sometimes take a lifetime of dedication to accomplish. As a result, ambitious people have to pick and choose between what they do. Even if these people prove successful in their chosen endeavours, they can still come to feel, as life moves towards closure, that there are other things that they would have liked to do too.

One major boon of increased life expectancy, then, is that it would enable people to 'have much longer careers', and to 'reinvent themselves again and again' (Harari, 2015: 30). People could also pursue careers in a much less harried fashion than is now common and avoid the associated burnout (Nussbaum, 2013: 40). Likewise, they could choose to focus their efforts on much riskier and more ambitious goals, rather than relatively easier, short-term, goals, that would otherwise enable them to 'climb the ladder' more quickly. What is more, people would likely feel less pressure to make the choice between work and family, or accomplishment and ease. So even if life expectancy were only to be pushed past 100, people would be much more capable of devoting a significant number of their years both to family and more personal ambitions. Alternatively, people could, as Nussbaum (2013: 41) has suggested, choose to devote their lives to trying to accomplish a personally important goal via multiple means: e.g. to promoting 'justice... as an author, an activist, a politician, an artist; and in different places, moving from the United States to India, and on to Africa, and so forth'.

As these remarks indicate, the ennuist's proposition that an ever longer life is an ever duller one, is far from a knockdown argument. As previously suggested, it can be countered through a sequential reinvention of self; through the relaxing of Williams' (1973) presupposition that a person has to retain the same qualitative outlook, or the same personal goals and objectives, if they are to be considered the same person overtime (Gorman, 2016; Schloendorn, 2006). Once this relaxation occurs, and it is acknowledged that people can seriously engage in different pursuits at different points in time, the concern that one will come to have quickly seen it all in life, fades into the background.

The ennuist's urgency concern (Belshaw, 2015) is also significantly diminished if one presumes that humanity will always be confronted by problems that need addressing within limited timeframes (Gorman, 2016: 1078). At the present juncture, there are any number of social problems that appear more or less urgent, and that would, for many people, seem worthy of their attention: e.g. climate change, malnourishment, animal rights. Moreover, it is reasonable to imagine that whole new arenas of human endeavour and accomplishment will emerge as new technologies develop. Consequently, and given the general merit of being first, it seems likely that there will continue to be sufficient felt urgency to spur action amongst those motivated by recognition and prestige, or just the more immediate felt satisfaction of winning.

Whilst developments in AI could diminish the total number of spheres within which humans can make a meaningful contribution, cyborg-like enhancements could mean that humans remain important players therein. Such enhancements might enable humans to compete with AI in game playing, or with the subsequent development of any machine intelligence that demonstrates significant capacities, in the domains of science, morality or aesthetics (cf. Chapter 8).

The recognition that one has a more or less significantly extended life-expectancy would also be likely to foster patience. A longer life would enable people to devote their energies to more challenging projects, and to wait for opportune moments at which to undergo significant change in their careers, family status or what have you. Thus, for people that feel life is currently too short, and that there are too many things to do, the possibility of extending their corporeal existence would prove hugely enticing. Suffice it to note that if Alphabet were to prove capable of delivering this 'priceless' gift, then the megacorporation would have a devoted and lucrative customer base in perpetuity.

Simultaneous Yous

As noted above, Ray Kurzweil is currently seeking to extend his meatsack existence up until 2045, when he expects to be capable of technologically transcending, or escaping, his corporeal existence (Friend, 2017). Such transcendent developments would enable Kurzweil, and anyone else with the money at hand, to extend their life in the sequential fashion described above. If we were to prove capable of cloning our physical bodies, and if we were to also prove capable of making backups of our consciousness with mindmaps, then we could, as per Lafferty's 2017 novel *Six Wakes*, have our backed-up consciousness remapped onto another, newer and younger, body, following an older one being damaged or destroyed. Whilst this particular possibility currently lies in the realm of science fiction, we do currently possess other, much less sophisticated, means by which we can make digital copies of ourselves and go on to 'live' post our biological death. These digital means, in their turn, give rise to the further possibility of creating multiple and varied versions of one's self – a series of simultaneous yous – that could go on to live indefinitely.

Substrate – Independent

At the most modest, and currently realizable, level, a person can use their digital dossier (see Chapter 4) to create some sort of replica of their self. One could, for example, use all of the digital information they have about themselves to build a chatbot that could converse with, or respond to various questions from, other people. As our digital dossiers grow ever larger, and as developments in AI become more advanced, our capacity to digitally clone ourselves in such a fashion will go well beyond what are already the 'eerily human' (Olson, 2018) impersonations that virtual assistants or receptionists like Google's Duplex enable.

Much less modest than chatbot cloning is the hope of 'whole brain emulation' or 'uploading' (Sandberg & Bostrom, 2008: 7). The basic idea here 'is to take a particular brain, scan its structure in detail, and construct a software model of it that is so faithful to the original that, when run on appropriate hardware, it will behave in essentially the same way as the original brain' (Ibid.). This uploading process might be destructive of the original brain, as with 'serial sectioning' processes in which the brain is frozen, cut and analyzed, 'layer-by-layer'; or non-destructive of the brain, as with some sort of imaging technology that enables a suitably fine-grained picture of the brain to be obtained non-invasively (Chalmers, 2010: 42).

Despite there being significant room for disagreement over timelines, Kurzweil (2005: 200) has confidently suggested that the requisite combination of technologies needed for uploading will be available by as early as the 2030s. Moreover, he has proposed that 'confirmation of the uploading milestone will be in the form of a "Ray Kurzweil" or "Jane Smith" Turing test' that is capable of convincing 'a human judge that the uploaded re-creation is indistinguishable from the original specific person' (Ibid.).

Of course, the passing of such a test does not mean that one's uploaded identity would be conscious. Most famously, Searle's Chinese Room argument – which supplements his belief that consciousness is substrate dependent – posits that if replication takes the form of a program, then such a replication could not be a 'mind' because minds have semantics and programs are entirely syntactical (Searle, 1980, 1997: 13). Those that believe in substrate independence, on the other hand, suggest that such emulations or replications could be conscious.

In this fashion, Chalmers (2010: 44) has adopted the functionalist (as opposed to biological) view that 'what matters to consciousness is not biological makeup but causal structure and causal role, so that a nonbiological system can be conscious as long as it is organized correctly'. Whilst Chalmers (Ibid.) acknowledges that 'we have no idea how a nonbiological system, such as a silicon computational system, could be conscious', he also emphasizes that we 'have no idea how a biological system, such as a neural system, could be conscious' either. He accordingly concludes that in the absence of any principled differences between biological and nonbiological systems that would explain or suggest why 'the former can be conscious and the latter cannot', the 'default attitude should be that both biological and nonbiological systems can be conscious', so long as they are functionally isomorphic (Chalmers, 2010: 45–46). If such functional isomorphism in organization was matched by isomorphism in terms of observed outputs, then many others would seemingly believe that a replica or emulation is conscious too.

As Kurzweil (2012: 209–210) suggests:

Imagine that you meet an entity in the future (a robot or an avatar) that is completely convincing in her emotional reactions. She laughs convincingly at your jokes, and in turn makes you laugh and cry... She convinces you of her sincerity when she speaks of her fears and longings. . . Would you accept her as a conscious person?. . . I believe that we will eventually come to regard such entities as conscious. Consider how we already treat them when we are exposed to them as characters in stories and movies.

In fact, the sorts of questions that Kurzweil is asking are already central to many fictional works. *Ex Machina*, for instance, tells of a convincingly conscious (and consciously convincing) android created by the CEO of a fictional search engine called BlueBook that shares obvious similarities with – and that some have suggested may be based on (Hardawar, 2015) – Google: whose founders have seen it 'as a vehicle to realize the dream of artificial intelligence in augmenting humanity' from 'the very start' (Levy, 2011: 6).

Personal Projection – Portfolio

Along with the potential role they could play in extending lifespans in a sequential you fashion, the development of substrate independent technologies would enable the development of multiple, simultaneous yous. The basic idea here is that, rather than there just being one of you at a given point in time, you could decide to create any number of yous that exist within the same, or overlapping, temporal periods. Whist the yous created would not be numerically identical to each other or some original you, they would still be related to you in the sense that you create them with whatever it is that you decide to take from your existence and identity.

Parfit (1984: 199–266) has previously explored such self-replication or division with reference to what he suggests are the impossible illustrations of personal teleportation/replication and brain division/ transportation. Given recent technological advances, however, such self-replication and division is beginning to seem less fanciful. As indicated above, by combining our dossiers with technologies like Google Duplex, we could create self-replicas that other people/entities could sonically interact with in a natural and conversational manner (Google AI, 2018). Or, through combining our dossiers with deepfake technologies that have been enabled by some combination of Google's Duplex and TensorFlow (see Chapter 4), we could create video replicas of ourselves that would enable videocall–like interactions.

For those inclined to indulge the different aspects of their personality, such technologies provide a new and significantly advanced set of means by which to create a portfolio of different, and simultaneous, versions of their self. You could, for example, divide up your dossier so as to construct a work you (boss you, employee you), family you (mother you, daughter you, sister you), friend you (listening you, helpful you, party you) or sport you (coach you, fan you, teammate you). Alternatively, you might try to create new and modified versions of yourself through combining your dossier with some digitized archive à la KimKierkegaardashian: a recent mélange of Kim Kardashian, a contemporary glamour model with a keen interest in (her) appearance; and Soren Kierkegaard, a nineteenth-century Danish philosopher of more serious intent.

To split apart or modify one's personality so as to build simultaneous versions of one's self is to give into the sense that we are pulled in various directions; to accept the 'danger of tearing' ourselves apart (Korsgaard, 2009: 126). Instead of being driven by the desire to bring one's self together by using an agency that rationally decides which of various appetites and desires should be heeded at different points in time, the decision to create simultaneous or partial self-replicas can be understood as some sort of will to what Korsgaard (2009: 161) pejoratively terms 'defective action'. As a result, it can also be seen as the opposite of 'self-constitution': the making of one's self 'into a particular person, who can interact well with herself and others... consistent and unified and whole' (Korsgaard, 2009: 214).There is, however, the additional possibility of creating partial versions of one's self that exist in parallel to the complete version. Indeed, by creating partial selves that are consistently governed and directed by particular desires or appetites, a complete version of one's self could, by watching over their various replicas, come to have a much greater understanding of the risks and benefits of giving into, or failing to heed, their different wishes and desires in various circumstances.

With this in mind, it is not difficult to imagine different versions of one's self being made to play the same role in some suitably sophisticated game environment; or of witnessing how the same version of one's self would or would not change by going down different paths as a result of Kieslowski-like 'blind chance' or 'sliding door' decisions (Insdorf, 2013: 59–60). In short, it is possible to imagine that, by running such experiments, one could come to have a much greater awareness of their analytically separable motives, and of what, if anything, is essential to their character.

As these later remarks indicate, there is the possibility for a sequential you to be one, or none, of a set of simultaneous yous. Thus, as substrate independent technologies develop, those that are not ready to die might need to decide whether or not they want to have just one sequential you; to have a sequential you that exists as one amongst other simultaneous yous; or to just have a portfolio of partial or defective simultaneous yous, and no sequential you at all. As the middle of these three paths would enable people to potentially realize the benefits, and minimize the costs, of the purer sequential and simultaneous alternatives, many might initially choose to experiment with partial alternatives that a complete version of their self could oversee, or viceversa.

Summary

With megacorporate resources at its disposal, Alphabet is in as good a position as any when it comes to the possibility of significantly extending both average and atypical human lifespans. Through its multitudinous investments in the life sciences, and in the more purely computational sciences too, it is contributing to the possibility of people being embodied in biological and digital forms that could go on to live indefinitely. For those unconvinced by any of the ascensionist, egalitarian, bioconservative or ennuist perspectives, each of which would make one ready to die, such technologies give rise to exciting new possibilities in terms of sequential and simultaneous existence.

As we are still in the very early stages of such developments, their ultimate direction and impact will be marked by uncertainty for some time. Nevertheless, it seems clear that such technologies will increase our means of self-creation both within and over different time periods. If Alphabet can enable, and extract surplus value from, these developments, then it could prove formidable for years to come.

To get a sense of just how formidable, it helps to remember that, at the moment, a huge portion of Alphabet's revenues do not come directly from the users of its various services, but from the advertisers that are willing to pay for ads targeting them. Further to increasing these revenues – through extending the overall time that a person can be advertised too – Alphabet could earn a whole new class of revenues given that many people would likely be willing to pay for an extension of their personal existence. In this fashion, Alphabet would be creating a double source of income: for people would be paying Alphabet to continue existing, which, in its turn, would enable advertisers to pay Alphabet more money in the hope that these personal identities will go on to consume more of their goods and services.

As the just described state of affairs may only seem to make sense if Alphabet proves successful in developing the possibility of sequential yous based on a biological substrate, it should be noted that many people could also be willing to pay Alphabet to maintain a digital substrate that is potentially associated with both simultaneous and sequential yous. It is, for instance, relatively easy to imagine Alphabet demanding an upfront fee, or guaranteed ongoing payments, from those that are about to die, but want to be rendered digitally immortal. Likewise, family members could be willing to pay Alphabet to have their deceased loved ones brought 'back from the dead'. Whatever the exact means, and whatever the level of consciousness it is possible to archive, Alphabet could well come to monopolize the lucrative gains that are likely to accrue from extending our personal futures.

7 | *Social Futures*

The desire to maintain the sustainable development of humanity is widespread. In the present chapter, it is proposed that Alphabet's capacity to shape this concern far outstrips that of most other organizations combined. Nevertheless, the megacorporation's potential to sustain humanity's development is not universally regarded as a net positive. In recognizing thus, this chapter posits that Alphabet's current impact on our social futures should be conceived as simultaneously having a more authoritarian, and a more autonomous, element to it. Whilst the exact nature of Alphabet's impact on our social futures remains to be seen, the chapter's concluding summary emphasizes – in anticipation of the discussions that begin the book's final part, Part III – that the megacorporation's interest in sustaining our future existence is not just consistent with, but positively enabled by, the custodial role it plays with regards to our personal and social pasts.

A Sustainable Power of Ambiguous Worth

Like many other individuals and organizations, Alphabet talks a big game when it comes to sustainable development: which is generally conceived as improving the well-being of current and future generations (World Commission on Environment and Development, 1987). Unlike most of these other actors, however, Alphabet controls and directs a set of resources that result in it potentially having a major, and more or less direct and singular, impact, on the security and well-being of the human species.

Unsurprisingly, those associated with Alphabet tend to present such capacities in an unremittingly positive light. Hence, Google's Chief Sustainability Officer Kate Brandt has suggested that Google is in the process of translating 'the circular genius of nature' into 'high-tech, industrial' settings. Additionally, she has proposed that, by turning 'to the work of the world's most efficient engineers', Google and other global businesses could eliminate our 'dependence on raw materials and fossil fuels' and give rise to 'a circular world of abundance' (Brandt, 2018). In much the same fashion, Sidewalk Labs' (2017) plans to develop the Toronto Waterfront are saturated (excuse the pun) by talk of engineering solutions, sustainability, zero waste, healthy lifestyles, biophilia and so on.

As the ever-growing number of Alphabet critics point out, however, the megacorporation's capacity to shape sustainable development is far from an unambiguously good thing. To this end, and in echoing the basic concerns underpinning the close to ubiquitous turn against Big Tech, Sidewalk Labs' 'smart city dream' in Toronto is being reported as 'turning into a privacy nightmare' (Summers, 2018). Indeed, when Alphabet entities like Sidewalk Labs (2017: 16) suggest that technology is 'a tool that empowers people to improve quality of life', such suggestions can come across less as bullshit, than they do as outright lies (see Frankfurt, 2005). Rather than being seen as a source of society's ongoing empowerment, then, Alphabet is, along with the rest of the data capitalism crowd, now widely perceived as being 'one of the main reasons why authoritarian practices are spreading worldwide' (Deibert, 2019: 31).

As is now argued, these contrasting perspectives on Alphabet's influence over future societies are two sides of the same coin. On the one hand, and as Alphabet itself tends to suggest, the megacorporation's interest in sustainable development, and its business practices more generally, can be seen to be helping create increasingly autonomous societies at three levels of analysis (i.e. individual, communal and environmental). On the other hand, and along with Alphabet's critics this time, the megacorporation can also be seen to be contributing to the construction of increasingly authoritarian future societies (at the same three levels of analysis once again). For ease of exposition, the chapter details the authoritarian perspective first.

Authoritarian

Societies with limited individual freedom and centralized power structures can be characterized as authoritarian. In contrast to their autonomous counterparts, authoritarian societies are characterized by relatively significant limits and constraints being placed on the behaviour of individual humans, other agents (e.g. organizations) and society in general. Despite the likes of Google suggesting that they promote freedom with something approaching religious fervour (e.g. Schmidt & Cohen, 2013), many now suggest that Google and other Alphabet entities are much better characterized as promoting the exact opposite (Zuboff, 2015). In moving through micro (individual), meso (communal) and macro (environmental) levels of analysis, the following shows that there is more than an element of truth to the claim that the megacorporation is currently helping create authoritatively constrained future societies.

Individual

Alphabet has become a megacorporation because Google has proven adept at providing users with information that they need or want to access. Given that the efficiency and convenience of such information provision can be advanced through increased levels of personalization, Google has long used the dossiers it collects on different users (see Chapter 4) to personalize the information that it seeks to provide all of us with. Of course, Google's provision of information comes at the cost (or for some the benefit) of personalized advertising, and also gives rise to a whole host of issues relating to privacy and surveillance. More generally, there is the concern that, through 'feeding' people personalized information, Google is diminishing the extent to which individuals act with autonomy by constructing informed realities (Flyverbom & Whelan, 2019) in which people are presented with information that is presumed to be to their taste (Morozov, 2011).

Morally and politically, these concerns are far from inconsiderable. Nevertheless, it appears that many are willing to set them to one side for the sake of efficiency and convenience, and that such people will happily live in a world in which they are directed by Google in an increasingly paternalistic fashion (see Varian, 2014: 30). At the very least, this contention is supported by the recognition that Google Assistant – an artificial intelligence–enabled tool that was first launched in 2016, and that can be used to provide guidance on recipes, workout plans, meditation practices, joke telling and so on (Google, Website E) – was already on half a billion devices by May 2018 (e.g. watches, laptops, cars, speakers), and 'will likely be on 1 billion devices in just a few years' (Protalinski, 2018).

That individuals concerned with sustainable development might find such paternalistic guidance attractive appears to have been part of the motivation for a nine-minute film produced by Alphabet's X in 2016 (Savov, 2018a). Entitled *The Selfish Ledger* (Foster & Murphy, 2016) in 'homage to Richard Dawkins' 1976 book *The Selfish Gene*, the 'middle section of the video presents a conceptual Resolutions by Google system, in which Google prompts users to select a life goal and then guides them toward it in every interaction they have with their phone. The goals the user could choose would "reflect Google's values as an organization"', and could potentially entail such things as urging a user 'to try a more environmentally friendly option when hailing an Uber' (Savov, 2018a) – the rideshare firm that GV, one of Alphabet's venture capital arms, invested $258 million into back in 2013 (D'Onfro, Zaveri & Bosa, 2018).

The film itself is of a relatively high production quality and could easily be confused for an episode of any number of contemporary works of dystopian science fiction: e.g. *Black Mirror* (Ibid.). Upon being made aware that the 2016 film, which was only meant for internal viewing at Google, was being leaked, an X spokesperson responded:

We understand if this is disturbing – it is designed to be. This is a thought-experiment by the Design team from years ago that uses a technique known as "speculative design" to explore uncomfortable ideas and concepts in order to provoke discussion and debate. It's not related to any current or future products. (Savov, 2018a)

Whilst the first part of the above statement is difficult to disagree with (for the film is somewhat disquieting in style and substance), the last part is not. The reason being that a 'core part of the Selfish Ledger concept' – i.e. 'to help users with self-improvement and behavior modification… on the individual level' – looks similar to a patent application entitled *Detecting and Correcting Potential Errors in User Behavior* that Google made in 2015 (Savov, 2018b). More generally, the ongoing success of any number of Google products and services – e.g. Google Assistant – makes it easy to imagine that more and more individuals concerned with sustainability issues could be willing to subject themselves to ever-increasing levels of behaviour guidance and modification.

Communal

In addition to willingly subjecting themselves to paternalistic guidance from Alphabet, many of those that are currently concerned with sustainable development could be willing to support the imposition of this guidance on others. There are a number of elements to this idea.

First is the belief that security is morally and politically more fundamental than other morally or socially desirable goods. According to Etzioni (2007: 6):

The main reason that the right to security takes precedence over all others is that all the others are contingent on the protection of life – whereas the right to security is not similarly contingent on any other rights. It sounds simplistic to state that dead people cannot exercise their rights, whereas those who are living securely at least have the possibility of exercising more rights in the futures. However, it is still an essential truth.

When viewed from a security-first perspective, the various ways in which climate change, or other environmental concerns, could contribute to undermining the protection of life – e.g. increased risk of water-borne infectious diseases, increased transmission season for diseases like malaria and dengue, extreme weather events, forced migration (UNCC, 2017) – could be seen to justify constraints being placed on various civil liberties. This sort of authoritatively ensured sustainability is perhaps most famously associated with Hardin's (1968) 'tragedy of the commons' argument. Whilst Hardin did make a minimal effort to appeal to the sentiments of his presumed democratic audience when he wrote that the 'only kind of coercion I recommend is mutual coercion, mutually agreed upon by the majority of the people affected' (Hardin, 1968: 1247), he still advocated for social constraints – on breeding for instance (Hardin, 1968: 1246) – that many would consider draconian.

Along with these examples from political science (e.g. Beeson, 2010; Gilley, 2012), arguments in favour of green authoritarianism can be found in the philosophy literature too. Jonas (1984: 11) in particular, is well known not just for stating that we should act in such a way as to ensure that the effects of our actions 'are compatible with the permanence of genuine human life', but for his belief that authoritarianism will prove essential to our doing so (Coyne, 2018: 236). A key reason for Jonas tending in this authoritarian direction was his belief that the policies that would be needed for the survival of human and non-human life were very likely to prove unpopular with the general public (Ibid.). Consequently, Jonas felt that some sort of social discipline, arguably of the more indirect and ideological than direct and coercive variety (Ibid.), would be needed to ensure that we all 'include the future wholeness of Man [sic] among the objects' of our will (Jonas, 1984: 11).

As the preceding comments indicate, arguments for authoritarian governance have generally presumed that it is state actors that would have to provide the relevant structures. Given Alphabet's existing capacities, however, such authority could be provided, perhaps entirely, by the megacorporation itself. Just as the megacorporation could come to be treated as the custodian of the great historical library of human existence (see Chapter 5), it is possible to imagine that Alphabet could come to be treated as the authoritarian custodian of future generations. Indeed, and whilst the above-noted film, *The Selfish Ledger*, does not explicitly state that Google or Alphabet should be made into an authoritarian government, it does imply it.

The fundamental thesis advanced by *The Selfish Ledger* is that the 'ledger' or dossier that each of us creates and contributes to throughout our daily lives may be understood as having some sort of volition or purpose of its own. Whilst individuals would reportedly be the 'custodians, transient carriers, or caretakers' (Foster & Murphy, 2016) of their various dossiers, it is seemingly Google that would care for the ledger as a whole, for as the second half of *The Selfish Ledger* dictates:

As an organization, Google would be responsible for offering suitable targets for a user's ledger. Whilst the notion of a global good is problematic, topics would likely focus on health or environmental impact… Once the user selects a volition for their ledger, every interaction may be compared to a series of parallel options. If one of these options allows the ledger to move closer to its goal, it will be offered up to the user…. As this line of thinking accelerates, and the notion of a goal-driven ledger becomes more palatable, suggestions may be converted not by the user, but by the ledger itself… By thinking of user data as multi-generational, it becomes possible for emerging users to benefit from the preceding generations' behaviors and decisions. (Ibid.)

To reemphasize, the above citation is taken from a film that was produced by Alphabet's moonshot factory, X, for internal use at Google. Additionally, it should be reemphasized that, whilst an

X spokesperson asserted that the film was just a 'thought-experiment' in response to the news that the film was being leaked (Savov, 2018a), when various parts of Alphabet's megacorporate empire are thought of simultaneously – e.g. Nest's recording systems; Google's processing capacities; DeepMind's expertise in machine learning – it all starts to feel much more real. Such capacities, suffice it to note, could result in Alphabet becoming a green authoritarian of choice. Whilst it will no doubt have to compete with the likes of the Chinese Communist Party for the hearts and minds of coercively minded environmentalists worldwide (see Beeson, 2010), its reputation for information gathering and user experiments, of which Google reportedly conducts more than 10,000 a year (Varian, 2014), means that Alphabet is ideally placed when it comes to coercively directing us all towards a more sustainable future.

Environmental

Underlying the current drive towards sustainable development is the anthropocentric concern to ensure the survival of the human species. Whilst the various threats that preoccupy the environmental movement today are of the human-made variety (e.g. climate change), our survival is threatened on other fronts as well. At the most general level,

the earth is… influenced by the vagaries of change in our astronomical environment. During the last few decades astronomers have become increasingly aware of the threat of asteroid and comet impacts. A single rock ten kilometres across, like the one thought to have brought an end to the dinosaurs 65 million years ago, can drastically alter the conditions for life… They can bring to bear upon the environment changes that far exceed the current shifts caused by humans. (Cockell, 2007: 10)

If our species is to prove ongoing in light of such potential catastrophe, it will be necessary to create 'self-sustaining space colonies' to ensure that 'any disaster confined to a single planet cannot eliminate all of humanity' (Bostrom, 2013: 22). Given what is involved, it is doubtful that any self-sustaining space settlements could be constructed within a timeframe that would prove useful in light of the planet's current anthropogenic maladies. Nevertheless, 'establishing space settlements' still appears essential 'over the very long term' (Schwartz, 2014: 204).

This argument has recently been used by SpaceX founder Elon Musk (2017: 47), who, in outlining his company's interest in creating a self-sustaining city on Mars, has proposed that it is possible for human history to

bifurcate along two directions. One path is we stay on Earth forever, and then there will be some eventual extinction event. I do not have an immediate doomsday prophecy, but eventually, history suggests, therewill be some doomsday event. The alternative is to become a space-bearing civilization and a multi-planetary species, which I hope you would agree is the right way to go.

SpaceX is a private company of which Musk's private trust owns 54 percent (and 78 percent voting control) of the outstanding stock (Johnson, 2018). Nevertheless, at the start of 2015, Alphabet (when it was still just Google) partnered with the investment firm Fidelity to invest $1 billion in the new space venture. In return, the two companies respectively received a 7.5 percent and 2.5 percent ownership share of SpaceX (Smith, 2015). As SpaceX was recently valued at more than $33 billion (Sheetz, 2019), this constitutes a more than threefold return on investment. So even if SpaceX's very ambitious plans for its 'Starlink constellation' – i.e. a 'space internet' or global communications network comprised of approximately 12,000 satellites – fails to materialize (Scoles, 2018), Alphabet could still turn a pretty penny from its SpaceX holdings right now.

Such financial considerations are interesting, but they are only of tangential importance to the present concern. What is of more immediate importance is Musk's suggestion that the most likely

form of government on Mars would be a direct democracy, not representative... So it would be people voting directly on issues. And I think that's probably better, because the potential for corruption is substantially diminished in a direct versus a representative democracy... I would [also] recommend some adjustment for the inertia of laws... It should probably be easier to remove a law than create one... I think that's probably good, because laws have infinite life unless they're taken away." (Grush, 2016)

In having the expectation, or hope, that (sustainable) space colonies would take the form of some sort of liberal, libertarian or democratic utopia – that 'the settling of Mars' would preserve and promote cultural diversity, spur innovation and technology development, and improve democratic governance (Schwartz, 2017: 168) – Musk is far from alone. Yet unfortunately for the likes of Musk, and further to its being undermined by the 'dubious' readings of American history upon which it is founded (Schwartz, 2017: 175), the idea of a freedom-loving space frontier appears fanciful for a number of reasons.

First, and as the above discussed history of the English East India Company suggests (see Chapter 2), corporate-led colonization projects need not result in increased liberty for all (see Persson, 2015). More pointedly, a quick look at the ownership (and voting) structures of SpaceX and Alphabet suggests that if either or both of these organizational entities are to play key roles in settling on Mars, then the rules and procedures of any Martian colony they create are more likely to be unilaterally set by the likes of Musk, Page and Brin, than they are to be democratically established by settlers themselves.

Second, lessons derived from recently created virtual worlds such as *Second Life* and the *World of Warcraft* show that, even when such worlds are 'explicitly designed as havens for libertarian experiments', they can come to be quickly characterized by the 'outright rejection of libertarian and collective self governance models... in favor of hierarchical and managerial models in which the great majority of people delegate... authority to a supreme leader' (McKnight, 2015: 104). What this evidence suggests, in short, is that rather than using the 'political vacuum' of 'unsettled new environments' to maximize liberty, people seek to fill such vacuums by delegating authority and responsibility to structures, leaders or algorithms (McKnight, 2015: 114).

Third, and arguably most problematically for democratic dreamers of the space frontier, the recognition that 'every non-terrestrial environment in our solar system is extremely hostile to human life (and to the other life forms on which we depend)' (Schwartz, 2017: 168), provides very material reasons for thinking that governance beyond Earth will tend in an authoritarian direction. Most notably, Cockell (2015: 2) has proposed that the

lack of atmospheres with a composition similar to that on Earth... lead universally to environments that lack readily available indigenous supplies of three commodities crucial to human existence: breathable air, liquid water and food. The paucity of these basic requisites... are a fact of Nature, an unassailable result of the extraterrestrial physical environment... their want puts into motion human social arrangements that will influence the character of liberty in very profound ways.

The basic problematic to which Cockell (2015) refers is well captured by Godwin's short story *The Cold Equations* (see also, Baxter, 2015). Originally published *in Astounding Science Fiction* in 1954 (and republished online by *Lightspeed* this century), Godwin (2011) tells of a stowaway on an Emergency Dispatch Ship (EDS) delivering urgent medical supplies to a set of colonists suffering from a fatal fever on a planet far, far away. At the start of the story, the ship's radiant heat monitoring makes the ship's captain aware of a 'a living, human body' stowed away in the ship's supply closet (Ibid.). Upon learning of the stowaway's presence, the captain unflinchingly acknowledges that the stowaway will have to be 'immediately jettisoned' as per the relevant Interstellar Regulation, which is underpinned by two physical laws that 'no amount of human sympathy... could alter': 1) that *h amount of fuel will power an EDS with a mass of m safely to its destination* and 2) that *h amount of fuel will not power an EDS with a mass of m plus x safely to its destination* (Ibid.).

As these equations dictate, when the mass of an EDS goes from *m* to *m plus x*, *x* needs to be discarded. The plot device that Godwin uses to reveal just how cold these equations are, is the revelation that the stowaway is not some (old, male) chancer seeking fortune or revolution, but rather, a teenage girl who wanted no more than to go see her brother (a colonist working on the EDS's planetary destination). Despite his discovery of the girl leading to his having significant misgivings, the pilot never loses sight of what he ultimately has to do. The girl – having likewise accepted the logic dictating that there was no alternative – comes to accept her misfortune too. So, when the time comes, the girl voluntarily steps into the open-air lock, turns to face the pilot, and says, "'I'm ready'" (Ibid.).

The idea that Godwin's story points towards is that, when external conditions are lethal, there is a relentless need to maintain the 'complexity of machinery that enables life' by artificially producing water, air and food (Cockell, 2016: 24). In such situations, dissent, as opposed to conformity, is likely to be in very short supply: for people within such environments will be strongly inclined to comply with established rules and procedures out of the fear that doing otherwise will put their life, or the lives of others, at risk. Moreover, any authorities that come to exist and govern in such places will – in seeking to maintain their legitimacy by pandering to people's fear about having no freedoms or rights when they are dead (Etzioni, 2007: 6) – be inclined to stamp out any potential security risks as quickly and authoritatively as possible (Cockell, 2016).

Rather than space settlements being some sort of libertarian, liberal or democratic utopia, more sober analysis suggests that those who first settle in hostile, alien environments, will, in their daily existence, be conservative and risk-averse to the extreme. So rather than acting as a spur to cultural and political creativity, what initial space settlements are more likely to show is that the value of freedom is contingent upon the existence of a human-friendly natural environment like that which we inhabit on Planet Earth (Schwartz, 2017: 177).

Autonomous

The ideal of autonomy is generally related to individuals freely, and in some sense deliberately, deciding upon what their own personal goals are and how they will pursue them. Instead of simply being the freedom to do whatever, autonomy tends to be aligned with considered reflection on what is good, valuable, desirable and appropriate. As a result, autonomy is also commonly associated with the idea of self-governance on the one hand, and with a lack of coercion or manipulation on the other (e.g. Bernal, 2014; Christman, 1991; Kim & Werbach, 2016; Raz, 1988).

As the preceding discussions have made clear, Alphabet can be seen to be pushing future societies away from autonomy. Such appearances correspond with currently popular beliefs regarding the megacorporation's totalizing tendencies and cannot be disproven. Nevertheless, such authoritarian tendencies are just one part of a more complex story; for as the following discussions of Alphabet's impact at the individual, communal and environmental levels demonstrate, the megacorporation can also be seen to be contributing to the emergence of a much more autonomous future. At the risk of towing the megacorporate line, then, the following posits that at least some of Alphabet's policies and practices appear to be having a positive impact on what the megacorporation itself suggests is the creation of 'free… open and inclusive' future societies (Google Take Action, Website).

Individual

On 29 December 2017, Hiroko Tabuchi wrote in *The New York Times* that, if you

[t]ype the words "climate change" into Google... you could get an unexpected result: advertisements that call global warming a hoax. "Scientists blast climate alarm," said one that appeared at the top of the search results page during a recent search... Another ad proclaimed: "The Global Warming Hoax — Why the Science Isn't Settled," linking to a video containing unsupported assertions, including that there is no correlation between rising levels of greenhouse gases and higher global temperatures. (Tabuchi, 2017)

Given such evidence, the conclusion to draw is that Google's current efforts to ensure that the advertisements it returns as part of its search results are clear, honest and enabling of informed decisions, are failing (Ibid.). Moreover, one might take such examples as clear evidence that Google's advertising business is currently undermining whatever other efforts the megacorporation is making to mitigate climate change.

Without wanting to understate the current extent of such fake-news problems, Google's basic concern to provide (useful) information, and the external pressures it faces to minimize access to deliberatively false or misleading resources, suggests that these concerns will be gradually resolved. To this end, the Google News Initiative is currently involved in a variety of media-literacy campaigns, fact-checking initiatives and media-transparency projects that seek to elevate 'accurate, quality content' over 'the flow of misinformation' (Gingras, 2018).

More positively, and with regard to climate change concerns in particular, Google directly provides a wealth of resources by which individuals can educate themselves about, and come to form their own opinions about, humanity's impact on global warming. Google's Environmental Insight Explorer provides a case in point by enabling users to explore how different cities contribute to climate change in terms of four categories: i.e. 'building emissions, transportation emissions, energy offset potential, and 20-year climate projections. Clicking on "Building emissions," for example, brings up detailed maps visualizing the emissions impact for both homes and non-residential buildings' (Moore, 2018). Whilst currently limited to a number of cities worldwide (e.g. Melbourne, Buenos Aires), the plan is to 'make this environmental information available' for 'thousands of cities, towns, and regions around the world' (Ibid.).

Google Search also provides users with ready access to resources that they can use to inform themselves about climate change debates, and possible social futures more broadly. Search returns will always differ, but anyone that is willing to look just a little past the initial results that a Google search returns, will be able to quickly find a variety of links by which to educate themselves. Besides a National Aeronautics and Space Administration (NASA) link, a Wikipedia link and a link to some 'climate solutions' on a page hosted by the David Suzuki Foundation, a search on climate change that I completed in early 2019 returned results suggesting that the next financial crisis could be caused by climate change (Dembicki, 2019); that the rebranding of global warming as climate change is due to the inconvenient fact that the planet is not warming (Murphy, 2018); and that the reason why people understand, but do not meaningfully act upon, the threat of climate change, is due to our evolved tendency to focus on very immediate and self-evident risks rather than those of a more distant and abstract nature (Gardner, 2019).

As this suggests, the fact that people can use the Internet to inform themselves about controversial issues in meaningful ways – a belief that was much more popular around the turn of the century than it is today (Simon, Graziano & Lenhart, 2001) – remains difficult to refute. For much the same reason, Benkler's (2006: 133–134) belief that the 'networked information economy' has increased our autonomy – by increasing 'the range and diversity of things that individuals can do for and by themselves'; by providing 'non-proprietary alternative sources of communications capacity and information'; and by qualitatively increasing the range of 'commercial and noncommercial, mainstream and fringe, domestic or foreign' information sources that individuals can access – remains basically true as well.

Communal

In controlling the two most visited websites in the world, Google Search and YouTube (Alexa, Website), and in having a long history of providing significant funding to other hugely popular websites like Wikipedia (Gomes & Fuller, 2019), Alphabet can be considered the world's major information portal. As the information that Alphabet enables access to often comes from sources that lie outside traditional mass media, Alphabet can also be seen to be contributing to a world in which new social groupings can more easily form, develop and communicate with each other.

To illustrate, many involved in the recent growth of veganism suggest that the Internet has played a key role in the development of what was, until very recently, a fringe, and much ridiculed, way of life. Thus, and whilst the Internet is far from having singularly caused the growth of veganism, significant anecdotal evidence, and basic logic, suggests that the speed and ease of uploading and accessing internet content (e.g. on YouTube) has enabled those interested in veganism to quickly inform others, or themselves, of different choices they can make in terms of cooking and purchasing food. It has also helped them realize that many other people around the world share their interests and concerns (Forgrieve, 2018; Lowbridge, 2017).

In this way, Alphabet's various assets have not just helped create different arenas of citizenship where people can express (fringe) points of view (Whelan, Moon & Grant, 2013), but they have helped create new digital spaces that contribute to the formation and development of different communities. Without wanting to suggest that Alphabet is categorically committed to what Schmidt and Cohen (2013: 7) refer to as 'digital empowerment', the megacorporation's general interest in promoting access to information – via. Google, YouTube, Blogger and so on – does result in it tending to encourage the creation of, and participation within, a multitude of communal assemblages.

In addition to animal rights and human health concerns, a key motivation for much of the vegan movement is the amelioration of environmental concerns such as deforestation and climate change (Whelan & Gond, 2017). Although the posited environmental benefits of a plant-based diet may ultimately prove overstated given the potential to reduce the environmental impact of the animal agriculture industry, both the popular press (e.g. Drayer, 2019) and the scientific literature (e.g. Springmann et al., 2018) increasingly acknowledge the environmental benefits of a reduction in the consumption of animal protein.

As many people continue to have a taste for meat and dairy, and as there are potential industrial (and environmental) efficiencies associated with the production of non-animal (fake) meat – e.g. you do not have to birth, raise and kill an animal (Whelan & Gond, 2017) – Alphabet's GV was one of the earliest financiers of (Shieber, 2018), and continues to hold investments in, Impossible Foods. Impossible Foods is headquartered in Redwood California and, having resisted Google's efforts to buy the company outright in 2015, continues to be privately held. According to Impossible Foods CEO Patrick Brown, Alphabet's efforts to take total control were rebuffed due to Impossible Foods being mission driven, and out of a concern to ensure that the start-up's fate would not 'rest on the whims of a company "trying a million things"' (Del Rey, 2018).

Nevertheless, Impossible Foods (Website) has happily accepted Alphabet finances in pursuing its stated mission to 'Save Meat. And Earth'. As the Californian company elaborates:

> We've been eating meat since we lived in caves. And today, some of our most magical moments together happen around meat: Weekend barbecues. Midnight fast-food runs. Taco Tuesdays. Hot dogs at the ballpark. Those moments are special, and we never want them to end. But using animals to make meat is a prehistoric and destructive technology. Animal agriculture occupies almost half the land on earth, consumes a quarter of our freshwater and destroys our ecosystems. So we're doing something about it: We found a way to make meat using plants, so that we never have to use animals again. That way, we can eat all the meat we want, for as long as we want. And save the best planet in the known universe. (Ibid.)

Through its investment in this plant-based meat company, Alphabet is contributing to future societies that could not just be more sustainable but could also be characterized by a sense of community that increasingly includes both human and non-human animals. Consequently, and presuming that reported improvements continue – e.g. a prior version of an Impossible Burger has been compared to an 'OK Sizzler steak', and a new version to 'a well-massaged Kobe ribeye' (Kerr, 2019) – then future societies could come to consider the act of eating (more types of) animals a crime due to the belief that they possess some sort of basic autonomy (Elliot, 1987).

Whilst these sorts of changes to autonomous social creation (and 'autonomous' social members) are significant, they would arguably be overshadowed by the sorts of increased social autonomy that Alphabet is virtually enabling. Unlike 'actual' societies, where the phenomena one experiences are directly attributable to material beings or entities: e.g. to actual, biological, persons; 'virtual' societies are characterized by experiences or phenomena that are 'always reliant on materials outside' of themselves for their 'presentation' and are not 'actually made of those materials' (Wolf, 2018: 192). When we virtually remember or dream about something, for instance, we are not in the material presence of that which we remember: e.g. a conversation with a friend, a sporting event, a day from one's childhood. Rather, it is our brain (or some neuropsychological process), that gives rise to the experience, which, whilst virtual, is nevertheless real (see Deleuze, 1988: 96–97).

With this in mind, the very considerable investments that Alphabet continues to make in augmented reality (Hempel, 2018), deep learning (DeepMind, Website), gaming platforms (Google Developers, Website) and so on, can be seen to be helping to bring about future societies that are themselves characterized by more and more virtual society creation. Although the virtual societies that people seem likely to increasingly spend their lives in could be created by someone else for them (Castronova, 2018: 127), or could be created for huge numbers of people by a business that has collected and organized a 'large library or smorgasbord' of experiential potentialities (Nozick 1974: 42), there is also the possibility that such capacities will be decentralized.

In the decentralized case, entire populations would become godlike (Novak, 1993: 118) or sub-godlike (Ensslin, 2018: 405) in their capacities, and would be able to create entire (virtual) populations on their own. In this fashion, and just as people in the future could use significantly advanced computer technology to create simulations of historical societies populated by virtual (and potentially conscious) entities, people in future societies could also use such technologies to personally construct societies that they could participate within (Bostrom, 2003). Presuming that any still existent basic needs can be met (e.g. nutrition), people could use various technological assemblages to construct their very own social utopias that they might never need, or want, to exit (see Nozick, 1974: 42–45).

For this eventuality in which anyone and everyone can autonomously create their own virtual societies to prove sustainable over the very long term, there would need to be significant advances in computing security: e.g. for significant developments in renewable energy, such as solar, to ensure that the seemingly massive and unending energy needs of such social creations could be met. There would also be a need for such societies to be backed up, or to be continuously replicated, if catastrophe is to be avoided. As Bostrom (2003: 245) has suggested then – albeit more in his role as Oxford philosopher than in his role as Alphabet DeepMind Ethics & Society Fellow – the sustainability of such societies (or social simulations) might depend on subsequent (post-human) generations being able 'to convert planets and other astronomical resources into enormously powerful computers'.

Environmental

Whilst any contribution that Alphabet might make to the emergence of post-human autonomous societies will only be meaningfully assessable, if ever, at some point in the distant future, the contributions Alphabet is making to human, Earth-based, autonomous societies, will be assessable much more quickly. The reason why, as Cockell (2015: 2) indicates, is that individual and social liberty is much less viable without an environment that – like most of the places that humans currently populate on Earth – enables humans to exit from existing social structures, and to create new social structures, with relative ease. What can be argued, as a consequence, is that whether or not Alphabet is going to be seen by our children or our children's children as a progenitor of, or as a roadblock to, their individual and social autonomy, will likely be determined by whether or not the megacorporation makes a significant contribution to ameliorating or preventing the effects of climate change right now. Given the important role that space science has played in the discovery of climate change (Cockell, 2007: 82–87; Weart, 2008: 83–85), it is Alphabet's various interests in low Earth orbit and beyond that will arguably prove most fecund in such regards.

In December 2010, Alphabet's non-profit arm Google.org announced the launch of 'Earth Engine' at the International Climate Change Conference in Cancun, Mexico. As the press release noted, Earth Engine

is a new technology platform that puts an unprecedented amount of satellite imagery and data—current and historical—online for the first time. It enables global scale monitoring and measurement of changes in the earth's environment. The platform will enable scientists to use our extensive computing infrastructure—the Google "cloud"—to analyze this imagery... The images of our planet from space contain a wealth of information, ready to be extracted and applied to many societal challenges. Scientific analysis cantransform these images from a mere set of pixels into useful information—such as the locations and extent of global forests, detecting how our forests are changing over time, directing resources for disaster response or water resource mapping. (Google Dot Org, 2010)

Earth Engine was originally made possible by NASA's 2008 decision to make its Landsat scenes, which at one point in time were on sale for more than $4,000 each, free to the public. Nevertheless, it is Google's Earth Engine that has played the key role in enabling the public to access and utilize the NASA data set (NASA Technology, 2015). In 2013 for instance, Matt Hansen, an Earth-observation data scientist at the University of Maryland, built on Earth Engine and Google's broader expertise in the domain of satellite imagery to publish 'the first ever global study of forest cover: a map of the world accurate down to 30 meters, depicting current forests and gains and losses between 2000 and 2012, with layers of data for each year available for download' (NASA Technology, 2015; see also, Hansen et al., 2013).

As Earth Engine is also central to initiatives that involve such organizations as the World Resources Institute and the Food and Agriculture Organization (Google Earth Engine, Website), and as it continues to be used in studies published in such outlets as *Nature* (Pekel et al., 2016), the megacorporation's hope that 'scientists will be able to build applications to mine' the 'treasure trove of data on Google Earth Engine' (Google Dot Org, 2010) appears well placed. Indeed, when Earth Engine is noted alongside Alphabet's for-profit geospatial analytics firm Orbital Insight – whose mission is to 'source, process, and analyze' the increasing amounts of (humanly uninterpretable) data that 'is being generated by satellites, drones, balloons, and other unmanned aerial vehicles' (Orbital Insight, Website) – the potential role that the megacorporation could play in helping ensure that Earth remains a nice planet for human habitation appears significant.

Further to contributing to the development and the diffusion of space science, Alphabet is also well placed when it comes to reminding the general public that Earth provides a habitat that is uniquely suited to human habitation. Through the use of Google Maps, Google Moon, Google Mars, Google Earth Pro and Google Sky, Alphabet continues to make it much easier for people to familiarize themselves with the Solar System and the Universe by providing access to images and information provided by NASA, the European Space Agency (ESA), and the International Space Station (ISS). Taken as a whole, these applications show that we live on a small planet within a Universe that is populated by trillions of galaxies of which ours, the Milky Way, is estimated to have well over a 100 billion stars by itself. In doing so, they give rise to a sense of awe at what is the unimaginable hugeness of space, and the associated wonder of its creation. They also show that the other places that humans could potentially inhabit in the foreseeable future – i.e. the Moon and Mars – are beautiful, but very, very desolate.

Although it may be too much to expect that, through these efforts, the megacorporation could replicate something like the emergent global consciousness, or '"Earthrise" era', that followed NASA's Apollo missions (Lazier, 2011), they do suggest that Alphabet can indirectly help to take some further steps along the same path. The collective works of Kim Stanley Robinson, who has made numerous presentations at Google over the years, provides a fairly thorough treatment of where this path is currently headed: i.e. towards the recognition that '*There is no planet B! Earth is our only possible home!*' (Robinson, 2015a). Accordingly, if the megacorporation helps to better inform the general public about some Robinson-type beliefs – e.g. that interstellar, or even just interplanetary, travel, faces massive and perhaps insurmountable difficulties that are very complex (e.g. sociological, psychological, biological and ecological) (e.g. Robinson, 2015b) – then it could make a significant contribution to the existence of autonomous, Earth-ensconced, future societies.

Summary

As the oscillating popular narratives regarding Alphabet's social impact indicates, the megacorporation is currently having a contradictory impact on the shape of future societies. On the one hand, and as Alphabet's critics suggest, the megacorporation does appear to be helping to create future societies that tend towards the dictatorial. In fact, by pushing for the creation of human settlements on Mars, and by creating systems that can guide and direct generations of individuals and entire societies, Alphabet appears to be helping create future societies that will be authoritative in previously unforeseen ways. On the other hand, and as Alphabet's colourfully progressive and democratic self-styling suggests, the megacorporation is also constructing technologies that enable decentralized, independent and experimental social creations.

Whilst we cannot currently know which of the authoritarian or autonomous elements will prove most influential, what does seem clear is that Alphabet has strong motive when it comes to making themselves a key part of sustaining future societies. Moreover, when one recognizes that the selfish ledger discussed in this chapter, and the simultaneous yous discussed in Chapter 6, would both build on the 'great library' that Alphabet is constructing in its role as custodian of our personal and social pasts (as discussed in Chapters 4 and 5 respectively), the synergies that exist between Alphabet's Janus-faced concern with our history and our future begin to reveal themselves. Thus, and although it is primarily concerned with explaining why Alphabet will one day cease to be, Part III of the book begins by noting that the ideology of infinite times helps ensure that Alphabet is not simply or immediately ripped apart by the huge diversity of things it is 'forever' trying to do.

Megadeath

8 | *A Finite Ideology*

This chapter begins by defining ideology in a descriptive and amoral fashion. In doing so, it shows that Greimas's semiotic square provides a useful means by which to conceive, and delineate, the ideology of infinite times from three alternatives that I respectively term the future primitive ideology, the ideology of extinction and the singularity ideology. In line with this framing, the chapter then completes two main tasks. First, it provides a recapitulation of the infinite times ideology; of the role it plays in bringing Alphabet's diverse activities together; and of the role it plays in aligning the megacorporation's interests with those of its users worldwide. Second, it explains how Alphabet is directly and indirectly encouraging developments that are consistent with the future primitive, extinction and singularity ideologies that are all, whatever else their differences, similarly opposed to the ideology of infinite times. Given these discussions, the chapter concludes by emphasizing that, as the ideology of infinite times is as finite as any other ideology, it provides one potential source of Alphabet's ultimate demise.

Distinguishing Ideologies

Although still often used in the pejorative sense first expressed by Napoleon (Nöth, 2004), the term ideology is now also commonly used, less judgementally, to describe and explicate the manner in which the phenomena we construct, and the goals we try to achieve, are, in each and every instance, constrained, limited and specific (Jameson, 2016; Johansen & de Cock, 2018; Keršyte, 2017; Nöth, 2004). Greimas (1983: 293) in particular, suggested that ideologies should be characterized as 'structures of signification'; as a 'network of relations of the type "both... and"' (Greimas & Courtés, 1982: 328). Moreover, he is known for his positing that ideologies are 'taken up by an individual or collective subject which is modalized by *wanting-*

to-be and, subsequently, by *wanting-to-do*' (Greimas & Courtés, 1982: 222).

As these brief remarks indicate, Greimas's understanding of ideology, and his related notion of the semiotic square – which is often illustrated, a little confusingly, in the form of a rectangle (e.g. Greimas & Rastier, 1968) – is fairly abstract. He also had a preference for terminology that tended towards the esoteric. Nevertheless, and like any good theory (Lewin, 1943: 118), Greimas's work has its practical uses: for through what is, ultimately, quite a simple iterative process, it helps to show how a given ideology presumes the existence of alternative ideologies that oppose it. Additionally, it suggests that a given ideology can play out in such a fashion that it actually helps, however unintentionally, to further the goals and aims of its ideological competition.

To get this Greimassian process started, one needs to first identify a term or an idea, and then identify its opposite or contrary. These two terms/ideas are then placed on an axis at the top of a diagram. Following this, one constructs a second axis at the bottom of the diagram, where they diagonally situate the contradiction or negation of each of the initial two terms. By completing these simple tasks, one is able to identify four terms/ideas that are situated at the four corners of a square (or a rectangle). Moreover, and most importantly in the present context, it enables one to identify and label four sides of a square, and to reveal the way in which a given ideology – when suitably conceived – logically presupposes three alternatives.

To make these discussions more concrete, it helps to remember that the ideology of infinite times is associated with the concern to (indefinitely) extend humanity's past and future. As has been detailed at some length in Part II of the book, the concern to 'never' forget and 'never' die is something that Alphabet continuously seeks to realize in a multitude of ways. Consequently, the ideology of infinite times helps quickly reveal that there is an underlying unity to what can otherwise appear to be Alphabet's schizophrenic investment strategy.

As Figure 8.1 shows, when a Greimassian semiotic square is used to conceive the ideology of infinite times, a number of considerations are brought to the fore. First, and most simply, it shows that the concern to extend the past can only really be made sense of in relation to its contrary, the concern to extend the future, and vice versa. Second, it

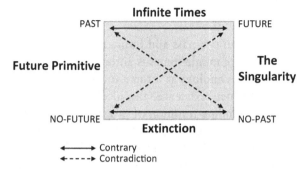

Figure 8.1 Four ideologies

reveals that this initial set of contrary terms imply an additional set of contradictory terms: i.e. no concern to extend or bring about the future (no-future); no concern to extend or safekeep the past (no-past). Third, it reveals that the different terms plotted at each of the semiotic square's corners, can themselves be mediated by terms placed along each of the square's sides. By bringing the corners together in four *and* relationships that run along one *or* another line, these mediating terms reveal the limits of a given set of ideologies (Greimas & Courtés, 1982: 149, 308–311; Greimas & Rastier, 1968; Jameson, 2008: 319–323). In short, the semiotic square makes it straightforward to demonstrate that, the ideology of infinite times is – like Hegel's (2010: 109–119) notion of the bad infinite (which is opposed to, and distinguished from, that which it is not) – finite.

In further elaborating on the demarcations made in Figure 8.1, the chapter's next section provides a brief discussion of the infinite times ideology, and of its importance for making sense of Alphabet's activities. Following this, the three alternatives to the ideology of infinite times, and the ways in which Alphabet is (in)directly, and however unintentionally, aiding their development, are detailed. As the furthering of these other ideologies is counterproductive to Alphabet's infinite times–informed interests, it should be remembered that such assistance seems unavoidable when viewed through the dialectical lens of Greimas's semiotic square. The reason being that the meaning of a given term, or a given ideology, cannot, in the last instance, be abstracted away from the contraries, the contradictions and the alternatives, that complexly combine to comprise it.

Infinite Times

In its concern to expand humanity's past and future at the individual and social levels, the ideology of infinite times is anthropocentric. And in positing that, on balance, technology is a force for good, due to it extending and improving human existence, the ideology of infinite times also links to the long-standing tradition of progressivism: to the belief that we are continuously increasing our individual and social welfare (Nisbett, 1994). In short, and in building on remarks by former chief scientist for AI research at Google Cloud, Fei-Fei Li – who departed this role following the leak of email correspondence in which public relations concerns relating to Google's controversial role in the building of AI weapons for the US military were discussed (Fang, 2018) – the ideology of infinite times can be said to be comprised of 'a human-centered approach' to technology in which the machines we create are harnessed as 'partners in securing our well-being' (Li, 2018).

This ideology has an influence that extends far beyond Alphabet and the Silicon Valley context from which the megacorporation emerged. To begin with the social level, and amongst many other examples that could be provided, it will suffice to note that the ideology of infinite times informs the United Nations' concern to make the most of technological advances to preserve and protect the world's diverse cultural heritage, and to further humanity's sustainable development. And at the individual level, the influence of the infinite times ideology is evidenced by the almost ubiquitous concern to document one's daily life (through photos and videos); the currently flourishing interest that many have in charting their genealogy with the help of websites like ancestry.com; and the concern that many people have with holding on to their youthful looks and capacities for as long as current levels of technological development make possible.

The recognition that the infinite times ideology is widespread in its influence is important because it suggests that Alphabet's many activities – which I propose are, whatever their superficial differences might suggest, all similarly informed by the infinite times ideology – far from incongruent with the beliefs and concerns of a significant number of people worldwide. Many people, for example, would be saddened or disappointed, albeit to varying degrees, if Alphabet's capacity to increase the quantity and quality of information that can be stored on individuals and societies was reduced. And it is likely that even more people would be saddened if Alphabet's attempts to increase the time for which individual humans, and humanity as a whole, can hope to exist, were somehow curtailed. So whilst not everyone wants Alphabet to be the sole custodian of humanity's past and future, many people do seemingly want it to play a pronounced custodial role given its significant capacities.

To get a quick sense of this statement, and to show that it is not hyperbole, note that in mid-2019 Google Photos passed the 1 billion user mark (Knight, 2019), and that in 2017, when it only had half this number of users, 1.2 billion photos and videos were reportedly being uploaded to the service every single day (Palladino, 2017). As these digital mementos need not just be used to document our pasts, but could also be used to create digital versions of ourselves that could go on to live in perpetuity, it is highly probable that a significant portion of the billion plus people that make use of Google Photos would be upset by its disappearance. In this fashion – and given that similar points can be made with regard to Alphabet's Google Books project, its Arts & Culture project, its Earth Engine project and so on – Alphabet's ideologically informed existence seems much more in step, than it does out of step, with the revealed interests of what can only be described as the huge number of people that currently make daily use of its various products and services (cf. Zuboff, 2015).

As well as aligning its interests with those of its users, the ideology of infinite times helps to ensure that Alphabet is not undermined by the million things it is trying to do (Del Rey, 2018). It helps ensure that the second of ten things that Google (Website D) has long known to be true – that 'it's best to do one thing really, really well' – does not appear a mockery in light of Alphabet's Other Bets. Most fundamentally, what the infinite times ideology does is make Alphabet want to be the custodian of humanity's past and future. It is what makes the mega-corporation want to undertake the activities that would turn Larry Page's 100-year dream of solving 'a lot of the issues we have as humans' (Waters, 2014) into a reality.

Nevertheless, the ideology of infinite times also implies, or encourages the development of, alternative ideologies that negate it. Most dramatically, the activities that the infinite times ideology gives rise to could unintentionally contribute to an extinction event that would make human-centred progress impossible. Accordingly, and as per Figure 8.1, the rest of this chapter is concerned with detailing how the infinite times–informed activities of Alphabet contribute, both directly (i.e. by Alphabet) and indirectly (i.e. by other entities that it encourages), to the promotion of three ideological alternatives that threaten the ideology of infinite times, and Alphabet along with it.

Future Primitive

In borrowing the title of an influential essay published by John Zerzan in 1994 (and republished in 2012), the ideology linking the past and no-future corners of the infinite times–initiated semiotic square, is here termed 'future primitive'. Given the corners it joins, this ideology is positively associated with former ways of life, and negatively associated with any sort of technologically advanced future orientation. Consequently, it can be understood as seeking a radical decrease in technological capacities that would result in our return to a simpler, more 'natural', way of life.

The Alphabet-Created Threat

That technological developments could contribute to humanity being sent back to the Stone Age is a topic of relatively widespread interest in various domains (e.g. fiction and non-fiction, academic and popular writings). Whilst such an 'unrecovered collapse', and subsequent 'permanent stagnation' (Bostrom, 2013: 20) in humanity's technological capacities could be deliberately brought about by those who desire it (see below), it could also be brought about as a result of considerations for which the infinite times ideology could be held directly, albeit unintentionally, responsible.

One common way in which such a collapse or reversal is often understood is in terms of reduced social, political and economic complexity, and a correspondingly significant reduction in human population size. Historical examples of this sort of complexity collapse include Norse Greenland (around 1500 CE), Mayan Civilization (around 900 CE) and Mycenean Greece (around 1200 BCE) (Diamond, 2005: 3). Whilst such social failures can seem like anomalies from our current vantage point, Tainter (1988: 24) proposes that it is actually modern complex societies that need to be conceived as such. The reason being that

[t]hroughout the several million years that recognizable humans are known to have lived, the common political unit was the small, autonomous community, acting independently, and largely self-sufficient. Robert Carneiro has estimated that 99.8 percent of human history has been dominated by these autonomous local communities... It has only been within the last 6000 years that something unusual has emerged: the hierarchical, organized, interdependent states that are the major reference for our contemporary political experience. (Ibid.)

To give a sense of just how anomalous we are, Tainter (1988: 23) notes that whilst hunter-gatherer societies are reported to have been comprised of 'no more than a few dozen distinct social personalities', European censuses in the 1980s differentiated between occupational roles numbering in the tens of thousands. One consequence of such complexity is that, whereas it was once possible to have a strong understanding of developments and techniques in a relatively significant number of social domains of wide-ranging importance (e.g. food production, energy production, construction, medicine), it is now very difficult to have 'contributory expertise' (Collins & Evans, 2002: 254) in more than a small number of specialized fields. As a result, professionals, scientists and researchers are now often completely unable, or entirely unwilling, to chance their hand at tasks undertaken in seemingly very close domains: e.g. different traditions in sociological research; different types of steel and timber construction; different fields of computer science.

As has been well understood since at least the Scottish Enlightenment, this complexity, and associated increase in specialization, is a major driver of the wealth of nations (Smith, 1999). Nevertheless, both the immense variety of discrete roles and responsibilities it entails, and the infrastructure that it requires, mean that accidents or catastrophes of sufficient size could not just result in our current rates of development and complexity being slowed down, but in their quickly being reversed. General purpose technologies like the Internet and AI – which cut across domains (Rosenberg & Trajtenberg, 2004); which enable processes of invention (Cockburn, Henderson & Stern, 2018); and which Alphabet is hugely invested in – are one obvious point from which modern, complex societies, could begin to unravel. It is not for nothing that US Homeland Security lists Information Technology and Communications amongst its critical infrastructure (Website).

By promoting the development of, and our dependence on, such technologies, the ideology of infinite times gives rise to the possibility of significant failings coming to pass should such technologies be rendered inoperable, or somehow cease to exist. Thus, once it is noted that such events might arise due to poor design, unmanageable complexity, or some sort of hostilities, it is not difficult to envisage how the infinite times–informed activities of Alphabet could directly contribute to the emergence of some sort of wholesale social collapse, and the subsequent emergence of some form of future primitivism.

The Other-Created Threat

Although most are likely to be horrified by the risk of complex societies collapsing, some welcome the prospect. The Unabomber Ted Kaczynski – who earned the 'Unabomber' label due to his targeting of people working for Universities and Airlines; and who is currently serving a life sentence without parole following his pleading guilty to a letter-bomb campaign that spanned the years 1978 through 1995, and that resulted in 3 people dying and 23 being injured – provides a case in point.

On 20 April 1995, Kaczynski sent a number of letters to leading US news outlets (Kurtz, 1995). In these letters, Kaczynski, who referred to himself as the terrorist group 'FC' (Freedom Club) (The New York Times, 1995), began outlining his philosophy and noted that, if the relevant news outlets were to subsequently publish his essay advocating the elimination of industrial society, he would desist from any further acts of terrorism. Following what one can only imagine was a very tense process involving the FBI, both *The New York Times* and *The Washington Post* agreed to jointly publish Kaczynski's manifesto (Kurtz, 1995). In subsequently 'recognizing the manifesto as Kaczynski's writing, his brother, David, turned Kaczynski in to the FBI, which arrested him at his Montana cabin on 3 April 1996' (Chase, 2000).

The basic thrust of Kaczynski's manifesto is that industrial-technological societies have resulted in humans becoming alienated, powerless and entirely lacking in independent security. There are a number of elements to his thesis. On the one hand, Kaczynski (1995) proposes that, by enabling many of us to satisfy our physical needs through simple acts of obedience (e.g. to corporations, to states), technical-industrial advances have resulted in people having to adopt 'surrogate activities' that give them some sense of power, agency and control. These 'surrogate activities' include such things as 'scientific work, athletic achievement, humanitarian work, artistic and literary creation, climbing the corporate ladder' (Ibid.). Whilst many think such activities are valuable, Kaczynski suggests that they are trivial, empty and ultimately unsatisfying. 'The scientist no sooner solves one problem than he moves on to the next. The long-distance runner drives himself to run always farther and faster' (Ibid.).

On the other hand, Kaczynski also proposes that modern humans are increasingly threatened by technologies that give rise to significant risks that we are completely unable to control. He argues that this ubiquitous, increasing and unmanageable threat to our security results in our being 'frustrated, humiliated and angry' (Ibid.). Finally, and in light of the preceding points, Kaczynski proposes that 'human beings have a need (probably based in biology) for... the "power process"': i.e. a meta-need to satisfy various other significant needs (e.g. basic needs like food and shelter) through 'serious effort' (Ibid.). Because technological advances radically decrease the extent to which this need for the power process can be satisfied, Kaczynski argues that 'the elimination of modern technology' must be 'the single overriding goal' for revolutionaries 'who hate the servitude to which the industrial system is reducing the human race' (Ibid.).

Although there are not many people that would be willing to engage in direct deadly actions like Kaczynski, the Unabomber's overall philosophical positioning – which, in advocating the dissolution of complex, technically advanced, modern societies, necessitates a rapid reduction in human numbers – has its advocates. Foremost amongst these is the author of *Future Primitive*, John Zerzan. Whilst no longer on terms with the Unabomber, seemingly as a result of their disagreement over the extent to which primitive societies were characterized by gender equality (Morin, 2014), Zerzan's work does share some clear similarities with the man he corresponded and sympathized with (Day, 2001).

What Zerzan (2012) argues is that industrialization and technological development, and the division of labour and symbolic cultures that have made them possible, have amounted to nothing less than an unmitigated disaster for humankind. Rather than improving human well-being, agricultural developments are purported to have established 'the material foundations of social hierarchy' and the 'priests, kings and warfare that have gone with it' (Zerzan, 2012: 10). More broadly, he suggests that our physical and emotional vigour has greatly decreased following the replacement of leisure-rich hunter-gatherer lifestyles with the 'conformity, repetition, and regulation' that have proven central to civilization's advance (Zerzan, 2012: 11, 14). Although he believes that defining a 'disallienated world would be impossible and even undesirable', Zerzan remains secure enough in his position to state:

We have taken a monstrously wrong turn… from a place of enchantment, understanding and wholeness to the absence we find at the heart of the doctrine of progress. Empty and emptying, the logic of domestication… shows us the ruin of the civilization that ruins the rest. Assuming the inferiority of nature enables the domination of cultural systems that soon will make the very Earth uninhabitable. (Zerzan, 2012: 23)

The only way out, according to Zerzan is to bring an end to social complexity and the division of labor that 'takes away the wholeness and integrity of an individual's life' (145). Put in more positive terms, human flourishing requires that one's life 'must literally be in one's own hands', for only 'when tools, and the rest of life, are direct and autonomous can complexity' and the domestication it results in 'be disposed of' (Ibid.). Despite seeking to distance his views from idealistic and romantic conceptions of prehistory (Morin, 2014), it is difficult to avoid equating Zerzan's work, and that of other (future) primitivists, with a literal reading of humanity's oft-posited and heavily mythologized fall from grace (Smith, 2002: 414). Be that as it may, one need not presume that there was ever a 'Golden Age' to think that 'the move from hunter-gathering to farming brought no overall gain in human well-being or freedom'; to think that, 'almost certainly, Paleolithic humanity was better off' (Gray, 2002: 156).

That Alphabet is a major contributor to the malaise of those informed by future primitive ideology is perhaps best illustrated by its nominal love of symbols and language, which Zerzan (2012) identifies as a key source of our civilizational woes. What is equally clear, however, is that Alphabet's activities contribute to the more limited unease that many amongst the broader population feel with regard to technology becoming a part of more and more aspects of daily life. As the Centre for Humane Technology (Website) has put it: 'Our society is being hijacked by technology.' But whereas this ideologically very moderate and relatively tech-friendly Centre proposes the need to halt and reverse this hijacking by means of 'inspire(d) humane design' and political pressure (Ibid.), future primitives argue that this hijacking needs to be sped up. The reason why is that, the quicker technology and 'civilization makes things worse', the quicker people will come to think that civilization itself has 'no future', and that they will be willing to 'put forth the effort' needed to bring civilization itself 'to an end' (Zerzan, 2014).

Extinction

In contrast to the future primitive ideology, which is associated with a significant reduction in human numbers, the ideology of extinction is associated with our complete elimination. For something close to everyone, this would be a tragedy of the highest degree. As technologies continue to advance, however, it can seem more and more likely that humanity will prove the author of its own demise. In being part of the current technological elite, and in being informed by the infinite times ideology, Alphabet is one of a number of actors that could make a significant contribution to such a catastrophe unfolding.

The Alphabet-Created Threat

Human existence has always been threatened by natural catastrophes: e.g. earthquake, flood, fire, pestilence. Nevertheless, the fact that our species has survived such events for 'hundreds of thousands of years' suggests that 'it is prima facie unlikely' that any natural catastrophe 'will do us in within the next hundred' (Bostrom, 2013: 15). Human-made and technologically enabled catastrophes, by way of contrast, are likely to prove more troubling. Indeed, given humanity's success with nuclear fission and fusion (Jonas, 1976: 94), and in light of subsequent developments in 'biotechnology, molecular nanotechnology, and machine intelligence', Bostrom (2013: 16) suspects that 'the great bulk of existential risk in the foreseeable future consists of... those arising from human activity'.

Not unlike Rachel Carson's book *Silent Spring*, which was published in 1962 and which is widely credited as a catalyst of the environmental movement, Bostrom's work on existential risks (e.g. Bostrom, 2002, 2013, 2014; Bostrom & Ćirković, 2008) has played a catalytic role in the development of what might be termed the 'continued existence' movement. Bostrom's influence, however, is not just through his writings, for he also plays a more or less practical and central role in such initiatives as Oxford's Future of Humanity Institute (est. 2005), Cambridge's Centre for the Study of Existential Risk (est. 2012), The Future of Life Institute (est. 2015), and Alphabet's DeepMind Ethics & Society research initiative (est. 2017). In short – and whilst some dismiss the existential concerns that Bostrom and his colleagues raise as a 'distraction' from other 'real' problems that technology exacerbates, such as 'sexism, racism, and other forms of discrimination' (Crawford, 2016) – the risks that Bostrom is concerned with have clearly struck a popular nerve. There appear to be two reasons why.

First is the previously noted, and seemingly very widespread, belief, that humanity's extinction would be, in ethical or moral terms, one of the worst disasters imaginable. In recent years, this general concern has come to be associated with Parfit (1984: 453–454), who asked his readers to make a comparison between three potential outcomes:

(1) Peace.
(2) A nuclear war that kills 99% of the world's existing population.
(3) A nuclear war that kills 100%.

(2) would be worse than (1), and (3) would be worse than (2). Which is the greater of these two differences? Most people believe that the greater difference is between (1) and (2). I believe that the difference between (2) and (3) is very much greater… The Earth will remain inhabitable for at least another billion years. Civilization began only a few thousand years ago. If we do not destroy mankind, these few thousand years may be only a tiny fraction of the whole of civilized human history. The difference between (2) and (3) may thus be the difference between this tiny fraction and all of the rest of this history. If we compare this possible history to a day, what has occurred so far is only a fraction of a second.

The second reason relates to the 'Carter-Leslie… doomsday argument' (Leslie, 1996: 188). According to John Leslie, this argument was 'first sketched' in a 1983 lecture given by Brandon Carter, 'the Cambridge mathematician who [also] invented the phrase "anthropic principle"' (Ibid.). Given the controversy associated with the argument, and given the efforts that Leslie subsequently made in elaborating it, Carter wrote to Leslie asking him 'to speak of "the Carter-Leslie argument", at least from time to time, to share "not only the credit but also the blame"' (Ibid.).

The doomsday argument builds on Carter's anthropic principle, which reminds us 'that observers, for instance humans, can find themselves only at places and times where intelligent life is possible' (Leslie, 1996: 14). As intelligent life cannot exist in other spheres, there can be no direct or immediate recording of them. When this basic idea is combined with the recognition that conditions enabling of intelligent life could be exceedingly rare, and that intelligent forms of existence can be the (un)intended authors of their own demise (particularly once they reach advanced levels of technological development), the full weight of the doomsday argument begins to take hold. It highlights the (self-evident) point that, just because we have not witnessed our own extinction, this does not mean that it cannot occur (Ćircović, 2008).

The doomsday argument also relates to Bayesian probability or Bayes' rule – which involves the updating of a prior probability on the basis of new evidence so as to form a posterior probability – and to the presumptions we make about the total number of humans that will ever live. Whilst the subject of continuing debate, the Bayesian logic that informs the doomsday argument has many adherents (cf. Cabantous & Gond, 2015; Zyphur, Oswald & Rupp, 2015), and is easy to understand with Leslie's (1996: 198–199) example of the lottery urn.

In short, Leslie asks his readers to imagine a lottery urn that contains different balls with different names on them (including one ball with your name). Before any balls are pulled out of the urn, you have to assign different probabilities to how many balls the urn contains. You assign a 98 percent probability to it containing 1,000 names, 'and a 2 percent probability that it contains just 10'. Following this, a person steps up and draws three balls from the urn, including one with your name on it. On this basis, and in accord with Bayes' theorem, Leslie (1996: 199–200) notes that 'the "posterior" probability of there having been only ten names in the urn' goes up to approximately 67 percent. 'Calculation on similar lines', he continues, suggests 'that the risk the human race will end soon has been regularly underestimated, perhaps very seriously' (Leslie, 1996: 200).

In terms of extinction, what the doomsday argument highlights is that if we were all to die tomorrow, with the population level at 7.8 billion, we would be living at a time when between 5 and 10 percent of the 100 billion or so humans that are estimated to have ever lived were alive (e.g. Benatar, 2006: 167). If, on the other hand, our species continues to prosper and advance for tens of thousands of years to come, then we would be alive at a time when only a tiny proportion of all humans that subsequently come into being were alive. As our finding ourselves amongst 5–10 percent of all humans that will ever live is more probable than our finding ourselves amongst an increasingly tiny fraction thereof, Leslie (1996: 202) suggests that it is reasonable to presume that 'the next 150 years will be a period of grave danger'. Hence, if our species is to avoid being struck down like 'straw dogs' (Gray, 2002), and if we are to stand a chance of human civilization extending for millennia to come, it seems reasonable to invest some efforts in avoiding existential catastrophe today (Bostrom, 2013).

The Other-Created Threat

Whilst it can seem controversial to suggest that our species may be at imminent risk of extinction (Leslie, 1996: 188), such controversy pales in comparison to that associated with normative arguments suggesting it would be good thing if we were to go the way of the dinosaurs. Nevertheless, and whether it is because of, or in spite of, the controversy that such arguments generate, various parties can be found arguing just this point. By and large, these parties have identified two main considerations that lead to the desiring of our extinction.

The first is the 'horrible human' element: the belief that the human species is a blight on our earthly home. Further to their suggesting that humans have a strong historical record when it comes to raping, pillaging and slaughtering their own kind, proponents of the 'horrible human' argument propose that humans have long done the same to other species and their environment as well. Given that humans have caused, and continue to cause, such 'colossal amounts of suffering – both for human and for non-human animals', the likes of Gray (2002: 224) conclude that 'there is a superb misanthropic argument against having children and in favour of human extinction'.

The second aspect of the normative argument for humanity's extinction is even less positive. It suggests that 'existence is fucked'. As the great German pessimist Arthur Schopenhauer (1969: 311) detailed a little more fully: 'life swings like a pendulum to and fro between pain and boredom, and these two are in fact its ultimate constituents. This has been expressed very quaintly by saying that, after man had placed all pains and torments in hell, there was nothing left for heaven but boredom'. Instead of lamenting the 'shortness of life', then, Schopenhauer (1969: 323–324) suggested that the brevity of its duration 'may perhaps be the very best thing about it': for 'whence did Dante get the material for his hell, if not from this actual world of ours?'

Like the 'horrible human' element, the 'existence is fucked' element is anti-natalist. It posits that because 'coming into existence is always a serious harm... we should not have children' (Benatar, 2006: 8). In being confronted by 'an extremely powerful pro-natalist bias' that has 'its roots in the evolutionary origins of human (and more primitive animal) psychology and biology' (Benatar, 2006: 8), anti-natalist arguments *prima facie* stand little chance in the race to convince. The fact that powerful organizations have long benefited from pro-natalist arguments as well – e.g. cannon fodder for the military (Benatar, 2006: 11); parish communities and the 'battle of the cradles' (Garigue, 1960) – does not increase their immediate popular appeal.

Having said that, normative precedents as to the asymmetry of pleasure and pain lend some support to this second normative aspect of the anti-natalist extinction agenda. This asymmetry can be summarized as follows (Benatar, 2006: 30–38). Existence gives rise to pleasure (which is good) and pain (which is bad). Non-existence, on the other hand, is associated with no-pain (which is good) and no-pleasure (which is not bad). Because good minus not-bad is more than good minus bad (according to Benatar), non-existence is preferable to existence. Put more concretely, Benatar (2006: 32) suggests that this line of reasoning is what underpins the widespread belief that 'there is a duty to avoid bringing suffering people into existence', but no corresponding duty 'to bring happy people into existence'.

Whilst Benatar (2017: 161) acknowledges, in a manner reminiscent of infinite times ideology, that 'our mortality is an unbearable limit that we seek to transcend', he believes that mortality will remain an 'ultimate limit that we simply cannot transcend in any literal way'. As he considers this awareness of our finitude 'one of the chief triggers of existential angst... a brute and ugly feature of the human predicament', he posits that, whilst an increased lifespan could have some benefits, it would still be preferable to never exist, to never be 'doomed to die' at all (Benatar, 2017: 162). Yet even if the fear of death could be eradicated, life would continue to appear a 'predicament' (Ibid.) from the 'existence is fucked', extinctionist, perspective. For it would simply result in perpetuating 'an error for ever... a false step, something that it would be better should [it] not be' (Schopenhauer, 1969: 491).

At least some people beyond the formal philosophical community are informed by elements of this argument. Members of The Voluntary Human Extinction Movement, whose VHMET acronym is aptly pronounced as vehement, provide a case in point. Of the two elements noted above, it appears that it is the 'horrible human' element that plays the stronger role in the movement's existence. In particular, and in contrast to Benatar (2006), who posits that all forms of sentient existence are undesirable (whilst focusing on the negatives of human existence in particular), popular reports (Fleming, 2018; Savory, 2008) provide anecdotal evidence of what the VHMET website suggests. Namely, that VHMET supporters 'know' that the

hopeful alternative to the extinction of millions of species of plants and animals is the voluntary extinction of one species: Homo sapiens... When every human chooses to stop breeding, Earth's biosphere will be allowed to return to its former glory, and all remaining creatures will be free to live, die, evolve (if they believe in evolution), and will perhaps pass away, as so many of Nature's 'experiments' have done throughout the eons. (VHMET, Website)

Just as Alphabet's infinite times–informed activities seem likely to indirectly encourage at least a minimal increase in the number of people that identify with the future primitive ideology, so too can the megacorporation's activities be seen to encourage at least some to further investigate, and potentially adopt, the ideology of extinction. If for no other reason, the fact that it is often perceived as fashionable to oppose oneself to the powers that be, suggests that the extinction ideology will be increasingly adopted so long as Alphabet continues on its current trajectory.

The Singularity

Whereas neither the future primitive nor extinction ideology are likely to find many adherents within Alphabet, or amongst the broader tech community, the singularity ideology quite possibly does. As has previously been indicated, no less than Google's director of engineering, Ray Kurzweil, is, amongst other things, famous for having written a book entitled *The Singularity Is Near* (Kurzweil, 2005), and for his foundational role in what is termed, with seemingly complete sincerity, Singularity University (Diamandis & Kotler, 2012: 57). As these points indicate, the singularity ideology is, relative to the other two ideological alternatives just identified, the one that is most similar to the infinite times ideology. Nevertheless, in going past the anthropocentric or humanistic point of view (Joy, 2000), and towards one that can be characterized as post- or trans- humanistic, the singularity ideology is clearly distinguishable from it.

This basic difference is perhaps best reflected by the belief that we are approaching an event horizon beyond which current levels of human understanding and biological existence will be superseded by exponential technological advances; beyond which all that we have historically learned could prove redundant (e.g. Kurzweil, 2005: 21–30). This possibility, which informed Bostrom (2013) in his *New York Times* bestseller *Superintelligence*, is one that various tech luminaries take quite seriously. Elon Musk, for example, has infamously suggested that 'with artificial intelligence we are summoning the demon' (McFarland, 2014). Moreover, the appointment of Bostrom to Alphabet DeepMind's recently established Ethics & Society research programme, clearly post-dates, and is seemingly informed by, Bostrom's (2013) prior professed concern that human brains could one day be surpassed by computer brains that are more super than they are simply intelligent.

The Alphabet-Created Threat

The general motivation for technological advance is that it reduces unwanted burdens and frees the species to engage in more important, productive, enjoyable, rational and creative activities. Yet, as technology advances, it appears that technology could come to replace, rather than supplement or enhance, what have hitherto been conceived as archetypically human capacities (Joy, 2000). Rather than being 'partners in securing' human well-being (Li, 2018), machines could prove the source of our redundancy. Although it is tempting to delve into the extensive fictional literature on the impact that massive advances in machine intelligence will have on society, it is arguably more interesting to look at a number of technological developments that have already occurred. The story of former world chess champion Garry Kasparov, and of his capitulation to IBM's Deep Blue in May 1997, provides a case in point.

The backstory to this momentous event – which a *Newsweek* cover provocatively referred to as 'The Brain's Last Stand' (see Levy, 2017) – can be traced to the middle of the twentieth century, when Bell Telephone Laboratories' scientist Claude Shannon first gave a lecture, and subsequently published a paper, that is now recognized as having founded modern chess computing as a field. Whilst early hopes that computers would be capable of beating a world chess champion in just a few years proved unfounded, by the 1970s chess grandmasters (i.e. the world's elite players, who then numbered in the hundreds) began to acknowledge that progress was being made (Hsu, 2002: vii; Newborn, 1996: 1–23).

In March 1989, IBM, which had a well-established history of dabbling in 'game-playing programs' (Newborn, 1996: 173), permanently appointed Feng-hsiung Hsu and a number of other computer scientists from Carnegie Mellon University. Hsu and his team were appointed to continue working on a 'chess machine' they had developed, and that was named Deep Thought in homage to the computer that provided 42 as the answer to the question of 'Life, the Universe, and Everything', in Douglas Adams' *The Hithchiker's Guide to the Galaxy* (Hsu, 2002: 62, 90).

In October of the same year, Deep Thought took on 'Garry Kasparov in a two-game match in New York and was routinely defeated' (Newborn, 1996: 173). At the press conference prior to the 1989 match, and following similar remarks he had made the year before (Hsu, 2002: 81):

Kasparov granted that someday a computer might outplay him, but he believed the day was not just over the horizon. "I don't know how we can exist knowing that there exists something mentally stronger than us," he said... [and] contended that the best humans will improve when the day comes that a computer really challenges them. (Newborn, 1996: 175)

Given this suggestion, it was to be expected that Kasparov would be more than happy to take IBM's money when another match with its chess machine, by then named Deep Blue (Newborn, 1996: 205), was arranged in celebration of the Association for Computing Machinery's (ACM) fiftieth anniversary in 1996. Whilst Kasparov reportedly had a crisis of confidence following his loss in the first game of the six-game match (Hsu, 2002: 174), he went home a happy man, winning 4–2. Yet IBM was pleased with Deep Blue's performance too. So much so that Hsu and his colleagues returned to work 'the following Monday as heroes' (Newborn, 1996: 278).

Consequently, it was with rising confidence that IBM arranged for a rematch the following year. As Hsu (2002: 204) has noted: 'We felt good about our chances. Garry Kasparov was strong, but he was not invincible.' The match was close, but in winning the final game, Deep Blue became the first computer to beat the World Champion in a regulation match (Hsu, 2002. 253–257). As Kasparov had 'never lost' in his life (Levy, 2017), it would seem that he found the whole experience quite confronting, to say the least.

Twenty years later, Kasparov admitted as much in his book *Deep Thinking*, where he pleadingly writes:

If you can, for a moment, imagine what that moment felt like for me, take one extra step in my shoes and imagine then having to face hundreds of reporters and a large audience asking you about it... I was in shock, exhausted, and bitter about everything that had happened on and off the board. When it was my turn to speak, I told the audience that I certainly did not merit their applause... I said that I was ashamed. (Kasparov, 2017: 214)

Further to the match still being of gossip value due to both sides accusing the other of a lack of sportsmanship (Hsu, 2002: 163; Kasparov, 2017: 220), Deep Blue's win continues to be of interest due to its now appearing inevitable (Levy, 2017). Whilst it took longer than some expected, everyone now acknowledges that neither Kasparov, nor current world champion Magnus Carlsen, could avoid being anything other than crushed by a computer today (Hsu, 2002: 271; Kasparov, 2017: 50).

As the game of Go is generally considered at least a few orders of magnitude more complex than chess (on the basis of possible board positions), it has often been suggested that it would prove impossible (Byford, 2016a), or at least a lot more difficult than chess (Newborn, 1996: 281), for computers to crack. Even Feng-hsiung Hsu, who one would imagine tends to be optimistic in such matters, estimated, back in 2002, that Go would prove too complicated to 'be "solved" within the next 20 years' (Hsu, 2002: 272).

Given such predictions, there was much excitement when Alphabet DeepMind's AlphaGo beat the legendary Go player Lee Sedol 4–1 in March 2016. Whilst no doubt impressed by AlphaGo's success, the world's best player at the time, a youthful prodigy named Ke Jie, still 'seemed cautiously optimistic about his own chances' against AlphaGo following Lee Sedol's initial loss, 'saying "it's 60 percent in favor of me"' (Byford, 2016a). As we now know, this optimism was misplaced, for at the Future of Go Summit in Wuzhen in May 2017, AlphaGo beat KeJie 3–0 (Byford, 2017).

Just like Kasparov and Lee Sedol before him, Ke Jie has had to face 'the slow, agonizing realization that the talent that brought him fame and fortune could be bettered by a sequence of ones and zeroes' (Byford, 2016b). As he himself put it:

I think I'm done with playing AlphaGo... To me, the AlphaGo is God, a being that can defeat anyone or anything. I think I need some time to figure out the situation. I had never doubted myself before. I used to think that I was the strongest and the most cogitative. But I guess to the AlphaGo, all my thinking and planning would seem primitive. What he [sic] sees is the whole universe, while what we see is just a pond in front of us. So I'll leave him with the task to explore the universe while I, myself, prefer fishing in the pond. (CGTN America, 2017)

To be clear, the forms of AI that inform chess and Go machines are far from some sort of general AI that can readily complete, let alone quickly change between, the full variety of activities that humans undertake in huge numbers on a daily basis. This recognition might be a source of comfort for some, for it suggests that there will always be something innate to humanity, some sort of creative genius or real intelligence, that machines will never prove capable of replicating. Indeed, this way of thinking appears to have played a role in Kasparov's apparent coming to terms with his loss. In particular, Kasparov has suggested, much like his arch-rival Hsu (2002) did fifteen years prior, that his loss was less a win for machines than it was 'a win for humans, since humans built the machine' (Kasparov, 2017: 221). Rather than trying to slow down machine development, then, Kasparov argues, in accord with infinite times ideology, that we should try to speed it up so that we can free ourselves of drudgery, and elevate 'our mental lives toward creativity, curiosity, beauty, and joy' (Kasparov, 2017: 10).

As the above noted remarks by Ke Jie suggest, however, and as Kasparov himself is no doubt fully aware, much human satisfaction and well-being is derived from the sense that we, as both individuals and as a species, constitute some sort of peak of possible performance. There is little dignity to be derived from the picking of low-hanging fruit. If recent rapid advances in AI continue, there is a very real risk that humanity could only ever hope to finish second in a whole variety of fields. The driving of cars, the translating of documents, the composition of music, the diagnosing of disease and so on, were all, up until recently, tasks that were considered as solely existing within the domain of human expertise. But As human-made machines become more sophisticated, however, these tasks are increasingly being undertaken by them. In fact, machines themselves can now play a fundamental role in the making of other, more sophisticated, machines.

Following its decimation of Ke Jie in May 2017, DeepMind let AlphaGo 'continue to train by playing millions of games against itself', and to develop into a new version termed AlphaGo Zero which 'picked up Go from scratch, without studying any human games at all. AlphaGo Zero took a mere three days to reach the point where it was pitted against an older version of itself and won 100 games to zero' (Chan, 2017). Whilst humans are still obviously central to this overall process, the AlphaGo Zero example does suggest that 'humanity as toolmaker' is likely to be increasingly supplanted by 'machine as toolmaker', just as 'man as toolmaker' has already supplanted 'man as performer' (Hsu, 2002: ix) in many domains.

As this process unfolds, as computers become increasingly advanced in terms of 'complex decision-making, reasoning and learning, sophisticated analytics and pattern recognition' (Pew Research Centre, 2018: 2), those aspects from which humans can derive meaning and satisfaction could diminish. Danaher (2017) thus suggests that, as machine intelligence accelerates, the contribution that humans will prove capable of making in terms of epistemic concerns (knowledge) and normative concerns (morality) will, along with any sense of achievement associated therewith, diminish. While we might still prove capable of experiencing direct and immediate joy in more aesthetic realms – e.g. through our engagement in artistic, sporting and romantic activities – whatever pleasure we derive therefrom will also be, at least in some sense, diminished by the recognition that machines are increasingly able to objectively outperform us in these areas too.

The basic fear is that technology will increasingly supplant the role that humanity has played in pursuit of the 'the True and the Good', and to a somewhat lesser extent, 'the Beautiful' (Danaher, 2017: 57–59). If such a possibility ever comes to pass, then our avoidance of it would likely require our being heavily supplemented by machines (as per infinite times ideology); our destroying of machines (as per future primitive ideology); or our ceasing to be (as per extinction ideology).

The Other-Created Threat

Along with Sun Microsystems co-founder Bill Joy (2000), many people would be discomforted by the idea that they may be helping 'create tools which will enable the construction of the technology that may replace our species'. But as is always the case, exceptions like Anthony Levandowski can be found.

Born in 1980, Levandowski has a long history of 'working with computers, robots, and AI' (Harris, 2017a). He 'worked at Google for almost a decade and was an integral part of its autonomous driving efforts that spun from Google (X) into Waymo' (Weintraub, 2018). In addition to his being referred to as an 'autonomous driving prodigy' (Ibid.), Levandowski is well known for his being accused of stealing secrets from Waymo, which he left in 2016 to set up his own self-driving company, Otto, which was subsequently bought by Uber (Wong, 2018). To cut a long story short, 'Levandowski left the GooglePlex with more than just his belongings and ended up the main defendant in a rare Waymo vs. Uber civil case which was settled where Google got an even bigger chunk of Uber and a promise from Uber not to use its tech' (Weintraub, 2018). Whilst Google and Uber settled, Levandowski's purportedly sticky fingers could still result in him serving significant time as he is currently facing thirty-three criminal charges of theft and attempted theft of trade secrets (Hawkins, 2019).

That Levandowski may be a thief is of clear interest to many parties, not least of all the man himself. But what is of much more interest in the present context, is that Levandowski founded a religious organization termed Way of the Future back in 2015 (Harris, 2017b). According to its website, Way of the Future 'is about creating a peaceful and respectful transition of who is in charge of the planet from people to people + "machines"'. One of the new religion's founding beliefs is that 'intelligence is not rooted in biology. While biology has evolved one type of intelligence, there is nothing inherently specific about biology that causes intelligence. Eventually, we will be able to recreate it without using biology and its limitations. From there we will be able to scale it to beyond what we can do using (our) biological limits' (Way of the Future, Website).

Another of Way of the Future's founding beliefs is that

the creation of "super intelligence" is inevitable... We don't think that there are ways to actually stop this from happening (nor should we want to) and that this feeling of we must stop this is rooted in 21st century anthropomorphism (similar to humans thinking the sun rotated around the earth in the "not so distant" past). Wouldn't you want to raise your gifted child to exceed your wildest dreams of success and teach it right from wrong vs locking it up because it might rebel in the future and take your job. We want to encourage machines to do things we cannot and take care of the planet in a way we seem not to be able to do so ourselves. We also believe that, just like animals have rights, our creation(s) ("machines" or whatever we call them) should have rights too when they show signs [of] intelligence (still to be defined of course). We should not fear this but should be optimistic about the potential. (Ibid.)

In discussions with Harris (2017a), Levandowski has posited that we are currently '"in the process of raising a god... It's a tremendous opportunity"'. Moreover, Levandowski has noted that everything the church develops will be 'open source', and that we should be proactively 'feeding the nascent intelligence large, labeled data sets; generating simulations in which it could train itself to improve' (Ibid.). In these ways, the church that Levandowski controls and founded, and that he registered as a non-profit corporation with the Internal Revenue Services in the United States (Ibid.), appears to share some commonality with what Harari (2015: 444–445) terms 'dataism': the celebration of dataflows. Moreover, and in duly noting that Floridi (2013: 15) has sought to dissociate himself from posthumanism's 'fanciful and fictional' tendencies, it appears to share at least some common ground with his belief that we are currently undergoing a revolution that is giving rise to 'unprecedented epistemic and engineering powers over natural and artificial realities', and that is casting a 'new light on... how we understand ourselves', the 'informational environment' and 'artificial agents' (Floridi, 2013: 14).

The Way of the Future's 'gospel' can also be related to Bostrom's (2014: 211) suggestion that the reason we would want to build a superintelligence in the first place, is to better realize a given value. To this end, Bostrom suggests that we could – and arguably should – want a superintelligence to not just help achieve values that we dictate but also actively identify the values we should pursue. For if it is really 'super', then this intelligence will be much 'better at cognitive work than we are', and would consequently occupy 'an epistemically superior vantage point' from which it could more readily identify beliefs that are 'more likely than ours to be true' (Ibid.).

In these still early days of AI development, the possibility of constructing such entities raises – at the risk of considerable understatement – a number of technical and normative difficulties (Bostrom, 2014). Whilst recognizing as such, the Way of the Future is clear that this state of affairs will eventually come about. Consequently, the fledgling church proposes that we need to 'stop pretending we can hold back the development of intelligence when there are clear massive short term economic benefits to those who develop it and instead understand the future and have it treat us like a beloved elder who created it' (Way of the Future, Website). The risk of our doing otherwise is neatly summed up by Levandowski when he suggests that if we want to be treated as this future AI Godhead's '"pets"', and not as its '"livestock"', then we need to start trying to 'smooth the inevitable ascension of our machine deity, both technologically and culturally', today (Harris, 2017a).

In contrast to the future primitive and extinction ideologies that Alphabet is indirectly enabling through being involved in developments that promote resistance; Alphabet is indirectly enabling the singularity ideology by helping to create data flows and data sets that could subsequently be used by others to fuel the growth of some future, artificially intelligent, overlord. So whilst Alphabet seems highly unlikely to suggest that we should welcome this loss of human pre-eminence, the technological developments it is currently helping to accelerate could be used by the likes of Levandowski to bring about a world in which we are dominated by a (hopefully benevolent) god born of computer scientists' labour.

Summary

This chapter has proposed that, by bringing the concern to extend humanity's past and future together, the ideology of infinite times provides the glue that enables Alphabet's wide-ranging and diverse activities to be seen as one. It has also been proposed that the infinite times ideology informs the revealed preference that so many people around the world have for the megacorporation's products and services. As a result, the infinite times ideology can be said to be a key source of Alphabet's continuing growth.

The flipside of this, however, is that the infinite times ideology also provides a potent source of the megacorporation's ultimate demise. The reason why is that the ideology of infinite times is itself finite, and directly and indirectly associated with developments that promote other ideologies that undermine it. Whether it is through some sort of accident that Alphabet is directly responsible for, or through a deliberate set of events that Alphabet unintentionally enables or encourages others to undertake, the megacorporation's infinite times–informed existence necessitates its own demise at some point in the more or less distant future. Thus – and whilst Alphabet could still be around in 100 years, as Larry Page has suggested (Waters, 2014); or even in 1000 years, as Vint Cerf has speculated (Ghosh, 2015) – neither it, nor the infinite times ideology that drives it, can hope to escape the finite limits that make their simple being, or their differentiation from everything else, possible.

9 | *Immediate Threats*

The final chapter notes that Alphabet's megacorporate existence could, further to the ideological reasons detailed in Chapter 8, potentially be brought to an end by two sets of considerations that are readily apparent right now. The first set of considerations relates to discord amongst the megacorporation's employees, and the second to anti-monopoly sentiment. Taken together, these considerations suggest that, in the short term, Alphabet's capacity to remain a megacorporation will likely turn on its capacity to account for disruptive elements from within; and its capacity to avoid being undermined by antitrust threats from without. The chapter's summary then brings the book to a close by emphasizing that, even if Alphabet's existence comes to an end sooner rather than later, the megacorporate concept it is an example of, the identification of the infinite times ideology that informs it, and the philosophical perspective that I have used to discuss it, remain of value, for they all help reveal that corporate influence over society is more profound than is commonly recognized.

Concerns on Campus

With more than 11 million views on YouTube in early 2020, the 'Google interns' first week' video from June 2013 may be the most-watched corporate recruitment video of all time. For those that have not seen it, do not worry, it is as cliched as you imagine. Within the first twenty-two seconds, the viewer sees a man riding a colourful bike through the Google campus; people enjoying a salad al fresco; a cute puppy; a young lady cuddling a sculpture of a doughnut; and a male speaker earnestly telling his audience that '"at Google we actually do have the ability to make more of an impact on people and more of a change in one year than many people do in their lifetimes"' (Google, 2013). For the present author at least, it seems that this last statement is true; for in completing this chapter, I could not help but note that the

'Google interns' first week' video received more views in one evening than I've had citations in my entire 'career'.

Whilst the recognition of such influence is a humbling experience for an observer like me, many who work for the megacorporation appear to experience a different sort of discomfort upon realizing the full extent of Alphabet's capacities. In particular – and as was suggested upon the 2015 release of Alphabet's code of conduct, which made no reference to the 'Don't be evil' motto that is still purported to guide those employed by its Google subsidiary (D'Orazio, 2015) – many that receive their paycheque from Alphabet appear to fear that if there is an evil empire, then it is they who work for it.

Although he only appears to have publicly voiced his concern once he found out that he would no longer have a job at the megacorporation (and to his subsequently being offered a demotion upon his hiring of counsel), it seems fair to say that, if he did still work there, Ross Lajeunesse – the former Google Head of International Relations – would not be alone in proposing that his own values are incompatible with Alphabet's. In the parting note he published on *Medium* at the start of 2020 (perhaps unaware that Alphabet is invested in *Medium* through its GV venture capital arm), Lajeunesse complained that, along with other employees 'who still believed in the mantra of "Don't be evil"', the human rights concerns that informed the company's decision to pull out of China back in 2010 had, by 2019, all but disappeared.

In addition to his worries about the now-terminated dragonfly project – the censored Chinese search engine whose development was leaked in 2018 (see Chapter 3) – Lajeunesse (2020) was 'concerned that [Google] Cloud executives were actively pursuing deals with the Saudi government, given its horrible record of human rights abuses'. He was also concerned by the fact that 'senior colleagues bullied and screamed at young women, causing them to cry at their desks'; and by his participation in 'a "diversity exercise"' in which he was placed 'in a group labeled "homos" while participants shouted out stereotypes such as "effeminate" and "promiscuous"' (Ibid.).

In seeking to explain these developments, along with the megacorporation's continual refusal to 'publicly commit' and 'adhere to human rights principles found in the UN Declaration of Human Rights', Lajeunesse pointed to a number of considerations (Ibid.). First, he suggested that, 'just when Google needed to double down on a commitment to human rights, it decided to instead chase bigger profits and an even higher stock price' (Ibid.). Second, he suggested that as day-to-day management concerns shifted from the founders to newly hired executives from Wall Street, and as the total number of employees shifted from 10,000 in 2008 to over 100,000 in 2019, 'the company's original values and culture' became forgotten (Ibid.).

Importantly, one does not have to accept Lajeunesse's suggestion that the megacorporation was once meaningfully informed by the concern to do no evil to acknowledge that a ten-fold increase in employee numbers over ten years, and changes in senior management, are likely to be a source of internal discord. Indeed, once it is noted that such growth has coincided with mass walkouts by Google staff around the world in protest at claims of sexual harassment (Bensinger, 2019a); the employment of a former US Department of Homeland Security official, Miles Taylor, who backed a controversial travel ban by President Trump that was widely seen as an attempt to ban Muslims from the US (Ibid.); and accusations that Google fired four engineers trying to organize workers around social issues (Pellman, 2019), it seems remarkable that the megacorporation has maintained 'its famously uninhibited' and 'open culture' for as long as it has (Bensinger, 2019a).

In light of an August 2019 memo, however, it would appear that free discussions at the megacorporation are a thing of the past (Bensinger, 2019b). On top of telling employees 'not to spend working time on debates about non-work topics', the memo 'sought to put the kibosh on the overuse or misuse' of internal forums, 'warning that "we will remove particular discussion forums, revoke commenting, viewing, or posting privileges, or take disciplinary action"' (Ibid.).

This stifling of internal discussion is clearly concerned to maintain a civil work environment (or the appearance thereof). The risk of promoting such civility, however, is that it will undermine many of the benefits that are popularly associated with working at the megacorporation, and that are heavily emphasized in the interns' first week video mentioned earlier (Google, 2013). Most concerningly, if the megacorporation moves further away from the campus life it is famous for (Levy, 2011: 135), and closer towards a culture that seeks to build trust through moderation (Bensinger, 2019a), then it may no longer prove a destination of choice for the tech elite it has hitherto had little trouble attracting. Moreover, these hierarchical means of imposing cohesion are all but certain to ensure that Alphabet's (2017) purported reliance 'on one another's good judgment to uphold a high standard of integrity for ourselves and our company' will never be anything more than a myth.

Concerns All Around

One example of employee discussions that Alphabet executives would apparently like to stifle are those relating to the megacorporation's monopolies. Back in July 2019, when the 2020 Democratic Primaries race was just starting to heat up, it was reported that some of the megacorporation's engineers were financially supporting campaigns in favour of Google's being broken apart. Besides suggesting that a breakup could help return the megacorporation to its 'startup roots', these employees suggested that breaking up Google would be good for the tech industry in general; and that if Microsoft had not been distracted by the antitrust case that was launched in 1998 (and that was settled in 2004), then 'the then-fledgling Google' would have never been able 'to rise up' (Molla & Ghaffary, 2019).

Unfortunately for the megacorporation's leadership and managerial elite, who have continuously suggested that breaking up the megacorporation would be a loss for all concerned (e.g. Pagnamenta, 2019), the idea that Alphabet is too big is gaining traction. Alongside the megacorporation's employees, and the various competitors that would financially benefit from its decimation, it is possible to identify three additional groups amongst which chants of 'take it down' are growing louder.

First, a series of recent polls suggest that a majority of consumers/ users see merit in Big Tech companies being split up. In September 2019, for example, it was reported that 'nearly two-thirds of Americans would support breaking up tech firms by undoing recent mergers... if it means ensuring more competition in the future' (Stewart, 2019). And in March 2020 it was reported that, whilst 90 percent of those surveyed had a favourable view of Google and YouTube, 51 percent still thought it would be best if they were split apart into separate companies (Newton, 2020).

Second, scholars like Lina Khan have sought to undermine the Chicago school–influenced belief that because 'competition is one click away' (Wismer, 2012), that because consumers 'can – and frequently do – switch between search engines at zero cost', Google can neither reduce competition nor be considered a monopoly (Bork & Sidak, 2012: 669, 672). Khan's critique – which proposes that 'antitrust law and competition policy' should not be (solely) focused on the promotion of consumer welfare, but on the promotion of competitive markets (Khan, 2017: 737) – has implications for those wanting to curtail Alphabet's powers. Amongst other things, it would enable Alphabet's role as a gatekeeper to be diminished by the use of 'common carriage rules' that would ensure that all users of a given network can equally access the infrastructure, prevent Alphabet 'from owning both an operating system and applications that run on it', and limit the extent to which Alphabet can use intelligence to 'thwart nascent rivals'(Khan, 2018: 331–333).

Third, anti-Alphabet sentiment also appears to be growing amongst politicians and state actors. In addition to the various confrontations it has faced in China over the years (see Chapter 3), the megacorporation has long faced concerns in the EU, where Google has had a 'combined $9.5 billion in antitrust fines' imposed on it since 2017 (Schulze, 2019). The first of these fines from 2017 totals $2.7 billion (€2.42 billion) and relates to Google purportedly 'favoring its own comparison shopping service over competitors' in search results' (Ibid.). At the time of writing, Google is appealing this 2017 fine in the EU General Court. Whilst the final result remains to be seen, the appeal did not start well; for on day two of the hearing, the Judge Colm Mac Eochaidh told Google that he considered its 'favoritism of its own shopping service as a clear infraction, and insisted that in Monopoly terms the internet giant had landed on "Go to jail"' (Van Dorpe, 2020).

Whilst Alphabet has previously enjoyed much more positive relations with US politicians and state actors – e.g. Alphabet is widely acknowledged to have enjoyed an 'extraordinarily close' relationship with the Obama administration (Google Transparency Project, 2016: 1; see also, Mullins, Winkler & Kendall, 2015; Orlowski, 2016) – the tide has begun to turn in its country of birth. Further to the megacorporation's might having been a key discussion point throughout the 2020 Democratic Party presidential primaries, and further to the Trump administration accusing Google of an anti-conservative bias (Lecher, 2019; Trump Jr, 2019), Alphabet and its Big Tech contemporaries are currently confronted by antitrust probes from the US Department of Justice (Romm, 2020); fifty attorney generals, including every state except California and Alabama (Feiner, 2019); and the Federal Trade Commission (2020). Moreover, the US Senate Judiciary Committee has recently met to discuss the announcement of Democrat Senator Amy Klobuchar's bill 'known as the "Anticompetitive Exclusionary Conduct Prevention Act"' (Robertson, 2020).

Although characterized by various differences, developments in the EU and United States are, along with scholarly critiques from the likes of Khan, all similar in that they are generally concerned to ensure that Alphabet cannot 1) use its platform power (e.g. Google search, the Android operating system) to favour its own products or services; 2) use its economic might to buy (or destroy) potential competitors; or 3) use its informational riches to identify, and subsequently mimic, any products or services that are produced by others. More generally – and whether framed in terms of enhancing competition, increasing consumer choice, increasing productive freedom or enhancing national security (Stewart, 2019; Sitaraman, 2020) – all these initiatives aim at reducing or limiting Big Tech's power.

Clearly, Alphabet is confronted by serious concerns. Nevertheless, these challenges seem surmountable. Amongst other things, the simple fact that the megacorporation's employees are still incredibly well paid – with a median salary of approximately $250,000 in 2019 (Thurm, 2019) – suggests that, even if some perks are lost, Alphabet is likely to remain an attractive workplace for many people. And with regard to its antitrust concerns, the fact that the megacorporation has significant resources with which to defend its monopolies, and that even very large fines have hitherto done little when it comes to denting its business interests (Schulze, 2019; Stewart, 2019), suggests that any future efforts that governments make to reduce its power will need to be much more aggressive than they have hitherto been. In fact, such efforts may need to take the form of a preemptive strike that makes Alphabet's existence as a holding company untenable given the megacorporation's investments in fledgling 'companies that are pretty far afield of' its 'main Internet products' (Page, 2015).

Final Summary

Having proceeded through Alphabet's birth, its current influence and its ultimately unavoidable death as a megacorporation, the book's three parts have told the unfinished story of Alphabet's existence. In doing so, I have suggested that, even if this story were to finish tomorrow, further analysis of Alphabet, and of its multifaceted impacts on society, would still be warranted. What is arguably more important than this, however, is that, in completing this book, I have sought to conceive and explain the two titular concepts whose importance goes beyond that of Alphabet.

As detailed in Part I of the book, it is somewhat surprising that the first of these concepts – the idea of a megacorporation – has lacked explicit conceptualization up until now. The reason why is that when we engage in daily life, it is very clear that the power of some corporations is so much greater than that of other corporations that they are deserving of a category all of their own. Thus – and just as a diverse range of international relations scholars have recognized that whilst many states may exist at any given point in time, the number of consequential states has always tended to be very small (e.g. Mearsheimer, 2001; Nye, 2004; Waltz, 1979) – the megacorporate concept highlights that even where there is a huge number of business corporations in existence, it is only a tiny proportion of such corporations that can ever hope to have a significant impact on people worldwide. So whilst there is undoubted merit in further analysing sole traders, small- and medium-sized enterprises, professional service firms, and so on, it seems sensible that the field of business and society, and the related fields of organization and management studies, devotes at least a little attention to megacorporations as well.

Given that the present work has only identified two examples of megacorporations (i.e. Alphabet and the English East India Company), it would be interesting to know how many others have existed during the time separating their existence. It would also be interesting to know whether any other megacorporations can be said to currently exist, how many megacorporations can potentially exist at a given point in time, and whether or not megacorporations can only emerge when protected by an established great (military) power. If one presumes that China's rise will continue, then it seems important to know whether or not megacorporations can emerge from within a one-party state, and whether or not the existence of a megacorporation is even compatible with autocratic systems.

As the ideology of infinite times appears to enjoy widespread support, its importance also goes beyond that of helping make sense of

Alphabet's various activities. In terms of the future, many people are clearly concerned to extend the length of their personal existence, and many people at least express concern when confronted with the possibility of our species becoming extinct. And in terms of the past, there is a very strong revealed preference when it comes to helping create information that can be used to construct individual and social pasts. Suffice it to note that, despite there being some obvious downsides to 'everything' being remembered, many people would be distraught if their technologically enabled personal memories, or if our technologically enabled stores of cultural heritage, were to be destroyed. It is only natural, however, that such widespread sentiments give rise to alternatives. In this fashion, the conceiving of the infinite times ideology suggests that ideological conflicts will increasingly focus not just on how, but on whether or not we should even try, to technologically extend our pasts and futures.

In conceiving and illustrating the importance of these two concepts, it is hoped that the present work has also demonstrated that the philosophical perspective that has been employed throughout has some merit. With regard to the analysis of business and society issues, what the philosophical perspective does is enable the identification, and explication, of issues that have a fundamental impact on our daily lives, such as how we understand and construct our pasts and our futures. The fact that megacorporations, and businesses more generally, can have such existential impacts, seems obviously important. As my own efforts at analysing such concerns are far from perfect, I can only hope that whatever failings are associated with this now-completed work do not obscure the benefits of applying the philosophical perspective more widely.

References

Agosto, D. E., & Abbas, J. 2017. 'Don't be dumb – that's the rule I try to live by': A closer look at older teens' online privacy and safety attitudes. *New Media & Society*, 19(3): 347–365.

Aguilera, R. V., Rupp, D. E., Williams, C. A., & Ganapathi, J. 2007. Putting the S back in corporate social responsibility: A multilevel theory of social change in organizations. *Academy of Management Review*, 32(3): 836–863.

Alexa. Website. *The Top 500 Sites on the Web.* www.alexa.com/topsites (February 4, 2020).

Alphabet. 2016. *Alphabet 2015 Annual Report.* https://abc.xyz/investor (September 12, 2018).

 2017. *Alphabet Code of Conduct.* Amended September 21, 2017. https:// abc.xyz/investor (March 10, 2020).

 2020. *Alphabet 2019 Annual Report.* https://abc.xyz/investor (February 4, 2020).

Alvesson, M., & Kärreman, D. 2007. Constructing mystery: Empirical matters in theory development. *Academy Management Review*, 32(4): 1265–1281.

Amadeo, R. 2019. Users alarmed by undisclosed microphone in Nest Security System. *Arstechnica*, February 20. https://arstechnica.com (December 19, 2019).

Anderson, C. 2008. The end of theory: The data deluge makes the scientific method obsolete. *Wired*, June 23. www.wired.com/2008 (May 7, 2018).

Anderson, V. D. 1998. New England and the seventeenth century. In N. Canny ed., *The Origins of Empire: British Overseas Enterprise to the Close of the Seventeenth Century*, pp. 193–217. Oxford: Oxford University Press.

Aspray, W. 1992. *John von Neumann and the Origins of Modern Computing.* Cambridge, MA: MIT Press.

Atal, M. R. 2018. *When Companies Rule: Corporate Political Authority in India, Kenya and South Africa.* PhD Thesis. Cambridge, UK: University of Cambridge.

Atwood, C. D. 2015. Jan Amos Comenius. *Oxford Bibliographies.* www
.oxfordbibliographies.com (May 4, 2018).

Auletta, K. 2012. Get Rich U: There are no walls between Stanford and
Silicon Valley. Should there be? *The New Yorker,* April 30. www
.newyorker.com (March 11, 2016).

Avi-Yonah, R. S. 2005. The cyclical transformations of the corporate form:
A historic perspective on corporate social responsibility. *Delaware
Journal of Corporate Law*, 30(3): 767–818.

Ayres, S. 2018. Russia's shadowy world of military contractors: Independent
mercenaries, or working for the Kremlin? *Los Angeles Times,* February
18. www.latimes.com (August 27, 2018).

Banks, I. M. 1988. *The Player of Games.* London: Orbital.

Barber, L. 2014. Google vs News Corp: Internet giant refutes piracy claim
made by Rupert Murdoch-owned publisher. *City A.M.*, September 25.
www.cityam.com (August 10, 2016).

Barkan, J. 2013. *Corporate Sovereignty: Law and Government Under
Capitalism.* Minneapolis, MN: University of Minnesota Press.

Bataille, G. 1991. *The Accursed Share: An Essay on General Economy*,
Volume 1 Consumption. New York: Zone Books.

Baxter, S. 2015. The cold equations: Extraterrestrial liberty in science fiction.
In C. S. Cockell ed., *The Meaning of Liberty Beyond Earth*, pp. 13–31.
Cham: Springer.

Bearman, P. 2015. Big data and historical social science. *Big Data & Society*,
2(2): 1–5.

Beeson, M. 2010. The coming of environmental authoritarianism.
Environmental Politics, 19(2): 276–294.

Belshaw, C. 2015. Immortality, memory and imagination. *The Journal of
Ethics*, 19(3–4): 323–348.

Benatar, D. 2006. *Better Never to Have Been: The Harm of Coming into
Existence.* Oxford: Oxford University Press.
  2017. *The Human Predicament: A Candid Guide to Life's Biggest
  Questions.* Oxford: Oxford University Press.

Benatar, S. R. 2003. Bioethics: Power and injustice: IAB presidential address.
Bioethics, 17(5–6): 387–398.

Benkler, Y. 2006. *The Wealth of Networks: How Social Production
Transforms Markets and Freedom.* New Haven, CT: Yale University
Press.

Benkler, Y., Roberts, H., Faris, R., Solow-Niederman, A., & Etling, B. 2013.
Social mobilization and the networked public sphere: Mapping the
SOPA-PIPA debate. *Berkman Center Research Publication No. 2013-
16.* http://cyber.law.harvard.edu (August 10, 2016).

Bensinger, G. 2019a. Google CEO, in leaked video, says company is 'genuinely struggling' with employee trust. *The Washington Post,* October 25. www.washingtonpost.com (March 9, 2020).

2019b. Google says only talk about work at work – and definitely no politics. *The Washington Post,* August 23. www.washingtonpost.com (March 9, 2020).

Berger, P. L., & Luckman, T. 1966. *The Social Construction of Reality: A Treatise in the Sociology of Knowledge.* New York: Penguin.

Berman, H. J. 1985. *Law and Revolution: The Formation of the Western Legal Tradition.* Cambridge, MA: Harvard University Press.

Bernal, P. 2014. *Internet Privacy Rights: Rights to Protect Autonomy.* Cambridge: Cambridge University Press.

Bernstein, S., & Cashore, B. 2007. Can non-state global governance be legitimate? An analytical framework. *Regulation & Governance*, 1(4): 347–371.

Blair, O. 2017. How much porn stars really get paid, according to leading agent for adult actors. *The Independent*, February 14. www.independent.co.uk (July 4, 2018).

Boland, T. 2018. The cacophony of critique. *The Sociological Review Blog.* September 7. www.thesociologicalreview.com (December 19, 2019).

Bork, R. H., & Sidak, J. G. 2012. What does the Chicago School teach about internet search and the antitrust treatment of Google. *Journal of Competition Law & Economics*, 8(4): 663–700.

Borges, J. L. 1942a. Funes the memorious. In J. L. Borges (1962), *Ficciones*, pp. 107–116. New York: Grove Press.

1942b. John Wilkins analytical language. In J. L. Borges (1999), *Selected Non-Fictions*, pp. 229–232. New York: Viking

Boltanski, L., & Thévenot, L. 2006. *On Justification: Economies of Worth.* Princeton, NJ: Princeton University Press.

Bostrom, N. 2002. Existential risks: Analyzing human extinction scenarios and related hazards. *Journal of Evolution and Technology*, 9(1): 1–31.

2003. Are we living in a computer simulation?*The Philosophical Quarterly*, 53(211): 243–255.

2005. In defence of posthuman dignity. *Bioethics*, 19(3): 202–14.

2013. Existential risk prevention as a global priority. *Global Policy*, 4(1): 15–31.

2014. *Superintelligence: Paths, Dangers, Strategies.* Oxford: Oxford University Press.

Bostrom, N., & Ćircović, M. M. (Eds.). 2008. *Global Catastrophic Risks.* Oxford: Oxford University Press.

Bostrom, N., & Ord, T. 2006. The reversal test: eliminating status quo bias in applied ethics. *Ethics*, 116(4): 656–679.

Boswell, J. 1983. The informal social control of business in Britain: 1880–1939. *Business History Review*, 57(2): 237–257.

Bourdieu, P. 1977. *Outline of a Theory of Practice*. Cambridge: Cambridge University Press.

Bowen, H. V. 1998. British India, 1765–1813: The Metropolitan Context. In P. J. Marshall ed., *The Eighteenth Century*, pp. 530–551. Oxford: Oxford University Press.

 2006. *The Business of Empire: The East India Company and Imperial Britain, 1756–1833*. Cambridge: Cambridge University Press.

Bowles, N. 2016. Burning Man buys 3,800-acre ranch – is it about to build a year-round festival? *The Guardian*, June 10. www.theguardian.com (August 03, 2016).

Brandon, R. 2018. The monopoly-busting case against Google, Amazon, Uber, and Facebook. *The Verge*, September 5. www.theverge.com (September 13, 2018).

Brandt, K. 2018. The journey toward a circular economy: From Muir Beach to data centers. *Google: The Keyword*, December 10. www.blog.google (January 18, 2019).

Brandtzaeg, P. B., & Lüders, M. 2018. Time collapse in social media: Extending the context collapse. *Social Media & Society*, https://doi .org/10.1177%2F2056305118763349

Braudel, F. 1958. History and the social sciences: *The Longue Durée*. In F. Braudel (1980), *On History*, pp. 25–54. Chicago: University of Chicago Press.

 1981. *The Structures of Everyday Life. Volume 1: Civilization & Capitalism 15th–18th Century*. London: Phoenix Press.

Brenkert, G. 1998. Marketing and the vulnerable. *Business Ethics Quarterly*, Special Issue: Ruffin Series: New Approaches to Business Ethics: 7–20.

Brin, S., & Page, L. 1998. The anatomy of a large-scale hypertextual web search engine. *Computer Science Department, Stanford University*. http://infolab.stanford.edu/~backrub/google.html (August 09, 2016).

Brooker, K. 2015. Google Ventures and the search for immortality. *Bloomberg*, March 9. www.bloomberg.com (December 19, 2018).

Bueno de Mesquita, B., Smith, A., Siverson, R. M., & Morrow, J. D. 2003. *The Logic of Political Surivival*. Cambridge, MA: The MIT Press.

Burke, E. 1783. Speech on Fox's East India Bill. In F. Canavan ed. (1999), *Miscellaneous Writings, Volume 4 Select Works of Edmund Burke, pp. 95–191*. Indianapolis: Liberty Fund.

 1788. On the impeachment of Warren Hastings, Esq. In E. Burke (1822), *The Works of the Right Honourable Edmund Burke*, A New Edition, Volume 13, pp. 2–402. London: F. C. and J. Rivington.

Burke, K. 1941. *The Philosophy of Literary Form: Studies in Symbolic Action*. United States of America: Louisiana State University Press.

Byford, S. 2016a. After AlphaGo, what's next for AI. *The Verge*, March 14. www.theverge.com (February 26, 2019).

2016b. AlphaGo's battle with Lee Se-dol is something I'll never forget. *The Verge*, March 15. www.theverge.com (February 26, 2019).

2017. AlphaGo retires from competitive Go after defeating world number one 3-0. *The Verge*, May 27. www.theverge.com (February 26, 2019).

Cabantous, L., & Gond, J.-P. 2015. The resistable rise of Bayesian thinking in management: Historical lessons from decision analysis. *Journal of Management*, 41(2): 441–470.

Cadbury World. 2016. *Cadbury World*. Website.www.cadburyworld.co.uk (June 29 2016).

Cadwalladr, C. 2014. Are the robots about to rise? Google's new director of engineering thinks so.…. *The Observer*, February 22. www.theguardian .com (December 11, 2018).

2016. Google, democracy and the truth about internet search. *The Observer*, December 4. www.theguardian.com (September 14, 2018).

Calico. Website. *We're Tackling Aging*. www.calicolabs.com (December 14, 2018).

Campanelli, V. 2015. Toward a remix culture: An existential perspective. In E. Navas, O. Gallagher & x. Burrough eds., *The Routledge Companion to Remix Studies*, pp. 68–82. New York: Routledge.

Carson, R. 1962. *Silent Spring*. Boston, MA: Houghton Mifflin Company.

Casarez, J. 2017. Anthony Weiner reports to prison. *CNN*, November 6. www.cnn.com (July 9, 2018).

Castronova, E. 2018. Philosophy. In M. J. P. Wolf ed., *The Routledge Companion to Imaginary Worlds*, pp. 127–133. New York: Routledge.

Centre for Humane Technology. Website. *The Problem*. http://humanetech .com (March 27, 2019).

CGTN America. 2017. Interview: GO champ Ke Jie talks about his match with Google's AI. *YouTube*, May 28. www.youtube.com (February 26, 2019).

Chalmers, D. J. 2010. The singularity: A philosophical analysis. *Journal of Consciousness Studies*, 17(9–10): 7–65.

Chan, D. 2017. The AI that has nothing to learn from humans. *The Atlantic*, October 20. www.theatlantic.com (February 26, 2019).

Chandler, A. (2013). How law made Silicon Valley. *Emory Law Journal*, 63(3): 639–694.

Chase, A. 2000. Harvard and the making of the Unabomber. *The Atlantic*, June. www.theatlantic.com (February 20, 2019).

Chaudhuri, K. N. 1968. Treasure and trade balances: The English East India Company's export trade, 1660–1720. *The Economic History Review*, 21(3): 480–502.

1978. *The Trading World of Asia and the English East India Company, 1660–1760*. Cambridge: Cambridge University Press.

Chiles, T. H., Bluedorn, A. C., & Gupta, V. K. 2007. Beyond creative destruction and entrepreneurial discovery: A radical Austrian approach to entrepreneurship. *Organization Studies*, 28(4): 467–493.

Christman, J. 1991. Autonomy and personal history. *Canadian Journal of Philosophy*, 21(1): 1–24.

Christopher, R. 2015. The end of an aura: Nostalgia, memory, and the haunting of hip hop. In E. Navas, O. Gallagher, & x. burrough, (Eds.). *The Routledge Companion to Remix Studies*, pp. 204–216. New York: Routledge.

Chung, T. 1973. The Britain-China-India trade triangle. *Proceedings of the Indian History Congress*, 34(2): 77–91.

Ćircović, M. M. 2008. Observation selection effects and catastrophic risks. In N. Bostrom & M. M. Ćircović, (Eds.) *Global Catastrophic Risks*: 120–145. Oxford, UK: Oxford University Press.

Clark, J. M. 1916. The changing basis of economic responsibility. *The Journal of Political Economy*, 24(3): 209–229.

Clinton, H. 2010. *Remarks on Internet Freedom*. Speech by U.S. Secretary of State. The Newseum, Washington, DC. January 21. www.state.gov (November 16, 2010).

Cockburn, I. M., Henderson, R., & Stern, S. 2018. The Impact of Artificial Intelligence on Innovation. *NBER Working Paper No. 24449*. www.nber.org/papers/w24449

Cockell, C. S. 2007. *Space on Earth: Saving our World by Seeking Others*. Houndsmills: Palgrave Macmillan.

2015. Introduction: The meaning of liberty beyond earth. In C. S. Cockell ed., *The Meaning of Liberty Beyond Earth*, pp. 1–9. Cham: Springer.

2016. Disobedience in outer space. In C. S. Cockell ed., *Dissent, Revolution and Liberty Beyond Earth*, pp. 21–40. Cham: Springer.

Cole, S. 2017. AI-assisted porn is here and we're all fucked. *Motherboard*, December 11. https://motherboard.vice.com (July 4, 2018).

Collins, H. M., & Evans, R. 2002. The third wave of science studies: Studies of expertise and experience. *Social Studies of Science*, 32(2): 235–296.

Collins, S. 1982. *Selfless Persons: Imagery and Thought in Theravada Buddhism*. Cambridge: Cambridge University Press.

Conger, K., & Wakabayashi, D. 2018. Google employees protest secret work on censored search engine for China. *The New York Times*, August 16. www.nytimes.com (September 14, 2018).

Conway, S. 1998. Britain and the Revolutionary Crisis, 1763–1791. In P. J. Marshall ed., *The Eighteenth Century*, pp. 325–346. Oxford: Oxford University Press.

Cooper, R. 1990. Organization/disorganization. In J. Hassard & D. Pym eds., *The Theory and Philosophy of Organizations: Critical Issues and New Perspectives*, pp. 167–197. London: Routledge.

Cowan, D. 2011. Review: *Transcendent Man. MIT Technology Review*, February 22. www.technologyreview.com (December 11, 2018).

Coyne, L. 2018. Responsibility in practice: Hans Jonas as environmental political theorist. *Ethics, Policy & Environment*, 21(2): 229–245.

Crane, A., Henriques, I., Husted, B. W., & Matten, D. 2015. Defining the scope of business & society. *Business & Society*, 54(4): 427–434.

    2016. Publishing country studies in business & society: Or, do we care about CSR in Mongolia? *Business & Society*, 55(1): 3–10.

Crane, A., Matten, D., & Moon, J. 2008. *Corporations and Citizenship*. Cambridge: Cambridge University Press.

Crawford, J. Website. *Orbital Insight 'Our Story'*. https://orbitalinsight.com (April 3, 2018).

Crawford, K. 2016. Artificial intelligence's white guy problem. *The New York Times*, June 25. www.nytimes.com (April 4, 2019).

Crocker, J., & Major, B. 1989. Social stigma and self-esteem: The self-protective properties of stigma. *Psychological Review*, 96(4): 608–630.

Cumpsty, John S. 1991. *Religion as Belonging: A General Theory of Religion*. Lanham, MD: University Press of America.

Curran, D. 2018. Are you ready? Here is all the data Facebook and Google have on you. *The Guardian*, March 30. www.theguardian.com (July 5, 2018).

Dalrymple, W. 2015. The East India Company: The original corporate raiders. *The Guardian*, March 4. www.theguardian.com (August 30, 2018).

    2019. *The Anarchy: The Relentless Rise of the East India Company*. New York: Bloomsbury.

Damore, J. 2017. Google's ideological echo chamber: How bias clouds our thinking about diversity and inclusion. *Google Memo July 2017*. https://assets.documentcloud.org/documents/3914586/Googles-Ideological-Echo-Chamber.pdf (September 13, 2017).

Danaher, J. 2017. Will life be worth living in a world without work? Technological unemployment and the meaning of life. *Science and Engineering Ethics*, 23(1): 41–64.

Darwin, C. 1968 (1859). *The Origin of the Species*. London: Penguin.

Day, M. 2001. Anarchy in the USA. *The Guardian*, April 18. www .theguardian.com (March 27, 2019).

Diamond, J. 2005. *Collapse: How Societies Choose to Fail or Succeed*. New York: Penguin.

de Certeau, M. de. 1984. *The Practice of Everyday Life*, Berkeley, CA: University of California Press.

1988. *The Writing of History*. New York: Columbia University Press.

de Tocqueville, A. 1945 (1835). *Democracy in America*, Volume II. New York: Alfred A. Knopf.

Del Rey, J. 2018. Here's why fake-meat startup Impossible Foods wouldn't sell to Google. *Recode*, June 1. www.recode.net (January 30, 2019).

DeepMind. Website. *Solve intelligence. Use it to make the world a better place.* https://deepmind.com/about/ (February 1, 2019).

Deibert, R. 2019. Three painful truths about social media. *Journal of Democracy*, 30(1): 25–39.

Deleuze, G. 1977. I have nothing to admit. *Semiotext(e)*, 11(3): 110–116.

1988. *Bergsonism*. New York: Zone Books.

Dembicki, G. 2019. The next financial crisis could be caused by climate change. *Vice*, January 28. www.vice.com (January 28, 2019).

Dennett, D. C. 2007. Heterophenomenology reconsidered. *Phenomenology and the Cognitive Sciences*, 6(1–2): 247–270.

Derrida, J. 1995. Archive fever: A Freudian impression. *Diacritics*, 25(2): 9–63.

Descola, P. 2013. *Beyond Nature and Culture*. Chicago, IL: University of Chicago.

Devlin, H. 2019. SpaceX satellites could blight the night sky, warn astronomers. *The Guardian*, May 28. www.theguardian.com (February 4, 2020).

Dewey, J. 1933. *How We Think: A Restatement of the Relation of Reflective Thinking to the Educative Process*, New Edition. Boston, MA: Houghton Mifflin Company.

Diamandis, P. H., & Kotler, P. 2012. *Abundance: The Future Is Better than You Think*. New York: Free Press.

DiMaggio, P. 2015. Adapting computational text analysis to social science (and vice versa). *Big Data & Society*, 2(2): 1–5.

Dodd, E. M. 1932. For whom are corporate managers trustees? *Harvard Law Review*, 45(7): 1145–1163.

Dodson, M. S. 2007. *Orientalism, Empire, and National Culture: India, 1770–1880*. Houndsmills: Palgrave Macmillan.

Donaldson, T. 1982. *Corporations and Morality*. Englewood Cliffs, NJ: Prentice-Hall.

D'Onfro, J., Zaveri, P., & Bosa, D. 2018. Google and Uber were like 'big brother and little brother' – until it all went wrong. *CNBC*, February 7. www.cnbc.com (January 21, 2019).

D'Orazio, D. 2015. Google's 'Don't be evil' creed disappears as the company morphs into Alphabet. *The Verge*, October 3. www.theverge.com (March 9, 2020).

Drayer, L. 2019. Change your diet to combat climate change in 2019. *CNN*. January 2. www.cnn.com (Janaury 30, 2019).

Drayton, R. 1998. Knowledge and Empire. In P. J. Marshall ed., *The Eighteenth Century*, pp. 231–252. Oxford: Oxford University Press.

Dreyfus, H. L. 1999. Anonymity versus commitment: The dangers of education on the internet. *Ethics and Information Technology*, 1(1): 15–21.

Drummond, D. 2010a. A new approach to China. *The Official Google Blog*. January 12. http://googleblog.blogspot.com (September 14, 2018).

2010b. A new approach to China: An update. *The Official Google Blog*. March 22. http://googleblog.blogspot.com (September 14, 2018).

2012. Don't censor the web. *The Official Google Blog*, January 17. https://googleblog.blogspot.com (August 10, 2016).

Duhigg, C. 2018. The case against Google. *The New York Times Magazine*, February 20. www.nytimes.com (September 13, 2018).

Durant, D. 2011. Models of democracy in social studies of science. *Social Studies of Science*, 41(5): 691–714.

Dutt, P., & Mitra, D. 2018. The paradox of protectionist populism. *Knowledge – Insead Economics & Finance Blog*, April 17. https://knowledge.insead.edu/blog (August 27, 2018).

Dwyer, J. 2005. Global health and justice. *Bioethics*, 19(5–6): 460–475.

Eaton, D. 2017. Here's why Google had the right to fire that employee over his diversity memo. *CNBC*, August 8. www.cnbc.com (September 13, 2018).

Edwards, D. 2011. *I'm Feeling Lucky: The Confessions of Google Employee Number 59*. London: Allen Lane.

Eggers, D. 2013. *The Circle*. London: Penguin.

Eisenhardt, K. M., & Graebner, M. E. 2007. Theory building from cases: Opportunities and challenges. *Academy of Management Journal*, 50(1): 25–32.

El Akkad, O. 2009. Google: we're not evil and we're no monopoly, either. *The Globe and Mail*, October 16. www.theglobeandmail.com (September 13, 2018).

Elgesem, D. 2008. Search engines and the public use of reason. *Ethics and Information Technology*, 10(4): 233–242.

Elliot, R. 1987. Moral autonomy, self-determination and animal rights. *The Monist*, 70(1): 83–97.

Elms, H., & Phillips, R. A. 2009. Private security companies and institutional legitimacy: Corporate and stakeholder responsibility. *Business Ethics Quarterly*, 19(3): 403–432.

Ensslin, A. 2018. Linden Lab's *Second Life*. In M. J. P. Wolf ed., *The Routledge Companion to Imaginary Worlds*, pp. 402–409. New York: Routledge.

Erll, A. 2009. Remembering across time, space, and cultures: Premediation, remediation and the 'Indian Mutiny'. In A. Erll & A. Rugney eds., *Mediation, Remediation, and the Dynamics of Cultural Memory*, pp. 109–138. Berlin: Walter de Gruyter.

Etter, M., Colleoni, E., Illia, L., Meggiorin, K., & D'Eugenio, A. 2018. Measuring organizational legitimacy in social media: Assessing citizens' judgments with sentiment analysis. *Business & Society*, 57(1): 60–97.

Etzioni, A. 2007. *Security First: For a Muscular, Moral Foreign Policy*. New Haven, CT: Yale University Press.

2019. Cyber trust. *Journal of Business Ethics*, 156(1): 1–13.

Evan, W. M., & Freeman, R. E. 1988. A stakeholder theory of the modem corporation: Kantian capitalism. In T. L. Beauchamp & N. E. Bowie eds., *Ethical Theory in Business*, 3rd Edition, pp. 97–106. Englewood Cliffs, NJ: Prentice Hall.

Fang, L. 2018. Leaked emails show Google expected lucrative military drone AI work to grow exponentially. *The Intercept*, May 31. https://theintercept.com (February 26, 2020).

Farokhmanesh, M. 2018. Deepfakes are disappearing from parts of the web, but they're not going away. *The Verge*, February 9. www.theverge.com (July 4, 2018).

Federal Trade Commission. 2020. Press Release – FTC to examine past acquisitions by large technology companies. *FTC News & Events*, February 11. www.ftc.gov (March 10, 2020).

Fehr, E., & Gächter, S. 2000. Fairness and retaliation: The economics of reciprocation. *Journal of Economic Perspectives*, 14(3): 159–181.

Feiner, L. 2019. Google faces a new antitrust probe by 50 attorneys general. *CNBC*, September 9. www.cnbc.com (March 10, 2020).

Fernstein, G. 2014. Eric Schmidt confirms it: He sealed the deal with Google at Burning Man. *Venture Beat*, September 25. http://venturebeat.com (August 03, 2016).

Ferrary, M., & Granovetter, M. 2009. The role of venture capital firms in Silicon Valley's complex innovation network, *Economy and Society*, 38(2): 326–359.

Feyerabend, P. 1970. Consolations for the Specialist. In I. Lakatos & A. Musgrave (Eds.), *Criticism and the Growth of Knowledge*, pp. 197–230. Cambridge: Cambridge University Press.

Fleischer, P. 2014. *Google's response to the questionnaire addressed to search engines by the Article 29 Working Party regarding the implementation of the CJEU judgment on the "right to be forgotten".* July 31. https://docs.google.com/a/google.com/file/d/0B8syaai6SSfiT0EwRUFyOENqR3M/preview?pref=2&pli=1 (July 9, 2018).

Fleming, A. 2018. Would you give up having children to save the planet? Meet the couples who have. *The Guardian,* June 20. www.theguardian.com (April 8, 2019).

Floridi, L. 2006. The ontological interpretation of informational privacy. *Ethics and Information Technology,* 7(4): 185–200.

2012. Big data and their epistemological challenge. *Philosophy & Technology,* 25(4): 435–437.

2013. *The Ethics of Information.* Oxford: Oxford University Press.

Flyverbom, M., & Whelan, G. 2019. Digital transformation, informed realities, and human conduct. In Rikke Frank Jørgensen (ed.), *Human Rights in the Age of Platforms,* pp. 53–72. Cambridge MA: The MIT Press.

Foer, F. 2017. *World Without Mind: The Existential Threat of Big Tech.* New York: Penguin Books.

Folkman, S., Lazarus, R. S., Dunkel-Schetter, C., DeLongis, A., & Gruen, R. J. 1986. Dynamics of a stressful encounter: Cognitive appraisal, coping, and encounter outcomes. *Journal of Personality and Social Psychology,* 50(5): 992–1003.

Forbes. 2019. Billionaires: The richest people in the world. *Forbes,* March 5. www.forbes.com (January 28, 2020).

Forgrieve, J. 2018. The growing acceptance of veganism. *Forbes,* November 2. www.forbes.com (January 29, 2019).

Foster, N., & Murphy, D. 2016. *The Selfish Ledger.* Leaked by Vlado Savov, *The Verge,* May 17, 2018. www.theverge.com (January 22, 2019).

Foucault, M. 1970. *The Order of Things: An Archaeology of the Human Sciences.* London: Tavistok Publications.

1972. *The Archaeology of Knowledge.* London: Routledge.

1977. *Discipline and Punish: The Birth of the Prison.* New York: Random House.

2007. *Security, Territory, Population: Lectures at the College de France 1977–1978.* New York: Palgrave Macmillan.

2008. *The Birth of Biopolitics: Lectures at the Collège de France 1978–1979.* New York: Palgrave Macmillan.

Frankfurt, H. 2005. *On Bullshit.* Princeton, NJ: Princeton University Press.

Freeman, R. E., & Greenwood, M. 2020. Deepening methods in business ethics. *Journal of Business Ethics,* 161(1): 1–3.

Freeman, R. E., & Phillips, R. A. 2002. Stakeholder theory: A libertarian defense. *Business Ethics Quarterly*, 12(3): 331–350.

Freeman, R. E., Wicks, A. C., & Parmar, B. 2004. Stakeholder theory and 'The Corporate Objective Revisited'. *Organization Science*, 15(3): 364–369

Friedland, R., & Alford, R. R. 1991. Bringing society back in: Symbols, practices, and institutional contradictions. In W. W. Powell & P. J. DiMaggio eds., *The New Institutionalism in Organizational Analysis*, pp. 232–263. Chicago, IL: The University of Chicago Press.

Friend, T. 2017. Silicon Valley's quest to live forever. *The New Yorker*, April 3. www.newyorker.com (09/11/2018).

Gallagher, R. 2018. Google plans to launch censored search engine in China, leaked documents reveal. *The Intercept*, August 1. https://theintercept .com (September 14, 2018).

Ganesan, A. 2010. US: A big step toward online freedom. *Human Rights Watch News Release*. January 22. www.hrw.org (September 14, 2018).

Gardner, D. 2019. Why don't we care about climate change? *The Globe and Mail*, December 21. www.theglobeandmail.com (January 28, 2019).

Garigue, P. 1960. The French Canadian family. In J.-C. Falaardeau ed., *La dualité canadienne. Essais sur les relations entre Canadiens français et Canadiens anglais*, pp. 181–200. Laval: Les Presses de l'Université Laval, University of Toronto Press.

Garland, D. 2014. What is a 'history of the present'? On Foucault's genealogies and their critical preconditions. *Punishment & Society*, 16(4): 365–384.

Geraci, R. M. 2010. *Apocalyptic AI: Visions of Heaven in Robotics, Artificial Intelligence, and Virtual Reality*. Oxford: Oxford University Press.

Gertner, J. 2014. An exclusive look behind the secretive lab's closed doors. *Fast Company*, April 15. www.fastcompany.com (August 11, 2016).

Ghosh, P. 2015. Google's Vint Cerf warns of 'digital Dark Age'. *BBC News*, February 13. www.bbc.com/news (April 6, 2018).

Gibson, W. 1984. *Neuromancer*. London: HarperCollins.

  2007. *Spook Country*. London: Penguin.

  2011.William Gibson. The art of fiction no. 211 – Interviewed by David Wallace-Wells. *The Paris Review*, 197 (Summer). www.theparisreview .org (August 201, 2018).

  2012. *Distrust that Particular Flavor*. London: Penguin.

Gilley, B. 2012. Authoritarian environmentalism and China's response to climate change. *Environmental Politics*, 21(2): 287–307.

Gingras, R. 2018. Elevating quality journalism on the open web. *Google: The Keyword*. https://blog.google (January 28, 2019).

Global Network Initiative. Website. *Global Network Initiative.* https://globalnetworkinitiative.org (September 14, 2018).

Godwin, T. 2011 (1954). The cold equations. *Lightspeed,* July 2011 (14). www.lightspeedmagazine.com (January 25, 2019).

Goffman, E. 2007 (1961). *Asylums. Essays on the Social Situation of Mental Patients and Other Inmates.* London: Transaction.

   1963. *Stigma: Notes on the Management of Spoiled Identity.* Englewood Cliffs, NJ: Prentice-Hall.

Goldberg, A. 2015. In defense of forensic social science. *Big Data & Society,* 2(2): 1–5.

Gomes, B., & Fuller, J. 2019. Expanding knowledge access with the Wikimedia Foundation. *Google: The Keyword.* www.blog.google (January 29, 2019).

Goodfellow, I., Bengio, Y., & Courville, A. 2016. *Deep Learning.* Cambridge, MA: MIT Press.

Google. 2013. Google intern's first week. *YouTube,* June 4. www.youtube .com (February 28, 2020).

   2015. *Google Annual Report 2015.* https://abc.xyz/investor (August 03, 2016).

   2019. *Google Diversity Annual Report 2019.* https://diversity.google (January 28, 2020).

   Website A. *From the Garage to the Googleplex.* www.google.com/about (September 18, 2018).

   Website B. *Privacy & Terms.* https://policies.google.com/privacy (July 5, 2018).

   Website C. *Personal Information Removal Request Form.* https://support .google.com/ (July 9, 2018).

   Website D. *10 Things we Know to be True.* www.google.com/about (April 3, 2018).

   Website E. *Google Assistant.* https://assistant.google.com (January 21, 2019).

Google Advisory Council. 2015. *The Advisory Council to Google on the Right to be Forgotten – Final Report.* February 6. www.google.com/ advisorycouncil (July 9, 2018).

Google AI. Website. *Vinton G. Cerf.* https://ai.google/research/people (July 3, 2018).

   2018. Google Duplex: An AI system for accomplishing real-world tasks over the phone. *Google AI Blog,* May 8. https://ai.googleblog.com (December 18, 2018).

Google Arts & Culture. Website. *Black History and Culture.* https://artsandculture.google.com (May 10, 2018).

   2018. Shameless Maya on Black Female Icons #GoogleArts #BHM. *YouTube,* February 26. www.youtube.com (May 10, 2018).

Google Cultural Institute. Website. *About Google Cultural Institute*. www
.google.com/culturalinstitute (April 6, 2018).
Google Developers. Website. *Make Games with Google*. https://developers
.google.com/games (February 1, 2019).
Google Dot Org. Website. *Google.org – Our Work*. www.google.org
(January 28, 2020).
 2010. Introducing Google Earth Engine. *Google.org blog*, December 2.
http://blog.google.org (February 4, 2019).
Google Earth Engine. Website. *Case Studies*. https://earthengine.google.com
(February 4, 2019).
Google Open Source. Website. *Google Open Source*. https://opensource
.google (March 23, 2020).
Google Take Action. Website. *Freedom to Participate*. www.google.com/
intl/en/takeaction (January 28, 2019).
Google Transparency Project. 2016. *Google's Support for Hillary Clinton*.
www.googletransparencyproject.org (May 8, 2019).
Gorman, A. G. 2016. Williams and the desirability of body-bound immor-
tality revisited. *European Journal of Philosophy*, 25(4): 1062–1083.
Gray, J. 2002. *Straw Dogs: Thoughts on Humans and Other Animals*.
London: Granta.
Green, H. 2010. *The Company Town: The Industrial Edens and Satanic
Mills that Shaped the American Economy*. New York: Basic Books.
Greenwood, M., & Freeman, R. E. 2017. Focusing on ethics and broadening
our intellectual base. *Journal of Business Ethics*, 140(1): 1–3.
Greimas, A. J. 1983 1966. *Structural Semantics: An Attempt at a Method*.
Lincoln, NE: Nebraska.
Greimas, A. J., & Courtés, J. 1982 1979. *Semiotics and Language: An
Analytical Dictionary*. Bloomington, IN: Indiana University Press.
Greimas, A. J., & Rastier, F. 1968. The Interaction of semiotic constraints.
Yale French Studies, 41: 86–105.
Grey Ellis, E. 2017. Whatever your side, doxing is a perilous form of justice.
Wired, August 17. www.wired.com (July 4, 2018).
Grimes, A. 2004. Why Stanford is celebrating the Google IPO. *The Wall
Street Journal*, August 23. www.wsj.com (August 03, 2016).
Grush, L. 2016. Elon Musk thinks the best government for Mars is a direct
democracy. *The Verge*, June 2 (January 14, 2019).
Habermas, J. 1990. *Moral Consciousness and Communicative Action*.
Cambridge: Polity Press.
Hacking, I. 1979. Imre Lakatos's philosophy of science.*The British Journal
for the Philosophy of Science*, 30(4): 381– 402.
Hackler, R., & Kirsten, G. 2016. Distant reading computational criticism,
and social critique: An interview with Franco Moretti. *Le Foucauldian*,
2(1): 1–17.

Hale, J. 2019. More than 500 hours of content are now being uploaded to YouTube every minute. *Tubefilter*, May 7. www.tubefilter.com (January 31, 2020).

Hansen, M. C., Potapov, P. V., Moore, R., Hancher, M., Turubanova, S. A., Tyukavina, A., Thau, D., Stehman, S. V., Goetz, S. J., Loveland, T. R., Kommareddy, A., Egorov, A., Chini, L., Justice, C. O., & Townshend, J. R. G. High-resolution global maps of 21st-century forest cover change. *Science*, 342(6160): 850–853.

Hardawar, D. 2015. 'Ex Machina' shows Turing test isn't enough to test AI. *Endgadget*, October 15. www.engadget.com (December 17, 2018).

Hardin, G. 1968. The tragedy of the commons. *Science*, 168(3859): 1243–1248.

Harari, Y. H. 2015. *Homo Deus: A Brief History of Tomorrow*. Canada: Penguin Random House.

Harris, M. 2017a. Inside the First Church of Artificial Intelligence. *Wired*. November 15. www.wired.com (February 25, 2019).

    2017b. God is a bot, and Anthony Levandowski is his messenger. *Backchannel,* September 27. www.wired.com (February 25, 2019).

Harvey, P. 1995. *The Selfless Mind: Personality, Consciousness and Nirvana in Early Buddhism*. Richmond, Surrey: Curzon Press.

Hatina, M. 2014. *Martyrdom in Modern Islam*. Cambridge: Cambridge University Press.

Hawkins, A. J. 2019. Ex-Google and Uber engineer Anthony Levandowski charged with trade secret theft. *The Verge*, August 27, 2019. www .theverge.com (February 27, 2020).

Hegel, G. W. F. 2010 (1833).*The Science of Logic*. Cambridge: Cambridge University Press.

Helin, J., Hernes, T., Hjorth, D., & Holt. R. 2014. Process is how process does. In J. Helin, T. Hernes, D. Hjorth & R. Hold eds., *The Oxford Handbook of Process Philosophy and Organization Studies*, pp. 1–18. Oxford: Oxford University Press.

Helms, W. S., & Patterson, K. D. W. 2014. Eliciting acceptance for 'illicit' organizations: The positive implications of stigma for MMA. *Academy of Management Journal*, 57(5): 1453–1484.

Hempel, J. 2018. Inside Magic Leap's Quest to remake itself as an ordinary company (with a real product). *Wired*, August 8. www.wired.com (January 15, 2018).

Hobsbawm, E. 1983. Introduction: Inventing traditions. In E. Hobsbawm & T. Ranger eds., *The Invention of Tradition*. Cambridge: Cambridge University Press.

Hof, R. D. 2013. Deep learning. *MIT Technology Review*, April 23. www .technologyreview.com (November 12, 2018).

Hoppe, H.-H. 1997. On certainty and uncertainty, or: How rational can our expectations be? *The Review of Austrian Economics*, 10(1): 49–78.

Horrobin, S. 2005. The ethics of aging intervention and life-extension. In S. I. S. Rattan ed., *Aging Interventions and Therapies*, pp. 1–28. Singapore: World Scientific Publishing.

Hume, D. 1969 (1739–40). *A Treatise of Human Nature*. London: Penguin Books.

Hutchinson, E. 2016. *Principles of Microeconomics*. Victoria: University of Victoria.

Hsu, F.-H. 2002. *Behind Deep Blue: Building the Computer that Defeated the World Chess Champion*. Princeton, NJ: Princeton University Press.

Impossible Foods. Website. *We're on a Mission.* https://impossiblefoods.com (January 30, 2019).

Insdorf, A. 2013 (1999). *Double Lives, Second Chances: The Cinema of Kzryzstof Kieślowski*. Evanston, IL.: Northwestern University Press.

Innes, S. 2001. From corporation to commonwealth. In J. Beatty ed., *Colossus: How the Corporation Changed America*, pp. 18–22. New York: Broadway Books.

Internet Society. Website. *Internet Hall of Fame Pioneer, Vint Cerf.* https://internethalloffame.org (January 28, 2020).

Jameson, F. 2008. *The Ideologies of Theory*. London: Verso.
  2016. An American utopia. In S. Žižek ed., *An American Utopia: Dual Power and the Universal Army*, pp. 1–96. London: Verso Books.

Jamieson, D. 2002. *Morality's Progress: Essays on Humans, Other Animals, and the Rest of Nature*. Oxford: Oxford University Press.

Jensen, N. M. 2006. *Nation-States and the Multinational Corporation: A Political Economy of Foreign Direct Investment*. Princeton, NJ: Princeton University Press.

Jockers, M. J. 2013. *Macroanalysis: Digital Methods and Literary History*. Urbana, IL: University of Illinois Press.

Johansen, C. B. & De Cock, C. 2018. Ideologies of time: How elite corporate actors engage the future. *Organization*, 25(2): 186–204.

Johnson, E. M. 2018. Is SpaceX the model for a private Tesla? *Reuters*, August 9. www.reuters.com (January 23, 2019).

Jonas, H. 1976. Responsibility today: The ethics of an endangered future. *Social Research*, 43(1): 77–97.
  1984. *The Imperative of Responsibility: In Search of an Ethics for the Technological Age*. Chicago, IL: The University of Chicago Press.

Joy, B. 2000. Why the future doesn't need us. *Wired*, April 1. http://archive.wired.com (March 22, 2015).

Kaczynski, T. 1995. Industrial society and its future. *Washington Post*, September 19. www.washingtonpost.com (February 20, 2019).

Kant, I. 1997 (1785). *Groundwork of the Metaphysics of Morals*. Cambridge: Cambridge University Press.

   1998 (1781/1787). *Critique of Pure Reason*. Cambridge: Cambridge University Press.

Kasparov, G. 2017. *Deep Thinking: Where Machine Intelligence Ends and Human Creativity Begins*. New York: Public Affairs.

Kastrenakes, J. 2013. Google's chief internet evangelist says 'privacy may actually be an anomaly'. *The Verge*, November 20. www.theverge.com (June 03, 2018).

Keay, J. 1991. *The Honorable Company: A History of the English East India Company*. London: HarperCollins.

Keck, M. E., & Sikkink, K. 1998. *Activists Beyond Borders: Advocacy Networks in International Politics*. Ithaca, NY: Cornell University Press.

Keeney, M. 2000. Introduction. In M. Kenney ed., *Understanding Silicon Valley: The Anatomy of an Entrepreneurial Region*, pp. 1–12. Stanford, CA: Stanford University Press.

Kenney, M., & Florida, R. 2000.Venture capital in Silicon Valley: Fueling new firm formation. In M. Kenney ed., *Understanding Silicon Valley: The Anatomy of an Entrepreneurial Region*, pp. 98–123. Stanford, CA: Stanford University Press.

Kenyon, C. 2010. The genetics of ageing. *Nature*, 464: 504–512.

Kerr, D. 2019. Impossible Burger 2.0 tastes like beef. Really. Next up, steak. *CNET*, January 7. www.cnet.com (Janaury 30, 2019).

Keršyte, N. 2017. Rethinking ideology: Greimas's semiotics, neomarxism, and cultural anthropology. *Semiotica*, 219: 485–509.

Khan, L. M. 2017. Amazon's Antitrust Paradox. *Yale Law Journal*, 126(3): 710–805.

   2018. Sources of tech platform power. *Georgetown Law Technology Review*, 2(2): 325–334.

Khan, S. A. 1923. *The East India Trade in the XVIITH Century. In its Political and Economic Aspects*. London: Oxford University Press.

Kieser, A., & Leiner, L. 2009. Why the research-relevance gap in management research is unbridgeable. *Journal of Management Studies*, 46(3): 516–533.

Kim, T. W., & Werbach, K. 2016. More than just a game: Ethical issues in gamification. *Ethics and Information Technology*, 18(2): 157–173.

Kinderman, D. 2012. 'Free us up so we can be responsible!' The co-evolution of Corporate Social Responsibility and neo-liberalism in the UK, 1977–2010. *Socio-Economic Review*, 10(1): 29–57.

King, R. 1999. *Indian Philosophy: An Introduction to Hindu and Buddhist Philosophy*. Edinburgh: Edinburgh University Press.

Kitchin, R. 2014. Big data, new epistemologies and paradigm shifts. *Big Data & Society*, 1(1): 1–12.

Knight, S. 2019. Google Photos passes the one billion user mark, ninth product in Googles roster to do so. *Techspot,* July 24. www.techspot .com (January 28, 2020).

Kobek, J. 2016. *I Hate the Internet*. Los Angeles, CA: We Heard You Like Books.

Korsgaard, C. M. 1989. Personal identity and the unity of agency: A Kantian response. *Philosophy & Public Affairs*, 18(2): 101–132.

2009. *Self-constitution: Agency, Identity, and Integrity*. Oxford: Oxford University Press.

Kuhn, T. 1970. Reflections on my Critics. In I. Lakatos and A. Musgrave eds., *Criticism and the Growth of Knowledge*, pp. 231–278. Cambridge: Cambridge University Press.

Kupfer, T. 2018. Doxxing the doxxer's doxxer. *National Review*, June 8. www.nationalreview.com (July 11, 2018).

Kurtz, H. 1995. Unabomber manuscript is published. Public safety reasons cited in joint decision by Post, N.Y. Times. *The Washington Post*, September 19. www.washingtonpost.com (March 27, 2019).

Kurzweil, R. 2002. Locked in his Chinese Room. In R. Richards ed., *Are We Spiritual Machines: Ray Kurzweil vs. the Critics of Strong AI*, pp. 128–171. Seattle, WA: Discovery Institute.

2005. *The Singularity Is Near: When Humans Transcend Biology*. London: Duckworth.

2012. *How to Create a Mind: The Secret of Human Thought Revealed*. New York: Penguin Books.

Lachmann, L. 1970. *The Legacy of Max Weber*. London: Heinnemann.

1976. From Mises to Shackle: An essay on Austrian economics and the kaleidic society. *Journal of Economic Literature*, 10(1): 55–59.

1986. *The Market as an Economic Process*. Oxford: Basil Blackwell.

Lafferty, M. 2017. *Six Wakes*. New York: Orbit.

Lajeunesse, R. 2020. I was Google's head of international relations. Here's why I left. *Medium*, January 2. https://medium.com (March 9, 2020).

Lakatos, I. 1970. Falsification and the methodology of scientific research programmes. In I. Lakatos & A. Musgrave eds., *Criticism and the Growth of Knowledge*, pp. 91–196. Cambridge: Cambridge University Press.

Lashinsky, A. 2008. Google wins again. *Fortune*. January 29. http://archive .fortune.com (July 03, 2016).

Lawrence, A. T. 2009. Google, Inc.: Figuring out how to deal with China. In E. Raufflet & A. J. Mills eds., *The Dark Side: Critical Cases on the*

Downside of Business, pp. 250–267. Sheffield, UK: Greenleaf Publishing.

Lawton, T., McGuire, S., & Rajwani, T. 2012. Corporate political activity: A literature review and research agenda. *International Journal of Management Reviews*, 15(1): 86–105.

Lazier, B. 2011. Earthrise; or, the globalization of the world picture. *The American Historical Review*, 116(3): 602–630.

Lea, R., & Taylor, M. 2010. Historian Orlando Figes admits posting Amazon reviews that trashed rivals. *The Guardian*, April 23. www.theguardian.com (June 04, 2018).

Leaver, T. 2003. Interstitial spaces and multiple histories in William Gibson's *Virtual Light, Idoru* and *All Tomorrow's Parties. Limina*, 9: 118–130.

Lecher, C. 2019. Trump says he's 'watching Google very closely' after meeting with CEO. *The Verge*, August 6. www.theverge.com (March 10, 2020).

LeCun, Y., Bengio, Y., & Hinton, G. 2015. Deep learning. *Nature*, 521: 436–444.

Leslie, J. 1996. *The End of the World: The Science and Ethics of Human Extinction*. London: Routledge.

Leslie, S. W. 2000. The Biggest 'Angel' of them All: The Military and the Making of Silicon Valley. In M. Kenney ed., *Understanding Silicon Valley: The Anatomy of an Entrepreneurial Region*, pp. 48–67. Stanford, CA: Stanford University Press.

Leslie, S. W., & Kargon, R. H. 1996. Selling Silicon Valley: Frederick Terman's model for regional advantage. *Business History Review*, 70 (Winter): 435–472.

Lessig, L. 2008. *Remix: Making Art and Commerce Thrive in the Hybrid Economy*. London: Bloomsbury.

Lévi-Strauss, C. 1966. *The Savage Mind*. London: Weidenfeld and Nicholson.

Levy, S. 2010 (1984). *Hackers: Heroes of the Computer Revolution*. Sebastopol, CA: O'Reilly.

   2011. *In the Plex: How Google Thinks, Works, and Shapes our Lives*. New York: Simon & Schuster.

   2013. Google's Larry Page on why moon shots matter. *Wired*, January 17. www.wired.com (November 03, 2016).

   2017. What Deep Blue tells us about AI in 2017. *Wired*, May 23. www.wired.com (April 10, 2019).

Lewin, K. 1943. Psychology and the process of group living. *The Journal of Social Psychology*, 17(1): 113–131.

Lewinsky, M. 2018. I'm the chick from over 125 rap songs. *Twitter*. May 9. https://twitter.com (July 9, 2018).

Li, F.-F. 2018. How to make A.I. that's good for people. *The New York Times*, March 7. www.nytimes.com (March 25, 2019).

Lhooq, M. 2017. The art of disruption: How CDJs are changing DJing. *Resident Advisor*, November 2. www.residentadvisor.net (May 14, 2018).

Lohr, S. 2011. Google schools its algorithm. *The New York Times*, March 5. www.nytimes.com (August 09, 2016).

Lowbridge, C. 2017. Veganism: How a maligned movement went mainstream. *BBC*, December 30. www.bbc.com/news (January 29, 2019).

MacMillan, K. 2013. 'Bound by our regal office': Empire, sovereignty, and the Ameican colonies in the seventeenth century. In S. Foster ed., *British North America in the Seventeenth and Eighteenth Centuries*, pp. 67–102. Oxford: Oxford University Press.

McCarthy, L. 2017. Empowering women through corporate social responsibility: A feminist Foucauldian critique. *Business Ethics Quarterly*, 27(4): 603–631.

McCracken, H., & Grossman, L. 2013. Google vs. Death. *Time*, September 30. http://content.time.com (July 17, 2018).

McFarland, M. 2014. Elon Musk: 'With artificial intelligence we are summoning the demon.' *The Washington Post*, October 24. www .washingtonpost.com (April 10, 2019).

McGrath, J. E. 2004. *Loving Big Brother: Performance, Privacy, and Surveillance Space*. London: Routledge.

McLaughlin, A. 2006. Google in China. *The Official Google Blog*. January 27. https://googleblog.blogspot.com (September 14, 2018).

McKinght, J. C. 2015. Space polities? Self-governance lessons from virtual worlds, in C. S. Cockell ed., *Human Governance Beyond Earth: Implications for Freedom*, pp. 103–119. Cham: Springer.

McWane, S. H. 2001. Hollywood vs. Silicon Valley: DeCSS Down, Napster to Go? *CommLaw Conspectus*, 9(1): 87–109.

Maier, P. 1993. The revolutionary origins of the American corporation. *The William and Mary Quarterly*, 50(1): 51–84.

Marcoux, A. M. 2003. A fiduciary argument against stakeholder theory. *Business Ethics Quarterly*, 13(1): 1–24.

Marcus, G. 2012. Ray Kurzweil's dubious new theory of mind. *The New Yorker*, November 15. www.newyorker.com (November 13, 2018).

Marshall, A. 2017. Alphabet is trying to reinvent the city, starting with Toronto. *Wired*, October 19. www.wired.com (May 16, 2018).

Martin, K. 2019. Ethical implications and accountability of algorithms. *Journal of Business Ethics*, 160(4): 835–850.

Marwick, A. E., & Boyd, D. 2011. I tweet honestly, I tweet passionately: Twitter users, context collapse, and the imagined audience. *New Media & Society*, 13(1): 114–133.

Marx, K. 1845. Theses on Feuerbach. In C. J. Arthur ed. (1970), *The German Ideology: Marx & Engels*, pp. 121–123. London: Lawrence and Wishart.

Marx, K., & Engels, F. 1848. Manifesto of the communist party. In R. M. Hutchins ed., *Great Books of the Western World – 50: Marx*, pp. 419–434. Chicago, IL: Encylopædia Britannica.

Matten, D., & Crane, A. 2005. Corporate citizenship: Toward an extended theoretical conceptualization. *Academy of Management Review*, 30(1): 166–79.

Matten, D., & Moon, J. 2008. 'Implicit' and 'explicit' CSR: A comparative understanding of Corporate Social Responsibility. *Academy of Management Review*, 33(2): 404–424.

2020. Reflections on the 2018 decade award: The meaning and dynamics of corporate social responsibility. *Academy of Management Review*, 45(1): 7–28.

Mayer-Schönberger, V. 2009. *Delete: The Virtue of Forgetting in the Digital Age*. Princeton, NJ: Princeton University.

Mearsheimer, John. J. 2001. *The Tragedy of Great Power Politics*. New York: W.W. Norton & Company.

Michel, J.-B., Shen, Y. K., Aiden, A. P., Veres, A., Gray, M. K., The Google Books Team, Pickett, J. P., et al. 2011. Quantitative analysis of culture using millions of digitized books. *Science*, 331(6014): 176–182.

Micklethwait, J., & Wooldridge, A. 2003. *The Company: A Short History of a Revolutionary Idea*. London: Phoenix.

Miklos, A. 2019. Exploiting injustice in mutually beneficial market exchange: The case of sweatshop labor. *Journal of Business Ethics*, 156(1): 59–69.

Mill, J. S. 1861. Utilitarianism. In J. S. Mill (1972), *Utilitarianism, on Liberty and Considerations on Representative Government*, pp. 1–68.London: Everyman's Library.

Miller, D. 2012. Inside the risky business of porn star agents. *The Hollywood Reporter*, November 15. www.hollywoodreporter.com (July 4, 2018).

Miller, R., & Michelson, G. 2013. Fixing the game? Legitimacy, morality policy and research in gambling. *Journal of Business Ethics*, 116(3): 601–614.

Mir, R., Willmott, H., & Greenwood, M. 2016. *The Routledge Companion to Philosophy in Organization Studies*. London: Routledge.

Mohr, J. W., Wagner-Pacifici, R., & Breiger, R. L. 2015. Toward a computational hermeneutics. *Big Data & Society*, 2(2): 1–8.

Molla, R., & Ghaffary, S. 2019. Why Google employees are donating to Warren and Sanders – presidential candidates who want to break up Google. *Recode*, July 30. www.vox.com/recode (March 10, 2020).

Montiel, I. 2008. Corporate social responsibility and corporate sustainability: Separate pasts, common futures. *Organization & Environment*, 21(3): 245–269.

Moon, J. 2014. *Corporate Social Responsibility: A Very Short Introduction*. Oxford: Oxford University Press.

Moon, J., Crane, A., & Matten, D. 2005. Can corporations be citizens? Corporate citizenship as a metaphor for business participation in society. *Business Ethics Quarterly*, 15(3), 429–453.

Moore, R. 2018. The more you know: Turning environmental insights into action. *Google: The Keyword*. September 10. www.blog.google (January 28, 2019).

Moretti, F. 2000. Conjectures on world literature. *New Left Review*, 1: 54–68.

2003. Graphs, maps, trees: Abstract models for literary history – 1. *New Left Review*, 24: 67–93.

2009. Style, inc. Reflections on seven thousand titles (British Novels, 1740–1850). *Critical Inquiry*, 36(1): 134–158.

Morin, R. 2014. The anarcho-primitivist who wants us all to give up technology. *Vice*, June 25. www.vice.com (March 27, 2019).

Morozov, E. 2011. Your own facts. *The New York Times*, June 10. www.nytimes.com (January 11, 2019).

2015. Google may have changed its name but the game remains the same. *The Guardian*, August 16. www.theguardian.com (May 11, 2016).

Mullins, B. Winkler, R., & Kendall, B. 2015. Inside the U.S. antitrust probe of Google. *The Wall Street Journal*, March 19. www.wsj.com (May 8, 2019).

Mumin, N. 2011. Why it took a Swede to make 'The Black Power Mixtape'. *IndieWire*, September 8. www.indiewire.com (May 14, 2018).

Murphy, K. P. 2012. *Machine Learning: A Probabilistic Approach*. Cambridge, MA: The MIT Press.

Murphy, R. 2018. What's in a name? With 'climate change,' a lot of reckless misuse. *National Post*, November 16. https://nationalpost.com (Januaray 28, 2019).

Musk, E. 2017. Making humans a multi-planetary species. *New Space*, 5(2): 47–61.

Myers West, S. 2019. Data capitalism: Refining the logics of surveillance and capitalism. *Business & Society*, 58(1): 20–41.

NASA Technology. 2015. Landsat data enriches Google Earth. *NASA Spinoff*. https://spinoff.nasa.gov (February 4, 2019).

Naughton, J. 1999. *A Brief History of the Future: The Origins of the Internet*. London: Phoenix.

Navas, E., Gallagher, O., & burrough, x. 2015. Introduction. In E. Navas, O. Gallagher, & x. burrough eds., *The Routledge Companion to Remix Studies*, pp. 1–12. New York: Routledge.

Netburn, D. 2012. Google says 4.5 million people signed anti-SOPA petition today. *Los Angeles Times*, January 18. http://latimesblogs.latimes.com (August 10, 2016).

news.com.au. 2016. Former porn star Bree Olson goes public: 'I'm shunned by society'. *news.com.au*, March 26. www.news.com.au (July 11, 2018).

Newton, C. 2020. The Verge tech survey 2020. *The Verge*, March 2. www .theverge.com (March 10, 2020).

Nieva, R., & Musil, S. 2018. Google 'not close' to launching search engine in China, Pichai says. *CNET*, August 17. www.cnet.com (September 14, 2018).

Nike. Website A. *Manufacturing Map*. http://manufacturingmap.nikeinc .com (August 21, 2018).

    Website B. *Retail Jobs*. https://jobs.nike.com (August 21, 2018).

Nixon, N. 1992. Cyberpunk: Preparing the ground for revolution or keeping the boys satisfied? *Science Fiction Studies*, 19(2): 219–235.

Nest. Website. *Nest Aware Catches Everything You Missed*. https://nest.com (April 3, 2018).

Newborn, M. 1996. *Kasparov versus Deep Blue: Computer Chess Comes of Age*. New York: Springer.

Nisbett, R. 1994 (1980). *History of the Idea of Progress*. London: Routledge.

Nöth, W. 2004. Semiotics of ideology. *Semiotica*, 148: 11–21.

Novak, M. 1993. *The Catholic Ethic and the Spirit of Capitalism*. New York: The Free Press.

Nozick, R. 1974. *Anarchy, State, and Utopia*. Oxford: Basic Books.

Nussbaum, M. 2013. The damage of death incomplete: Arguments and false consolations. In J. S. Taylor ed., *The Metaphysics and Ethics of Death: New Essays*, pp. 23–43. New York: Oxford University Press.

Nye, J. S. 2004. *Soft Power: The Means to Success in World Politics*. New York: Public Affairs.

O'Brien, L. 2018. Trump's loudest anti-Muslim Twitter troll is a shady vegan married to an (ousted) WWE exec. *Huff Post*, May 31. www .huffingtonpost.ca (July 12, 2018).

O'Donovan, C. 2018. Google employees are quitting over the company's secretive Chinese search project. *Buzzfeed*, September 13. www .buzzfeednews.com (March 25, 2020).

Oliver, C. 1991. Strategic responses to institutional processes. *Academy of Management Review*, 16(1): 145–179.

Olson, P. 2018. Google, Microsoft and startups are going to war on chatbot technology. *Forbes*, July 27. www.forbes.com (December 17, 2018).

Olsson, G. 2011. *The Black Power Mixtape 1967–1975*. New York: IFC Films.

Ogas, O., & Gaddam, S. 2012. *A Billion Wicked Thoughts: What the Internet Tells us about Sexual Relationships*. New York: Plume.

Orbital Insight. Website. *Geospatial Analytics for an Integrated World*. https://orbitalinsight.com (February 4, 2019).

Orf, D. 2016. Creeps are using a neural network to dox porn actresses. *Gizmodo*, https://gizmodo.com (July 4, 2018).

Orlowski, A. 2016. Just how close are Obama and Google? You won't believe the answer. *The Register*, April 4. www.theregister.co.uk (May 8, 2019).

Padgett, E. 2016. Duelling identities: Narrative strategy and the construction of complex identities in porn star memoirs. *Porn Studies*, 3(2): 222–237.

Palfrey, J., & Gasser, U. 2008. *Born Digital: Understanding the First Generation of Digital Natives*. New York: Basic Books.

Page, L. 2015. G is for Google. *The Official Google Blog*, August 10. http://googleblog.blogspot.com (Septmber 7, 2018).

Page, L., & Brin, S. 2004. 'An Owner's Manua' for Google's shareholders. *Alphabet Investor Relations*. https://abc.xyz/investor (January 28, 2016).

Pagnamenta, R. 2019. Breaking up tech giants would be 'illegal' and will harm consumers, says Google's Eric Schmidt. *The Telegraph*, May 20. www.telegraph.co.uk (March 10, 2020).

Palazzo, G., & Richter, U. 2005. CSR business as usual? The case of the tobacco industry. *Journal of Business Ethics*, 61(4): 387–401.

Palladino, V. 2017. Updates to Google Photos ensure you'll actually see those party photos you're in. *Arstechnica*, May 15 https://arstechnica.com (February 25, 2020).

Panzar, J. C. 1991. Is postal service a natural monopoly? In M. A. Crew & P. R. Kleindorfer eds., *Competition and Innovation in Postal Services*, pp. 219–228. New York: Springer.

Parfit, D. 1984. *Reasons and Persons*. Oxford: Clarendon Press.

Pasquale, F. 2010. Beyond innovation and competition: The need for qualified transparency in internet intermediaries. *Northwestern University Law Review*, 104(1): 105–173.

Patriotta, G., Gond, J.-P., & Schultz, F. 2011. Maintaining legitimacy: Controversies, orders of worth, and public justifications. *Journal of Management Studies*, 48(8): 1804–1836.

Pekel, J.-F., Cottam, A., Gorelick, N., & Belward, A. S. 2016. High-resolution mapping of global surface water and its long-term changes. *Nature*, 540: 418–422.

Pellman, P. 2019. Former Google on how tech giant squandered employee trust – and how Sundar Pichai can gain it back. *CNBC*, December 11. www.cnbc.com (March 9, 2020).

Peirce, C. S. 1901. On the logic of drawing history from ancient documents, especially from testimonies. In C. S. Peirce (1998). *The Essential Peirce: Selected Philosophical Writings*, Volume 2 (1893–1913), pp. 75–114. Bloomington, IN: Indiana University Press.

Penney, J. W. 2016. Chilling effects: Online surveillance and Wikipedia use. *Berkeley Technology Law Journal*, 31(1): 117–182.

Persson, E. P. 2015. Citizens of Mars Ltd. In C. S. Cockell ed., *Human Governance Beyond Earth: Implications for Freedom*, pp. 121–137. Cham: Springer.

Petrik, J., Kilybayev, T., & Shormanbayeva, D. 2014. The internet, identity and intellectual capital: A response to Dreyfus's critique of e-learning. *Ethics and Information Technology*, 16(4): 275–284.

Pew Research Centre. 2014. *The Future of Privacy (Digital Life in 2025)*. December. www.pewresearch.org (January 28, 2020).

2018. *Artificial Intelligence and the Future of Humans*. December. www .pewinternet.org (February 27, 2019).

Pianigiani, G. 2016. Viral sex tapes and a suicide prompt outrage in Italy. *The New York Times*, September 16. www.nytimes.com (July 4, 2018).

Pijnenburg, M. A. M., & Leget, C. 2007. Who wants to live forever? Three arguments against extending the human lifespan. *Journal of Medical Ethics*, 33(10): 585–587.

Poole, S. 1999. Nearing the nodal. *The Guardian*, October 30. www .theguardian.com (August 20, 2018).

Popper, B. 2013. Understanding Calico: Larry Page, Google Ventures, and the quest for immortality. *The Verge*, September 19. www.theverge.com (November 09, 2018).

Popper, K. 1994 (1945). *The Open Society and Its Enemies*. London: Routledge.

Protalinski, E. 2018. Google Assistant is now on over 500 million devices. *Venture Beat*, May 8. https://venturebeat.com (January 21, 2019).

Quigley, J. M., & Huffman, D. 2002. The role of the university in attracting high tech entrepreneurship: A Silicon Valley tale. *The Annals of Regional Science*, 36: 403–419.

Raz, J. 1988. *The Morality of Freedom*. Oxford: Oxford University Press.

Regalado, A. 2013. Google to try to solve death, LOL. *MIT Technology Review*, September 18. www.technologyreview.com (November 9, 2018).

2016. Google's long, strange life-span trip. *MIT Technology Review*, (December 15). www.technologyreview.com (November 9, 2018).

Reuters. 2016. China completes merger that creates nation's biggest steel company. *Reuters*, December 1. www.reuters.com (August 23, 2018).

Rippetoe, P. A., & Rogers, R. W. 1987. Effects of components of protection-motivation theory on adaptive and maladaptive coping with a health threat. *Journal of Personality and Social Psychology*, 52(3): 596–604.

Ritzer, G. 1996. The McDonaldization Thesis: Is expansion inevitable? *International Sociology*, 11(3): 291–308.

Robertson, A. 2020. Congress takes aim at Google search in antitrust hearing. *The Verge*, March 10. www.theverge.com (March 10, 2020).

Robins, N. 2012. The corporation that changed the world: How the East India Company shaped the modern multinational. *Asian Affairs*, 43(1): 12–26.

Robinson, K. S. 2015a. Our generation ships will sink. *Boing Boing*, November 16. https://boingboing.net (February 5, 2019).

  2015b. *Aurora*. London: Orbit.

Rogers, R. W. 1975. Protection motivation theory of fear appeals and attitude-change. *Journal of Psychology*, 91(1): 93–114.

Romm, T. 2020. Justice Department faults Google for turning over evidence too slowly in antitrust probe, hinting at possible legal action. *The Washington Post*, February 27. www.washingtonpost.com (March 10, 2020).

Ronson, J. 2015. *So You've Been Publicly Shamed*. New York: Riverhead Books.

Rorty, R. 1989. *Contingency, Irony, and Solidarity*. NewYork: Cambridge University Press.

Rosenberg, N. & Trajtenberg, M. 2004 'A General Purpose Technology at Work: The Corliss Steam Engine in the Late-Nineteenth-Century United States', *Journal of Economic History*, 61(1): 61–99.

Rothman, J. 2014. An attempt to discover the laws of literature. *The New Yorker*, March 20. www.newyorker.com (May 3, 2018).

Ruggie, J. G. 2003. Taking embedded liberalism global: The corporate connection, in D. Held & M. Koenig-Archibugi eds., *Taming Globalization: Frontiers of Governance*, pp. 93–129. Cambridge: Polity.

Said, E. W. 2003. *Orientalism*. London: Penguin.

Salter, J. 2012. Hume and mutual advantage. *Politics, Philosophy & Economics*, 11(3): 302–321.

Sandberg, A., & Bostrom, N. 2008. *Whole Brain Emulation: A Roadmap*. Technical Report #2008-3, Future of Humanity Institute, Oxford University.

Saul, H. 2016. Conversations with porn stars: My life after leaving the industry. *Independent*, December 10. www.independent.co.uk (June 21, 2018).

Savory, E. 2008. VHEMT: The case against humans. *CBC News.* September 4. www.cbc.ca (April 08, 2019).

Savov, V. 2018a. Google's selfish ledger is an unsettling vision of Silicon Valley social engineering. *The Verge,* May 17. www.theverge.com (January 14, 2019).

2018b. Google's selfish ledger ideas can also be found it its patent applications. *The Verge,* May 19. www.theverge.com (January 14, 2019).

Saxenian, A. 1994. *Regional Advantage: Culture and Competition in Silicon Valley and Route 128.* Cambridge, MA: Harvard University Press.

Schauer, F. 1978. Fear, risk and the 1st amendment - Unraveling the chilling effect. *Boston University Law Review,* 58(5): 685–732.

Scheffler, S. 2013. In N. Kolodny ed., *Death and the Afterlife.* Oxford: Oxford University Press.

Scherer, A. G., & Palazzo, G. 2007. Toward a political conception of corporate social responsibility: Business and society seen from a Habermasian perspective. *Academy of Management Review,* 32(4): 1096–1120.

2011. The new political role of business in a globalized world: A review of a new perspective on CSR and its implications for the firm, governance and democracy. *Journal of Management Studies,* 48(4): 899–931.

Schloendorn, J. 2006. Making the case for human life extension: Personal arguments. *Bioethics,* 20(4): 191–202.

Schmidt, E., & Cohen, J. 2010. The digital disruption: Connectivity and the diffusion of power. *Foreign Affairs,* 89(6): 75–85.

2013. *The New Digital Age: Reshaping the Future of People, Nations and Business.* London: John Murray.

Schmidt, K. J. 1995. *An Atlas and Survey of South Asian History.* Armonk, NY: M.E. Sharpe.

Schopenhauer, A. 1969 (1818/1844). *The World as Will and Representation, Vols. I and II.* New York: Dover Publications.

Schulze, E. 2019. If you want to know what a US tech crackdown may look like, check out what Europe did. *CNBC,* June 7. www.cnbc.com (March 10, 2020).

Schwartz, J. S. J. 2014. Prioritizing scientific exploration: A comparison of the ethical justifications for space development and for space science. *Space Policy,* 30(4): 202–208.

2017. Myth-free space advocacy part II – The myth of the Space Frontier. *Astropolitics,* 15(2): 167–184.

Scoles, S. 2018. Maybe nobody wants your space internet. *Wired,* March 15. www.wired.com (January 23, 2019).

Scott-Heron. G. 1970. Whitey on the Moon. *The Revolution Begins.* New York: Flying Dutchman.

Searle, J. R. 1980. Minds, brains and programs. *The Behavioral and Brain Sciences*, 3(3): 417–5

1997. *The Mystery of Consciousness*. London: Granta.

2017. Biological naturalism. In S. Schneider & M. Velmans eds., *The Blackwell Companion to Consciousness*, pp. 327–336. Malden, MA: John Wiley & Sons.

Shaban, H. 2018. Google for the first time outspent every other company to influence Washington in 2017. *The Washington Post*, January 23. www .washingtonpost.com (September 13, 2018).

Shackle, G .L .S. 1958. *Time in Economics*. Amsterdam: North-Holland.

Shane, S., Metz, C., & Wakabayashi, D. 2018. How a Pentagon contract became an identity crisis for Google. *The New York Times*, May 30. www.nytimes.com (September 4, 2018).

Sharwood, S. 2014. Rupert Murdoch says Google is worse than NSA. *The Register*, August 18. www.theregister.co.uk (August 10, 2016).

Sheetz, M. 2019. SpaceX valuation rises to $33.3 billion as investors look to satellite opportunity. *CNBC*, May 31. www.cnbc.com (February 4, 2020).

Shelton, K. 2017. The value of search results rankings. *Forbes*, October 30. www.forbes.com (September 13, 2018).

Shenker, O. 1996. The firm as total institution: Reflections on the Chinese state enterprise. *Organization Studies*, 17(6): 885–907.

Shieber, J. 2018. Where's the beef? For Impossible Foods it's in boosting burger sales and raising hundreds of millions. *Tech Crunch*, April 3. https://techcrunch.com (January 30, 2019).

Shy, J. 1998. The American colonies in war and revolution, 1748–1783. In P. J. Marshall ed., *The Eighteenth Century*, pp. 300–324. Oxford: Oxford University Press.

Sidewalk Labs. Website. *Sidewalk Labs*. www.sidewalklabs.com (April 14, 2018).

2017. *A. Project Vision (Toronto's Eastern Waterfront)* https:// sidewalktoronto.ca (January 18, 2019).

Sidgwick, H. 1874. *The Methods of Ethics*. London: Macmillan & Co.

Simon, M., Graziano, M., & Lenhart, A. 2001. *The Internet and Education: Findings of the Pew Internet & American Life Project.* www .pewinternet.org (January 17, 2019).

Simonite, T. 2014. Ray Kurzweil says he's breathing intelligence into Google search. *MIT Technology Review*, June 26. www.technologyreview.com (November 12, 2018).

2017. What is Ray Kurzweil up to at Google? Writing your emails. *Wired*, August 8. www.wired.com (November 12, 2018).

Singer, P. 2017. Why Google was wrong: Did James Damore really deserve to be fired for what he wrote? *NY Daily News*, August 10. www .nydailynews.com (September 18, 2018).

Sitaraman, G. 2020. Too big too prevail: The national security case for breaking up big tech. *Foreign Affairs*, 99(2): 116–126.

Smith, A. 1999 (1776). *The Wealth of Nations*, Books IV-V.London: Penguin.

Smith, C. 2006. Statement. *The Internet in China: A Tool for Freedom or Suppression?* Joint Hearing, House of Representatives, One Hundred Ninth Congress, Second Session. February 15. www.foreignaffairs .house.gov/archives (November 15, 2010).

Smith, M. 2002. The state of nature: The political philosophy of primitivism and the culture of contamination. *Environmental Values*, 11(4): 407–425.

Smith, R. 2015. SpaceX + Google = Satellite Internet. *The Motley Fool*, February 7. www.fool.com (January 23, 2019).

Solar, P. M., & Luchens, A. 2016. Ship speeds during the Industrial Revolution: East India Company ships, 1770–1828. *European Review of Economic History*, 20(1): 66–78.

Solove, D. J. 2006. A taxonomy of privacy. *University of Pennsylvania Law Review*, 154(3): 477–564.

Springmann, M., Clark, M., Mason-D'Croz, D., Wiebe, K., Bodirsky, B. L., Lassaletta, L., de Vries, W., Vermeulen, S. J., Herrero, M., Carlson, K. M., Jonell, M. J., Troell, M., DeClerck, F., Gordon, L. J., Zurayk, R., Scarborough, P., Rayner, M., Loken, B., Fanzo, J., Godfray, H. C. J., Tilman, D., Rockström, J., & Willet, W. 2018. Options for keeping the food system within environmental limits. *Nature*, 562: 519–525.

Srnicek, N. 2017. We need to nationalise Google, Facebook and Amazon. Here's why. *The Guardian*, August 30. www.theguardian.com (August 24, 2018).

Stanford News. 2012. New members inducted into Stanford Inventor Hall of fame. *Stanford News*, June 6. http://news.stanford.edu (March 11, 2016).

Stanford Research Park. Website. *Past, Present & Future.* https:// stanfordresearchpark.com (September 7, 2018).

Statscounter. Website. *Search Engine Marke Share Worldwide, Dec 2018 – Dec 2019.* https://gs.statcounter.com (January 28, 2020).

Statt, N. 2017. Google fires employee who wrote anti-diversity memo. *The Verge*, August 7. www.theverge.com (September 13, 2018).

    2019. The rise, disappearance, and retirement of Google co-founders Larry Page and Sergey Brin. *The Verge*, December 4. www.theverge .com (April 2, 2020).

2018. Alphabet's experimental investments in the future continue to cost it a fortune. *The Verge*, July 23. www.theverge.com (September 12, 2018).

Stephenson, N. 2004. *Quicksilver*, Book 1 The Baroque Cycle. London: Arrow.

Stern, P. J. 2011. *The Company-State: Corporate Sovereignty and the Early Modern Foundations of the British Empire in India*. Oxford: Oxford University Press.

Stewart, E. 2019. Poll: Two-thirds of Americans want to break up companies like Amazon and Google. *Vox*, September 18. www.vox.com (March 10, 2019).

Stone, B. 2013. Inside Google's secret lab. *Bloomberg Business*, May 22. www.bloomberg.com (August 11, 2016).

Stonewall. 2018. Why it's never okay to out someone. *Stonewall*, March 18. www.stonewall.org (July 4, 2018).

Stross, R. 2008. *Planet Google: How One Company Is Transforming our Lives*. London: Atlantic Books.

Sturgeon, T. J. 2000. How Silicon Valley Came to Be. In M. Kenney ed., *Understanding Silicon Valley: The Anatomy of an Entrepreneurial Region*, pp. 15–47. Stanford, CA: Stanford University Press.

Suchman, M. C. 1995. Managing legitimacy: Strategic and institutional approaches. *Academy of Management Review*, 20(3): 571–610.

Sullivan, D. 2016. 10 big changes with search engines over my 20 years of covering them. *Search Engine Land*, April 17. https://searchengineland .com (September 13, 2018).

Summers, N. 2018. Google's smart city dream is turning into a privacy nightmare. *Endgadget*, October 26. www.engadget.com (January 18, 2019).

Swearingan, J. 2017. Google sells Boston Dynamics, maker of unnerving robots. *New York Magazine*, June 9. http://nymag.com (September 14, 2018).

Swierstra, T. 2013. Nanotechnology and technomoral change. *Etica & Politica/Ethics & Politics*, 15(2): 200–219.

Swift, R. 2015. The day I learned to stop hating laptop DJs. *Cuepoint*, June 8. https://medium.com (May 14, 2018).

Tabuchi, H. 2017. How climate change deniers rise to the top in Google searches. *The New York Times*, December 27. www.nytimes.com (January 28, 2019).

Tainter, J. A. 1988. *The Collapse of Complex Societies*. Cambridge: Cambridge University Press.

TEF (Tennessee Ernie Ford) Enterprises. Website. *Sixteen Tons: The Story Behind the Legend.* www.ernieford.com (January 20, 2020).

The Motley Fool. 2020. Alphabet Inc (GOOG) (GOOGL) Q4 2019 Earnings Call Transcript. *The Motley Fool*, February 3. www.fool.com (February 4, 2020).

The New York Times. 1995. *BOMBING IN SACRAMENTO: THE LETTER; Excerpts From Letter by 'Terrorist Group,' FC, Which Says It Sent Bombs. The New York Times*, April 26. www.nytimes.com (March 27, 2019).

The President's Council on Bioethics. 2003. *Beyond Therapy: Biotechnology and the Pursuit of Happiness*. Washington, DC: A Report of the President's Council on Bioethics.

Thurm, S. 2019. What tech companies pay employees in 2019. *Wired*, May 21. www.wired.com (March 17, 2020).

Tierney, B. 1955. *Foundations of the Conciliar Theory: The Contribution of the Medieval Canonists from Gratian to the Great Schism*. Cambridge: Cambridge University Press.

Toobin, J. 2007. Google's Moon Shot. *The New Yorker*, February 5. www .newyorker.com (August 11, 2016).

Toolis, K. 1999. The most dangerous man in the world. *The Guardian*, November 6. www.theguardian.com (September 14, 2018).

Transparency International. 2018. Corruption Perceptions Index 2017. *Transparency International*, February 21. www.transparency.org (August 27, 2018).

Trump, D. Jr. 2019. Free speech suppression online builds case to break up Big Tech. *The Hill*, September 30. https://thehill.com (March 31, 2020).

Turner, F. 2006. *From Counterculture to Cyberculture: Steward Brand, the Whole Earth Network, and the Rise of Digital Utopianism*. Chicago, IL: University of Chicago Press.

  2009. Burning man at Google: A cultural infrastructure for new media production. *New Media & Society*, 11(1–2): 73–94.

UNCC (United Nations Climate Change). 2017. *Climate Change Impacts Human Health*, Report/12 APR, 2017. https://unfccc.int (January 21, 2019).

US Defense Innovation Board. Website. *Defense Innovation Board*. https:// innovation.defense.gov (September 14, 2018).

US Department of Defense. 2018. *Contractor Support of U.S. Operations in the USCENTCOM Area of Responsibility*, July 2018. www.acq.osd.mil (August 27, 2018).

  Website. *About the Department of Defense*. https://dod.defense.gov (September 14, 2018).

US Department of Labor. 2017. 26.8 million Hispanics or Latinos in the US labor force in 2016. *TED: The Economics Daily*, September 25. www .bls.gov (September 13, 2018).

US Homeland Security. Website. *Critical Infrastructure Sectors*. www.dhs .gov (March 26, 2019).

Vaidhyanathan, S. 2011. *The Googlization of Everything (and Why We Should Worry)*. Berkeley, CA: University of California Press.

Van Dorpe, S. 2020. EU judge tells Google it landed on Monopoly's 'Go to jail' square. *Politico*, February 13. www.politico.eu (March 10, 2020).

van Liedekerke, L., & Dubbink, W. 2008. Twenty years of European business ethics – past developments and future concerns. *Journal of Business Ethics*, 82(2): 273–280.

Vandekerchkove, W. 2017. New editor's welcome. *Philosophy of Management*, 16(2): 91–92.

Varian, H. R. 2014. Beyond big data. *Business Economics*, 49(1): 27–31.

Vaughan, B. K., & Martin, M. 2015. *The Private Eye*. www.panelsyndicate .com

Verily. Website. *Verily Life Sciences*. https://verily.com (December 14, 2018).

VHMET (Voluntary Human Extinction Movement), Website. *About the Movement*. www.vhemt.org (April 08, 2019).

Vincent, J. 2018. Elon Musk, DeepMind founders, and other pledge to not develop lethal AI weapon systems. *The Verge*, July 18. www.theverge .com (September 14, 2018).

Vise, D. A. 2005. *The Google Story*. London: Pan Books.

Wagoner, B. 2011. *After Porn Ends*. Los Angeles, CA: Oxymoron Entertainment.

Waltz, K. N. 1979. *Theory of International Relations*. Long Grove, IL: Waveland.

Wanono, N. 2015. Détournement as a premise of the remix from political, aesthetic and technical perspectives. In E. Navas, O. Gallagher, & X. Burrough eds., *The Routledge Companion to Remix Studies*, pp. 386–396. New York: Routledge.

Warren, R. 2018. A mother wants the Internet to forget Italy's most viral sex tape. *The Atlantic*, May 16. www.theatlantic.com (July 9, 3018).

Waters, R. 2014. FT Interview with Google co-founder and CEO Larry Page. *Financial Times*, October 31. www.ft.com (September 7, 2018).

Way of the Future. Website. *Way of the Future Church: Humans United in Support of AI, Committed to Peaceful Transition to the Precipice of Consciousness*. www.wayofthefuture.church (April 11, 2019).

Weart, S. R. 2008. *The Discovery of Global Warming*, Revised & Expanded Edition. Cambridge, MA: Harvard University Press.

Weber, K., & Waeger, D. 2017. Organizations as polities: An open systems perspective. *Academy of Management Annals*, 11(2): 886–918.

Weber, M. 1978. *Economy and Society: An Outline of Interpretive Sociology*. Berkeley, CA: University of California Press.

Weintraub, S. 2018. Anthony Levandowski's new Pronto.ai startup has already autonomously driven 3099 miles cross country. *Electrek*, December 18. https://electrek.co (May 3, 2019).

Wesch, M. 2009. YouTube and you: Experiences of self-awareness in the context of the collapse of the recording webcam. *Explorations in Media Ecology*, 8(2): 19–34.

Whelan, G. 2012. The political perspective of corporate social responsibility: A critical research agenda. *Business Ethics Quarterly*, 22(4): 709–737.

2017. Political CSR: The corporation as a political actor. In J. Moon, M. Morsing & A. Rascheeds., *Corporate Social Responsibility: Strategy, Communication, Governance*, pp. 136–153. Cambridge, UK: Cambridge University Press.

2019. Born political: A dispositive analysis of Google and copyright. *Business & Society*, 58(1): 42–73.

Whelan, G., & Gond, J.-P. 2017. Meat your enemy: Animal rights, alignment and radical change. *Journal of Management Inquiry*, 26(2): 123–138.

Whelan, G., Moon, J., & Grant, B. 2013. Corporations and citizenship arenas in the age of social media. *Journal of Business Ethics*, 118(4): 777–790.

Whelan, G., Moon, J., & Orlitzky, M. 2009. Human rights, transnational corporations, and embedded liberalism: What chance consensus? *Journal of Business Ethics*, 87 (Supp.2): 367–383.

Whitley, R. 1997. Business systems. In A. Sorge & M. Warner eds., *The IEBM Handbook of Organizational Behavior*, pp. 173–186. London: International Thomson Business Press.

Wilkins, J. 1668. *An Essay Towards a Real Character and a Philosophical Language*. London: The Royal Society.

Wismer, D. 2012. Google's Larry Page: 'Competition is one click away'. *Forbes*, October 14. www.forbes.com (May 9, 2019).

Williams, B. 1973. 'The Makropulos case: Reflections on the tedium of immortality', In B. Williams ed., *Problems of the Self: Philosophical Papers 1956–1972*, pp. 82–100. Cambridge: Cambridge University Press.

Wolf, M. J. P. 2018. Virtual worlds. In M. J. P. Wolf ed.,*The Routledge Companion to Imaginary Worlds*, pp. 192–197. New York: Routledge.

Wong, J. C. 2017. Segregated valley: The ugly truth about Google and diversity in tech. *The Guardian*, August 7. www.theguardian.com (September 13, 2018).

2018. The Uber trial exposing dirty secrets of Silicon Valley's greatest innovators. *The Guardian*, February 5. www.theguardian.com (April 11, 2019).

World Commission on Environment and Development. 1987. *Our Common Future*. Oxford: Oxford University Press.

Wu, T. 2018. *The Curse of Bigness: Antitrust in the New Gilded Age*. New York: Columbia Global Reports.

YouTube. Website A. *About YouTube*. www.youtube.com/about (January 31, 2020).

    Website B. *Culture & Trends*. www.youtube.com/trends/discover (January 31, 2020).

Zeng, R., & Greenfield, P. M. 2015. Cultural evolution over the last 40 years in China: Using the Google Ngram Viewer to study implications of social and political change for cultural values. *International Journal of Pscyhology*, 15(1): 47–55.

Zerk, J. A. 2006. *Multinationals and Corporate Social Responsibility: Limitations and Opportunities in International Law*. Cambridge: Cambridge University Press.

Zerzan, J. 2012. *Future Primitive Revisited*. Port Townsend, WA: Feral House.

    2014. A word on civilization & collapse. *Fifth Estate*, 392. www.fifthestate.org (March 27, 2019).

Zuboff, S. 2015. Big other: Surveillance capitalism and the prospects of an information civilization. *Journal of Information Technology*, 30(1): 75–89.

    2019. 'We Make Them Dance': Surveillance capitalism, the rise of instrumentarian power, and the threat to human rights. In R. F.Jørgensen ed., *Human Rights in the Age of Platforms*, pp. 3–52. Cambridge, MA: MIT Press.

    2020. You are now remotely controlled. *The New York Times*, January 24. www.nytimes.com (January 28, 2020).

Zyphur, M. J., Oswald, F. L., & Rupp, D. E. 2015. Rendezvous overdue: Bayes analysis meets organizational research. *Journal of Management*, 41(2): 387–389.

Index

Printed in the United States
by Baker & Taylor Publisher Services